THE MAKING OF
MODERN ZIONISM

Also by **Shlomo Avineri**

Herzl's Vision: Theodore Herzl and the Foundation of the Jewish State

Moses Hess: The Holy History of Mankind & Other Writings

Europe's Century of Discontent (with Zeev Sternhell)

The Law of Religious Identity (with András Sajó)

Communitarianism and Individualism (with Avner de-Shalit)

Arlosoroff: A Political Biography

Moses Hess: Prophet of Communism and Zionism

Varieties of Marxism

Marx's Socialism

Hegel's Theory of the Modern State

Israel and the Palestinians

Karl Marx on Colonialism and Modernization

The Social and Political Thought of Karl Marx

THE MAKING
OF MODERN
ZIONISM

The Intellectual Origins of the Jewish State

Updated with a New Preface and Epilogue

Shlomo Avineri

BASIC BOOKS
New York

Library of Congress Control Number: 2017930727
ISBN: 978-0-465-09479-0 (2017 revised paperback)
ISBN: 978-0-465-09480-6 (2017 revised e-book)
ISBN: 978-0-465-04328-6 (1981 hardcover)
ISBN: 978-0-465-04331-6 (1984 paperback)

10 9 8 7 6 5 4 3 2 1

CONTENTS

Great revolutions which strike the eye at a glance must have been preceded by a quiet and secret revolution in the spirit of the age (*Zeitgeist*), a revolution not visible to every eye, especially imperceptible to contemporaries, and as hard to discern as to describe in words. It is lack of acquaintance with this spiritual revolution which makes the resulting changes astonishing.

HEGEL

PREFACE TO THE 2017 EDITION

SINCE THE ORIGINAL PUBLICATION OF THIS BOOK IN 1981, a number of developments in Israel and the region have occurred which underline some of the successes and dilemmas of Zionism.

The disintegration of communism brought to Israel almost one million immigrants from the former Soviet Union. Civil war and internal disturbances in Ethiopia brought to the Jewish state around one hundred thousand members of its black Jewish community. Both immigrations, though as diametrically different in social, economic, and intellectual background as could be imagined, posed novel challenges to Israel, not all of which have been successfully overcome.

At the same time, both waves of immigration proved once again how crucial the very existence of a Jewish nation-state is to the fate of Jewish communities the world over. The fact that there is a country which will welcome Jewish immigrants if they feel persecuted or uncomfortable in their country of residence vindicates the moral foundation and *raison d'etre* of Zionism and of Israel's Law of Return, which enables every Jewish person to immigrate to the country. Never again will Jewish persons persecuted or expelled find out that there is no place for them under the sun.

On another level, the 1993 Oslo Accords between Israel and the Palestinian Liberation Organization have opened the way for an eventual historical compromise between the two national movements: Zionism and Palestinian nationalism. Yet the hopes implied in what was undoubtedly a historical breakthrough have not been fulfilled.

Both sets of developments will be discussed at length in the new Epilogue added to this new edition.

As stated in my original Preface, this volume is not a history of Zionism. Its aim is more limited: to delineate a number of aspects of Zionist *thought*, as expressed through the writings of selected nineteenth- and twentieth-century individuals. This approach is intended to bring out both the enormous richness and variety of the intellectual ferment that gave rise to the call for a Jewish state as well as to show how the Zionist movement drew on both the legacy of Jewish tradition and the challenges of the modern age. It was this coalescence of the *Sturm und Drang* of the forces unleashed by the European Enlightenment with a historical Jewish heritage going back thousands of years, which endowed Zionism with its extraordinary appeal and force. For this reason I included pre-Zionist thinkers like Nachman Krochmal and Heinrich Graetz, whose contribution to the transformation of Jewish identity from merely religious into a modern, mainly secular national discourse seems to me of historical importance.

Every selection can be challenged, and the critical reader may question my inclusion of Vladimir Jabotinsky while not mentioning Chaim Weizmann, or including David Ben Gurion while leaving out Berl Katznelson. My criteria for inclusion related both to the question whether the person could be seen as expressing a distinct and somewhat systematic set of ideas as well as what his impact has been. It is for the second reason that thinkers like Jacob Klatzkin or Martin Buber have not been included. I am well aware that another author might have decided otherwise.

Because Zionism rose as a secular, political movement under concrete conditions in nineteenth- and twentieth-century Europe but also drew on deep historical sources, some of them religious, it is in a way much more complex and pluralistic, and perhaps even baffling, than other modern national movements. Without confronting this complexity it is difficult to understand both its impact and the challenges faced by it, and it is this multifaceted texture that my study aims to elucidate.

As I did in the Preface to the first edition, I would like to thank my wife Dvora and my daughter Maayan Avineri-Rebhun who helped me in more ways than can be conveyed in words to prepare this volume.

The Hebrew University
Mount Scopus, Jerusalem

INTRODUCTION

ZIONISM AS A REVOLUTION

A T THE ROOT OF ZIONISM LIES A PARADOX.
On the one hand, there is no doubt about the depth and intensity of the bond between the Jewish people and the Land of Israel: there had always been a Jewish community, albeit a small one, living in Palestine, and there had always been a trickle of Jews coming to live and die in the Holy Land. Moreover, during eighteen centuries of exile, the link to the Land of Israel always loomed large in the value system of Jewish communities all over the world and in their self-consciousness as a group. Had this tie been severed and had the Jews not regarded the Land of Israel as the land of both their past and their future, then Judaism would have become a mere religious community and would have lost its ethnic and national elements. What singled out the Jews from the Christian and Muslim majority communities in whose midst they have resided for two millennia was not only their distinct religious beliefs but also their link—tenuous and nebulous as it might have been—with the distant land of their forefathers. It was because of this that Jews were considered by others—and considered themselves—not only a minority but a minority *in exile.*

On the other hand, the fact remains that for all of its emotional, cultural, and religious intensity, this link with Palestine did not change the praxis of Jewish life in the Diaspora: Jews might pray three times a day for the deliverance that would transform the world and transport them to Jerusalem, but they did not emigrate there; they could annually mourn the destruction of the Temple on *Tish 'ah be-Av* and leave a brick over their door panel bare as a constant reminder of the desolation of Zion, but they did not move there. Here and there individuals did go to Jerusalem; occasionally

1

messianic movements swept individuals or even whole communities in a fervor of a redemptive Return, but they fizzled out sooner or later. The belief in the Return to Zion never disappeared, but the historical record shows that on the whole, Jews did not relate to the vision of the Return in a more active way than most Christians viewed the Second Coming. As a symbol of belief, integration, and group identity it was a powerful component of the value system; but as an activating element of historical praxis and changing reality throughout history, it was almost wholly quietistic. Jewish religious thought even evolved a theoretical construct aimed at legitimizing this passivity by a very strong skepticism about any active intervention in the divine scheme of things. Divine Providence, not human intervention, should determine when and how the Jews will be redeemed from exile and return to Zion.

This, then, is the paradox: on the one hand, a deep feeling of attachment to the Land of Israel, becoming perhaps the most distinctive feature of Jewish self-identity; on the other hand, a quietistic attitude toward any practical or operational consequences of this commitment.

An active movement for Jewish return to Palestine does not appear until the second half of the nineteenth century. This movement, culminating in the emergence of Zionism as a political force and the establishment of the State of Israel, has radically changed the course of Jewish history and the nature of the bond between Jews and the Land of Israel. It requires an explanation other than the pious and sometimes apologetic phrases relating Zionism to the "deep link with the Land of Israel," true as they are. In particular, how did this link become active in the nineteenth century after having remained passive for eighteen centuries? Why was it precisely in the secularized atmosphere of the nineteenth and twentieth centuries that a link which was originally religious became a potent force for action?

The most common explanation, in textbooks and political propaganda (both Zionist and anti-Zionist), relates the emergence of Zionism in the nineteenth century to the outbreak of anti-Semitism: the appearance of racist theories in Germany and France, pogroms in Russia in 1881–82, the Kishinev killings in 1903, and the Dreyfus affair. But these examples only beg the question in more than one way. It was not only in the late nineteenth century that Jews began to experience feelings of enmity from the communities surrounding them. Jewish history is a chronicle of discrimination at the hands of Christians and Muslims alike long before the rise of racist anti-Semitism in the nineteenth century. Jews were persecuted under the Visigoths and Byzantines; massacred during the Crusades; expelled from England, France, and then traumatically from Spain and Portugal; not allowed to reside in imperial cities in the Holy Roman Empire; forcibly converted in Portugal and Persia alike; made to wear distinctive clothes and barred from holding public offices in Christian Italy and Muslim Morocco. In all these cases Jews reacted with resignation and by immigration to other countries but *not* to Palestine. What made them react to the persecution of the nineteenth century by turning toward Zion?

The Russian pogroms and anti-Semitic policies of the czarist government caused almost three million Jews to emigrate from Russia between 1882 and 1914. Yet only a small fraction of these, perhaps 1 percent, went to Palestine. The preponderant majority went to the United States, Canada, South America, Australia. Zionism was not the solution for the great majority of persecuted Jews, and even the 1 percent that went to Palestine could have been absorbed in this great immigration, which, after all, followed the traditional Jewish way of coping with the disasters of exile. The fact that an avant-garde minority opted for the Land of Israel rather than another exile cannot be explained just by the *push* which drove them out of Russia. There was also a *pull*, to Palestine. So the question remains: why did that *pull* operate in the nineteenth and twentieth centuries and not earlier?

From any conceivable point of view, the nineteenth century was the best century Jews had ever experienced, collectively and individually, since the destruction of the Temple. With the French Revolution and Emancipation, Jews were allowed for the first time into European society on an equal footing. For the first time Jews enjoyed equality before the law; and schools, universities, and the professions were gradually opened to them.

Indeed, if one compares the beginning of the nineteenth century to its end—perhaps 1815 and 1914 should be the points of comparison—then it becomes dramatically evident that economically, socially, politically, and intellectually, this was the most revolutionary century in history for the Jews. The European Jews in 1815 were a community still at the margin of gentile society: geographically and socially, most Jews still lived in the rural hinterlands of European society, in the *shtetls* of the Pale of Settlement in

Eastern Europe, and in rural districts like Hesse and Alsace. The great cities of Europe—Paris, Vienna, Berlin, London, Moscow, and St. Petersburg—were still predominantly *Judenrein*. Sociologically, Jews were still excluded, in accordance with Christian theology, from positions of public service. They were not allowed into schools and universities, could not be public officials or serve in the army, and were barred from most professions. Most Jews were still relegated to the humble life of the petty mercantile middleman, finding a living in the niches and crevices of a society which excluded them even when it tolerated their religious beliefs. Until 1815 hardly any Jewish person had had a major impact on European politics or philosophy, finance or medicine, the arts or the law. A history of Europe at that time need not contain more than a passing reference to the existence of the Jews, individually or collectively.

By 1914 the intervening hundred years of Emancipation had shifted Jewish life from the periphery to the center of European society. Geographically, Jews were now heavily concentrated in the metropolises of Europe. Berlin, Vienna, Budapest, Warsaw—and to a lesser degree London, Paris, and Odessa—had a disproportionately high percentage of Jewish inhabitants, as did the major urban centers in America. And Jews had achieved a prominence far beyond their numbers in the intellectual life of these cities. Universities, academies, and schools drew larger and larger numbers of Jews into their activities. Jews had achieved important positions in journalism, literature, music, science, painting, philosophy, and psychology; the world of finance was replete with Jewish magnates; and revolutionary movements abounded with Jewish leaders—from Karl Marx, Moses Hess, and Ferdinand Lassalle to the prominent Jewish names among the Russian Social Revolutionaries and Social Democrats. A history of Europe at this time cannot be written without pointing to the Jewish presence. Jews may not have been as prominent as some anti-Semites would have liked to believe in the commanding heights of political and industrial power, but if they were not at the height of society, they certainly were at its center—and very visible. From a marginal community they had become the great beneficiaries of the Enlightenment, Emancipation, and the Industrial Revolution. All of this had been achieved in less than a hundred years.

If this was the general picture (and there were, of course, nuances), to what dilemma could Zionism then address itself and try to provide an answer? If the nineteenth century was so good to the Jews, why did it, for the first time, give rise to a movement that attempted to uproot the Jews from the continents in which they had resided, albeit precariously, for two thousand years?

In the nineteenth century there was still a Jewish problem and a very acute one. It was not merely economic. Nor was it a continuation of the dilemmas faced by Jews in gentile society in pre-1789 days. Rather, the problem, as it appeared to Jews and Gentiles alike, was a product of the Enlightenment and of Emancipation. It was a specifically modern problem, requiring modern and innovative answers, and Jews were unable to find a solution in the traditional mechanism of Jewish accommodation and quietism.

What the Enlightenment and secularization did to the Jews was to change their perception of themselves as well as how they were perceived by the non-Jewish communities. Prior to the Enlightenment and to the French Revolution, in a world in which the non-Jewish majority viewed itself as belonging to the *gens Christiana* or to the *Dar el-Islam*, the Jew was characterized by his different and nonconforming religious beliefs. Until the late eighteenth century, if a Christian were asked what distinguished him from a Jew, he would have answered in terms of religious beliefs and so would a Jew if asked to define what distinguished him from the majority society. Identity for an individual and a group was perceived in religious terms, and the Jewish distinctiveness was viewed by Jews and non-Jews alike in a religious context.

Religion also determined the status of the Jew: being what he was by virtue of his religious commitment, he naturally could not be part of the body politic, which was defined in religious terms. Since Christian society viewed its political organization as expressing the religious tenets of a *Christian* state, the Jew had to be excluded. He could, of course, be tolerated in the sense that most Christian societies in most periods allowed Jews freedom of worship: but the price for that toleration was apartness and clearly defined and legitimized discrimination. In a Christian state, a person who did not believe in Christ could not hold public office, could not exercise authority over Christians, could not enter into the feudal bond, and hence could not possess land. (In Muslim countries, with some notable exceptions, like Muslim Spain, the situation was more or less parallel: anyone who was not a Muslim was legitimately excluded from power and had to pay the special tax levied on non-Muslims.) For the Jew integration into a Christian society was equally undesirable: being in exile, living under a non-Jewish yoke, benevolent as it occasionally may have been, the Jew had no wish to be a member of a society whose basic tenets he repudiated. Individual Jews could, of course, adopt the majority religion and become members of the Christian—or Muslim—majority society and polity, and many did. But those who remained Jews—and in a deep sense this was voluntary, since conversion was open to all and was generally encouraged—also opted for the marginal status thus allocated to them and their coreligionists. The Jewish community, the *kehilla*, organizing the religious and social lives of these marginal men and women, became the quasi-political organization of this minority.

In this unequal and hierarchical equilibrium, Judaism was able to exist for almost two millennia. The basic principles of this equilibrium and the apartness of the Jews as a distinctive religious community were internalized by both Jews and Gentiles. Persecution, forced conversions, pogroms, burnings at the stake, and expulsions often shattered this balance. But the theological underpinnings of Christianity's attitude toward the Jews ultimately legitimized this tolerance based on discrimination—a tolerance very different from the modern, liberal concept based on equality of all.

It was this equilibrium, even with all its occasional and horrifying breakdowns, that enabled the Jews to survive in a basically hostile environment. It also enabled them to internalize their inferior status—legitimized in the Christian community through triumphalism and in the Jewish community through the theology of exile.

Enlightenment and the reverberations of the French Revolution throughout most of Europe disrupted this equilibrium. Secularization and liberalism opened European society for Jews as equals. For the first time since the destruction of the Temple, schools, universities, the public service, politics, and the professions were opened to Jews as *citizens*. Equality before the law and the relegation of religion to the realm of private concerns meant that the state no longer viewed itself as Christian but as encompassing every citizen regardless of his religious beliefs or lack of them. It was this revolution that catapulted the Jews in most European countries from their marginal and peripheral status in the early part of the nineteenth century to their central and salient positions toward the end of the century. It was the most tremendous revolution in the position of the Jews since Vespasian's times.

Yet it was precisely this opening up of non-Jewish society which created a completely novel set of dilemmas and problems for which the traditional framework of the *kehilla* was wholly inadequate, based as it was on the legitimized and mutually accepted separation and discrimination of the Jews in a Christian society.

The area of education illustrates this problem well. Before the Enlightenment, schooling in non-Jewish society was a clerical affair. Hence Jews would not attend schools that aimed at a Christian education. Christians would not have Jewish children (unless they were ready to convert), and Jews would not dream of sending their children to Christian schools. Thus the only formal education for Jewish children was that of the traditional Jewish religious school, the *heder* and the *yeshiva*. The incredible result of this parallel Jewish education before Emancipation was a male Jewish community that was the most literate community in Europe compared to any other identifiable group, though this literacy was in a language that had been ironically called dead—Hebrew.

With Emancipation Jewish parents could now send their children to the general schools which became secularized. No longer were they Christian schools, and religious education, insofar as it was offered, was just one subject among many others; and Jewish children could be excused from these classes or separate religious teaching could be offered to them. But this apparently reasonable, decent, and liberal solution left some very basic problems of identity. Since the state schools were obviously open on Saturday (Sunday continued to be the public day of rest even in a secularized Christian society), Jewish parents and pupils were immediately confronted with the problem of coping with an educational system that conflicted with Jewish tenets about the Sabbath. Should the child go to school on Saturday? Should he write on the Sabbath—something that is expressly forbidden in the Jewish tradition? What if there were exams on Saturday? And what about the Jewish holidays, which were of course not recognized or noticed by the school system? Thousands of separate answers to these dilemmas were given by Jewish parents and Jewish pupils. Some preferred not to send their children to schools that were open on Saturday; others advised their children not to write on Saturday or perhaps to write only if there were a very important exam. Still others combined a religious atmosphere at home—a Sabbath meal, candles, and no work—with their children going or being driven to school. What matters is not the individual solutions arrived at but the fact that the problems of Jewish identity had not been solved by liberalism and tolerance but, in a way, had been exacerbated. Being Jewish no longer meant a single, sometimes heroic, decision to stand by one's conviction and not succumb through conversion to majority pressure. Rather, it now became a series of innumerable daily decisions, bringing out the difference and distinction *within equality* in hundreds of individual decisions.

Going to university only multiplied the problems. The young person, now severed from the parental home, had to make decisions about such issues as joining a student fraternity or eating at a *mensa* which was not, of course, kosher. Again, individual decisions varied tremendously from strict abstention to convoluted modes of accommodation. But whatever the decision, it only served to underline the existence of a dilemma.

With the young person's entry into professional life, now open to the Jews, the problems continued to accumulate. If he opened a doctor's practice, he had to decide whether to have his clinic open on Saturday and the Jewish holidays, and if he shared a clinic with gentile associates the dilemma became even more acute. If he became a clerk in a bank or a state employee or a teacher in the public school system, he had to solve the same problem. The necessity—and desire—to socialize with gentile colleagues again brought up the question of kosher food.

These may appear to be trivial issues: they are certainly not the sort of concerns which agitate moral philosophers or theologians *ex cathedra*. But they were problems of daily behavior, lifestyle, identity, and self-respect. Whatever the answers given by any individual Jew, these were dilemmas that his forefathers in the ghettos had never had to confront. A whole new universe of problems, to which traditional mores had no answer, opened before the liberated, emancipated, and secularized Jews.[1]

To this specifically modern dilemma of identity in the context of liberalism must be added another set of predicaments brought about by nationalism. The forces unleashed by the French Revolution were not only those of liberalism and secularization but of nationalism as well. The modern, secularized, and educated Jew, shedding much of his particular characteristics, was nonetheless faced with the difficulty of relating to a non-Jewish society that, for all its general adherence to universalistic principles, was viewing its own identity in terms of national integration and cohesion. The religiously oriented self-perception of gentile society was not replaced by an undifferentiated, universalist fraternity but by a new identity distinguished by nationalism, ethnicity, a common language, and past history, either real or imagined. If people ceased to view themselves primarily as Christians and their neighbors as Jews in the religious sense, they began to view themselves as Frenchmen, Germans, Russians, Poles, Hungarians.

It was into this world of growing nationalism that the modern, emancipated Jew entered, only to be confronted with completely new dilemmas of identity, both internal and external. No Jewish person had wanted to enter the old Christian society as a Jew, but now that society was opened on a universalistic base. Still there remained the question whether the Jewish person could regard himself, and be regarded by others, as French or Polish or German. When French children learned in school that their ancestors were the Gauls, could a Jewish child truly identify with Vercingetorix, and would his schoolmates truly view him as a descendant of the ancient Gauls? Would German students really view a Jewish colleague as a true descendant of Arminius?

The inclusivism of the universalistic principles of the French Revolution was tempered everywhere by the historicist exclusivism of much of modern nationalism. What ultimately shocked Theodore Herzl during the Dreyfus affair was not just the virulent anti-Semitism that swept over so many sectors of French society. What appeared so scandalous to Herzl was the fact that here was a completely emancipated, successfully integrated, and largely secularized Jewish person. One could hardly be more chauvinistically French, more militaristic, and more "un-Jewish," in the stereotyped sense, than Captain Alfred Dreyfus. Yet when a suspicion of treason arose and one of the suspects turned out to be Dreyfus, the public consensus tended to say, "Well, of course, yes, it must be him; after all he is not really French, he is Jewish." Nothing could have been a graver blow to the promise of Emancipation and assimilation than this gut reaction: do whatever you wish; to us, true Frenchmen, true descendants of the ancient Gauls, you are just Judas.

This dilemma of identity could not even be solved by religious conversion. Much of modern nationalism relates to origins and is suffused with cultural determinism and racism. Yet even if these extremes are overlooked, the cultural problem facing the modern, secularized Jew became almost unbearable. It became especially acute in Eastern Europe, where most Jews were then living, precisely because in these areas national movements were competing with each other—and the Jews found themselves in the cross fire.

Imagine the problem of a modern, emancipated Jew in the mid-nineteenth century living in Lithuania. He has a son whom he wants to send to school for a general education, having himself transcended the confines of traditional Jewish religious upbringing. But to which school? Politically, the area is part of the czarist empire, hence the state school is a Russian school. But there is a sizeable Polish minority in Lithuania, dating back to the old Polish-Lithuanian Commonwealth, and the local Polish school extols these glories. There is also a significant German minority, and its *Gymnasium* offers the best in German education and consciousness. Also the awakening nationalism of the Lithuanian population is on the ascendant, with an emerging school system of its own. Not wanting to give his son a "Jewish" education, the father discovers that he is unable to give him a general or universal education either. His choice is between giving him a Russian, Polish, German, or Lithuanian particular education.

It is then not surprising that the first attempt to write a modern, secular yet biblical-historical novel in Hebrew emerged in Lithuania in the mid-nineteenth century out of this dilemma of identity and crosscurrents of contending nationalisms. If Poles and Lithuanians could delve into their history and forge their own modern, national identity on the anvil of the past, why could the Jews not follow this modern and liberating example?

The political movement of Zionism was preceded in Eastern Europe by a revival of the Hebrew language as a nonreligious, literary medium. Jews always used Hebrew in their prayers and religious writings, but this was a revival of Hebrew as a language of novels and poems, polemical articles, and journalistic feuilletons. This development was an anathema to the rabbis who saw in it a desecration of the Holy Tongue. The origins of this movement are found in ethnically mixed Lithuania and later in Galicia, where the German *Kultursprache* of the Austrian rulers contended with both Polish and Ukrainian (Ruthenian) nationalism. Secularized, modern Jews began to ask for the origins of their culture, for the roots of their history; to extol the glories of Jerusalem; to ask whether they should not look into their own past just as members of other groups were doing.

Thus both liberalism and nationalism created in these Jews the beginning of a new self-awareness, no longer determined by any religious terms but coeval to the emergence of modern, secular nationalism in Europe. The development of a modern Hebrew literature, that of Jewish *Haskala* (Enlightenment), was the first step in that direction. The political Zionism of Leo Pinsker, Theodore Herzl, and Max Nordau followed, and it is significant that in all these founders of modern Zionism there appears again and again the same phenomenon: they did not come from the traditional, religious background. They were all products of European education, imbued with the current ideas of the European intelligentsia. Their plight was neither economic nor religious: they responded—just like black leaders in America a century later—to the challenge of their identity, looking for roots, acquiring self-respect in a society which had uprooted them from their traditional, religious background and had not provided them and their likes with adequate answers for this quest.

Those Jews who were seeking just survival and economic security emigrated to America in the wake of pogroms and pauperization. Those who, on the other hand, went to Palestine did not just flee from pogroms nor were they bent on economic safety and success—Ottoman Palestine was hardly an economic paradise. They were seeking self-determination, identity, liberation within the terms of post-1789 European culture, and their own newly awakened self-consciousness.[2]

Zionism, then, is a post-Emancipation phenomenon. While drawing on a historical bond with the ancestral Land of Israel, it made into an active, historical-practical focus a symbol that had lain dormant, passive though potent, in the Jewish religious tradition. Jewish nationalism was then one specific aspect of the impact of the ideas and social structures unleashed by the French Revolution, modernism, and secularism. It was a response to the challenges of liberalism and nationalism much more than a response merely to anti-Semitism, and for this reason it could not have occurred at any period before the nineteenth and twentieth centuries.[3]

Zionism was the most fundamental revolution in Jewish life. It substituted a secular self-identity of the Jews as a nation for the traditional and Orthodox self-identity in religious terms. It changed a passive, quietistic, and pious hope of the Return to Zion into an effective social force, moving millions of people to Israel. It transformed a language relegated to mere religious usage into a modern, secular mode of intercourse of a nation-state.

Pious reiterations of the links of Jews to Palestine do not suffice to explain the emergence of Zionism when it did. Conversely, Zionism is not just a reaction of a people to persecution. It is the quest for self-determination and liberation under the modern conditions of secularization and liberalism. As such it is as much a part of the Jewish history of dispersion and return as of the universal history of liberation and the quest for self-identity.

CHAPTER 1

KROCHMAL: THE HEGELIANIZATION OF JEWISH HISTORY

NACHMAN KROCHMAL'S *THE GUIDE TO THE PERPLEXED OF OUR Time* (Moreh Nevuchei Ha-zman) is one of the first and most intriguing intellectual attempts to confront the problems of modern Jewish existence within a conceptual framework drawn from the dominant European philosophical traditions of the nineteenth century. The title of the book consciously evokes echoes of Maimonides's *Guide to the Perplexed,* and the parallel is obvious. Maimonides's great achievement was to integrate a rational understanding of Judaism into the dominant medieval Aristotelian tradition. Similarly, Krochmal wished to guide the perplexed of his generation by the light of idealist philosophy from Kant to Hegel. His aim was to try to answer the problems besetting the first Jewish generation after Emancipation by referring to the general philosophical *Zeitgeist.* He attempted to show that maintaining a Jewish identity did not necessarily contradict universal philosophical imperatives; on the contrary, he attempted to vindicate the validity of Judaism through idealist philosophy, in some cases referring to the traditional philosophical objections to Judaism. Trying to prove the validity and legitimacy of Judaism according to Hegelian principles was the main achievement of Krochmal's impressive volume.

Nachman Krochmal (1785–1840) was born in Galicia, then under the Hapsburgs, and until his early death he witnessed the vicissitudes that overtook this region in the wake of the Napoleonic wars. Living in an area where most people spoke Polish but where the *Kultursprache* was German, Krochmal wrote his philosophical treatise in Hebrew—one of the first attempts to adapt modern philosophical discourse to this language. The book was published posthumously in 1851, and if Hegel once boasted that he had taught philosophy to speak German, one can say that Krochmal taught Hegelian philosophy to speak Hebrew.[1]

Krochmal was a typical progeny of the first generation of emancipated Jews. From his traditional background he received his religious Jewish education, and through his own efforts he became acquainted with general culture, mainly German letters and philosophy. According to a biographical sketch, written in Hebrew by his disciple Meir Halevi Letteris, Krochmal studied "Hebrew, Arabic and Aramaic, German and French; he learned the history of many nations and studied the philosophy of Spinoza, Mendelssohn . . . Lessing and especially Kant . . . until he arrived at the magnificent scholars of our own age, mainly Schelling, Fichte and Hegel."[2]

The structure of Krochmal's *Guide* is indeed Hegelian. Human history is not conceived as a series of meaningless occurrences; there is a structure and a *telos* to history. Man is a social animal, and man's achievements are expressed in collective entities possessing a common denominator. Society, the nation (*uma*), are the subjects of history. History is the story of these cultural entities, and this heritage common to groups of human beings is what creates culture. Following Herder and Hegel, Krochmal calls these cultural entities *ruah ha-uma*, the spirit of the nation.

Judaism also has to be considered within such a historical understanding. Judaism should not be viewed, as Orthodox rabbinical thinking has it, as an unchanging and frozen entity, existing in its crystallized form from time immemorial, but as an outcome of an unending chain of events, embedded in world history.

True to the Hegelian meaning of *Volksgeist*, Krochmal views the spirit of a nation not as a mystical and irrational force but as the aggregate of specific qualities common to a given group of men which distinguish this group from others. It is the spiritual root common to the historical creativity of any given human group. According to Krochmal, the observer who looks into the differences between nations will discover a key or a code which characterizes all the institutions and cultural expressions of any given entity:

> Just like the individual spirit, so the spirit of a nation has specific traits in every single entity, and it can be discerned in all its acts. In arts and crafts, in customs and laws, in the education and upbringing of children, in the knowledge of the divine and in religious worship—in all its acts in peace and war, in all its periods and vicissitudes, a nation could always be distinguished and differentiated from other nations. It is nevertheless true that sometimes it is difficult—and much understanding would be necessary—to discover the relationship between these spiritual phenomena, their value and their interconnections.[3]

Like Herder, Krochmal sees three stages in the development of all nations: growth, great historical achievement, and decline. These stages are linked dialectically with each other: out of a nation's struggles during its time of growth there emerges its historical significance in its apotheosis, and it is the elements of its power that bring about its internal corruption and decline, for "when splendour and glory abound in a nation, the love of luxury develops and art will be subjugated to mere sensual stimuli."[4] Thus it happens that every nation goes through a period of grandeur to be followed by decline and disintegration.

Yet the specific contribution of each nation becomes integrated into the totality of world history and lives on as the universal heritage of mankind even after the disappearance of a nation. Again following Hegel, Krochmal maintains that despite the disappearance of the Greeks and the Romans from the historical stage, their contributions persist. Greece endowed mankind with the aesthetic spirit, while Rome bequeathed a political and juridical tradition. Thus, while individual *Volksgeister* disappear, their contributions persist within the universal *Weltgeist*. Dialectically, every *Volksgeist* is thus only a moment in the ever-unfolding *Weltgeist*, itself an expression of the Absolute Spirit. This is the dialectical synthesis of the particular and the universal in the Hegelian tradition. National culture is not an end unto itself but only a step in the development of universal culture, and the mounting series of national cultures expresses also a mounting order of an ever-widening universality—from the *polis* in its closeness and apartness to the modern world with its universalistic structures and content.

The Jews are seen by Krochmal as a nation, as one of the many nations that contributed the world history. However, their historical existence spans much of known world history; while other nations have appeared on the world stage, made their contribution, and taken their bow and disappeared, the Jews continue to exist. Does this need a special explanation, or are the Jews, as the Orthodox rabbinical tradition maintains, living completely outside history, a nation unto itself, untouched by world history and thus also uncontaminated by it?

Krochmal rejects the Orthodox view. To him, the Jewish national spirit has characteristics similar to those of other national spirits, "a nation among the nations." Yet the question persists: why did the Jews not disappear like the ancient Egyptians and the Persians, like the Greeks and the Romans? The question goes back to Hegel himself. Both Herder and Hegel viewed the Jews as a nation, a *Volk*, not as a mere religious community. Yet Hegel's view allocated to the Jews a role described in terms of the historical past, and ultimately he did not give an adequate answer to the survival of the Jews into present times.

Krochmal develops his philosophy of history by going back to what Hegel said about the Jewish contribution to history, and out of it he develops his own, rather startling, synthesis of Judaism and Hegelianism. According to Hegel, the Jewish people introduced the concept of monotheism and made this belief in one God a historical reality. The chosenness and holiness of the Jewish people was the political and historical actualization of the idea of monotheism, and its objective historical reality was expressed in the notion of a Holy Nation, a people of priests.[5]

Yet, according to Hegel, this monotheism was still bound by the particular historical limitations of the Jewish people and did not have any impact outside its own very restricted boundaries. Moreover, because the monotheistic idea was so novel, it did not become implanted immediately in the active consciousness of the people of Israel—hence the frequent lapses, during the period of the Judges and Kings of the First Commonwealth, back into paganism. This tenuous and precarious monotheism therefore had to be buttressed and sustained by an intricate structure of rigid and formalistic legislation. The Mosaic code, with its numerous formalistic and highly technical commandments, was intended to serve as a substitute for the lack of real belief.

Hegel thus maintained that Jewish monotheism needed a complement that would both take it out of its particular attachment to the Jewish people as well as emancipate it from the thralldom of the Mosaic code and turn it into a creed based on internal, subjective conviction, not on external codification. This was, according to Hegel, what Jesus did. He emancipated Jewish monotheism from its tribal attachment to the Jewish people and turned it into a world religion. By anchoring it in the subjective belief of the individual soul he freed it from a crushing obedience to the formalistic Mosaic code.

It is at this turning point, when Judaism became—through its offspring, Christianity—a world religion, that Hegel also placed dialectically the end of historical Judaism. Once Israelite monotheism became, via Christianity, open to the whole of mankind, a separate and distinct existence of the Jewish people lost its justification. The rationale for the existence of the people of Israel was in its separation and apartness from a world of paganism. Now that the message of monotheism had been universalized through Christianity, what justification could there be for this distinctiveness? The New Testament, complementing the Old Testament, made the separate existence of the Jewish people superfluous. According to Hegel's dialectical reasoning, the victory of Jewish monotheism in the form of Christianity eliminated the raison d'être for the historical carrier of this idea—the people of Israel. Once the Jewish people had achieved its mission on a universal scale, *it* had to disappear from the historical scene as the Greeks and the Romans disappeared after their contributions had been integrated into the course of world history.

Here Krochmal discovers a problem which had faced Hegel and which he had been unable to solve. Anyone following Hegel's argument up to this point would have to deduce from it that the Jews did indeed disappear from the historical scene after the emergence of Christianity. However, unlike the Greeks and the Romans, the Jews did *not* disappear from history. In fact they continued to survive under extremely difficult conditions. Neither the Greeks nor the Romans had their political structures destroyed in a way similar to what had befallen the Jews with the destruction of their Temple. Yet despite losing every shred of political autonomy, having their holy places devastated, and being exiled from their country, the Jews continued to exist for two millennia. Traditional

Christian theology could, perhaps, find some explanation and even justification for the continued existence of the Jewish people even after the Jews rejected Jesus; yet for someone like Hegel, who viewed history as a succession of peoples contributing to world history and then disappearing, the continued existence of the Jews *after* making their historical contribution did pose a serious philosophical question.

Hegel had no answer to this problem. Krochmal suggests that if the whole Hegelian schema of world history has validity, it cannot overlook such a conspicuous case of a people not fitting into its overall pattern. Either this exception is an indication of a serious flaw in the whole argument, or there is need to supplement the general pattern by some special explanations about the deviation of the course of Jewish history.

Here Krochmal uses Hegel's own theories to refute him while constructing his argument within the Hegelian framework itself. Krochmal concurs with Hegel that the Jewish contribution to world history has been the idea of monotheism, yet he develops this idea in an original way. While all the contributions of other nations to world history have been of a *particular* nature, the Jewish contribution has been of a *universal* nature. The Greek contribution in the field of aesthetics, like the Roman contribution in the field of statecraft, basically relates to the world of externalities and, hence, is particular. The Jewish contribution of monotheism directly relates to the Absolute Spirit, which is the content of history itself. Thus the Jewish contribution is not bound by time and space because it is itself absolute and universal and not subject to the ebb and flow of historical development. The content of Judaism is therefore equal to the content of philosophy—the Idea—and this is the reason for the ability of the Jews to transcend time and place.

Like Hegel, Krochmal maintains that all religions try to confront the Absolute. Primitive religion tries to do it in an undifferentiated form, and only historical development brings forth more complex and more adequate expressions of this idea:

> You should know that all religion is grounded in the spiritual realm, so that even the basest religion of savages is not related to something material, which is particular, finite and perishable, but is ultimately related to its sustaining power: and this transcends the ephemeral changes of the particular and is universal and infinite. . . .
> [All nations have therefore spiritual elements in their religion,] yet they could not transcend particular spiritualities [and identify

them] with what is still particular, related to time and space, and therefore transient. These nations have not yet reached the truly universal, which has actuality in the Absolute Spirit: this is pure reason and cannot have an external form. . . .[6]

Only in Jewish monotheism is this spirituality, which is found in every religion but is still imprisoned within particularism, raised to the level of universality. Since the material and the particular are transient by their very nature, the nations which introduced such particular spiritualities (like the Greek and the Roman) disappeared in the course of history, whereas the bearer of Absolute Spirit, the people of Israel, can transcend the temporality of history:

> Such is the case with all nations whose spirituality is particular and hence finite and perishable. But in the case of our nation, though we too are subject to the laws of [finite] nature with regard to material aspects and sensuous externalities . . . our universal spirituality saves us from perishing. . . .[7]

Jewish history, because of its universal content, is thus different from other histories. Krochmal discovers in it not only the three stages of the historical development of all nations but also a cyclical pattern *in which the three stages are repeated again and again in every cycle.* Every time the third stage arrives, the Jews, rather than disintegrating and disappearing, start a new cycle and like the legendary phoenix, proceed again to a new first stage.

Jewish history appears, therefore, to Krochmal not as linear but as cyclical, and most of the second part of his *Guide* is dedicated to this dialectical periodization of Jewish history. Krochmal discerns three cycles in Jewish history, and each cycle encompasses within itself the three stages of youth, maturity, and decline that characterize all historical development. Jewish history in that way is the meeting point of the temporal and the transcendental, the finite and the infinite, the historical expression of the Absolute Spirit.

Krochmal's three cycles in Jewish history are (1) from Abraham to the destruction of the First Temple; (2) from the Return from Babylon through the destruction of the Second Temple to the death of Rabbi Akiva and the fall of Betar during Bar-Kochba's revolt against the Romans; and (3) from the composition of the Mishnah until the 1648–49 pogroms of Chmielnicki in the Ukraine. Since then, a new era has begun, heralded by the Enlightenment and Emancipation. What characterizes this periodization, true to the Hegelian tradition, is the rise and decline of *political* structures among the Jews. This is a highly politicized and national periodization of history, and Krochmal is the first Jewish modern thinker not only to propose an outline of Jewish history but also to make political criteria into the cornerstones of its structure. With minor modifications, Krochmal's construction of Jewish history would remain intact in later generations and would constantly accompany the Jewish national renaissance.

Krochmal's tour de force is intellectually brilliant and stimulating. He takes Hegel and judges him by his own criteria and finds him wanting in supplying a satisfactory answer to the survival of the Jewish people beyond the moment at which its contribution had been integrated into world history. The question is asked, and the answer proposed in Hegelian terms but through an internal *Aufhebung* of the qualities attributed by Hegel to the Jews. If Hegel viewed the Jews as having made a significant contribution to world history in the past, and in the past alone, and their continued existence remains for him an inexplicable aberration, Krochmal needs to prove the absolute essence of Judaism. While Hegel and the Left Hegelians could thus criticize the continued existence of the Jews as being particularistic and hence irrational and superfluous, in Krochmal's writings *the Jews themselves appear as the bearers of absolute universality.* The Jews, not the nations of the world, are truly universal; it is the Gentiles who are particularistic. For Krochmal, the people of Israel is elevated to the only historical phenomenon which is simultaneously metahistorical. Hence the very historical existence of the Jewish people, far from being an anachronism and an aberration, is itself of philosophical significance. The people of Israel link the eternal and the temporal, the philosophical and the historical. The roots of the Jewish people are, like those of all other people, in history, yet its *telos* transcends the temporalities and externalities of mere historical existence. The Jewish people is hence *am olam*—in the double meaning of the term—a universal as well as an eternal people.

The attribution of Hegelian qualities to the Jewish people thus becomes a key to Krochmal's restructuring of Hegel's own philosophy of history. It is not the gentile peoples, who reached their hegemony through material, terrestrial, and temporal means, who are the bearers of true universality: each of these world historical nations (*welthistorische Völker*) is transient. Only the Jewish people, whose power is the power of the spirit, is truly universal. Hence it could survive without political power, without a state. In the spirituality and continued existence of the Jewish people, the Absolute Spirit of Hegelian philosophy finds its true subject. The Jews are thus not to be seen as a historical quirk, drawing out their existence through mere stubbornness generations and millennia after their role has been exhausted; they have an eternal universal *telos* in the realm of the Absolute Spirit.

Such a Hegelianization of Jewish history, carried out through a dialectical *Aufhebung* of certain elements of Hegel's philosophy itself, is, undoubtedly, a highly original intellectual breakthrough in the Jewish self-consciousness in the era after the French Revolution. This integration of Jewish history into a revised reading of Hegel's philosophy of history, whose subjects are nations and their cultures (*Volksgeister*), views Jewish history as the history of a nation, not of a mere religious community. Hence there can be a Hegelian legitimacy to writing Jewish history, while no such legitimacy could be found for writing Christian history as such. In the emerging world of nations, Krochmal gives a universal significance to Jewish history much the same as Alexander Herzen did to Russian history. In this way Krochmal was one of the first to answer the problems of Jewish identity in a community of nations and to give that particular answer its universal dimensions.

CHAPTER 2

Graetz: Revolutionizing Jewish Historical Consciousness

EVERY NATIONAL MOVEMENT IN EUROPE WAS ACCOMPANIED—or even preceded—by the emergence of a new and revolutionary historical consciousness, through which the new or renascent nation expressed its self-awareness and its new image. A call for a national future was always voiced in the context of the discovery of a historical past or its reinterpretation. Hence the emergence of historical writing in the post-1789 era was a constant accompaniment to the rising nationalism.[1] Heinrich Graetz (1817–1891) was the most influential among Jewish writers in carrying out this historiographical revolution in Jewish thinking.

Like Krochmal before him, Graetz came from a border area between German and Polish cultures. He was born in the Posen (Poznan) district, which was then under Prussian rule and was similar to Galicia, where Krochmal was born, in its linguistic and cultural pluralism and the clash between two national entities. Between 1853 and 1876 he published eleven volumes of his *Geschichte der Juden von den ältesten Zeiten bis auf die Gegenwart* (History of the Jews from the Earliest Time to the Present),[2] in which he proclaims that Jewish history is free from theology and is to be judged according to general historical laws. More than any other piece of writing Graetz's work contributed to the emergence of a worldview of the Jews as a nation and Jewish history as a national history. No longer is Judaism considered an unchanging, dogmatic religious structure, as maintained by Orthodoxy, nor is it conceived as a religious community merely possessing a moral and spiritual vision, as claimed by the Reform movement. To Graetz, the Jews are a nation, possessing a historical continuity and a story unfolding in time and place, undergoing changes and transformations like all other nations.

The two major influences evident in Graetz are the Hegelian philosophical legacy combined with the tradition of German historical writing, mainly identified with Leopold Ranke. Just as these two traditions greatly influenced and enhanced most Central and East European national movements, so their impact can be traced in Graetz's work. Like Krochmal before him, Graetz derives his view of history as an unfolding structure from Hegel, and hence he considers the course of Jewish history as successive dialectical stages of Judaism's own awareness of its spiritual contents. From Ranke he derives the necessity to place historical developments into a meaningful structure. As in Ranke, the need to write "objective," detached history (*wie es eigentlich gewesen ist*) becomes itself a polemical enterprise. All historical writing is ultimately polemical—be it the Whig interpretation of history or Rankean research-oriented historiography—and Graetz's monumental historical effort is no exception.

What Krochmal tried to do in a philosophical context and in Hebrew—in his period still an outlandish medium—Graetz attempted to do in a much more popular vein in German, the *Kultursprache* of educated Jews in Central and Eastern Europe. Within a short time, his work was translated into most European languages spoken by Jews, and his book truly transformed the image Jews had of their own history. When the political Zionism of Herzl appeared at the turn of the century, the view of Jews as a nation among nations and not a mere religious community, had already been implanted mainly through Graetz's writings among many educated Jews.

Graetz expresses his view of history in a short essay published in 1846 called "Die Konstruction der jüdischen Geschichte,"[3] and from this essay follow the theoretical foundations which would guide him through his decades of work on the multivolume *History of the Jews*.

Graetz opens his essay with an attack on some of the dominant schools of thought then prevalent among educated Jews in Germany. Each of these schools tries to present Judaism as a religion characterized by definite content. For example, Judaism is presented in one as a rational religion, in another a religion of divine revelation. According to Graetz, all these schools are right—but not exclusively, only if they are presented as different moments in the continuous unfolding of the principle of Judaism in history. To Graetz, Judaism should not be explicated through any particular texts but through the concrete historical behavior of the Jewish people over time. Judaism, like any other human phenomenon, should be perceived only through the *totality* of its historical praxis and not through any single doctrinal moment of its teachings.

Following his Hegelian premises, Graetz does think that Judaism has a central idea, but this is not an abstract or merely hortatory idea of a moral desideratum. It can be grasped only through its historical manifestations, and mere biblical or talmudic quotations will not suffice to bring out this efficacy. "Every vital idea must create for itself a solid existence. It must work itself out of the monotonous, dormant state of the ideal into the changing, turbulent world of reality. Thus, history is not only the reflection of the idea but also the test of its power."[4] The historical forms are the moments of the idea turned concrete; hence historical study is also philosophical enquiry.

In trying to identify this central idea of Judaism that is evident in its historical development, Graetz echoes the general revolutionary climate of his time as well as some specific elements of the *Sturm und Drang* ambience in Germany. According to Graetz, at the moment Judaism entered history, it appeared as a protest, a negative force, a revolt against paganism; and this revolt is considered by Graetz the main historical characteristic of Judaism. In an excursus that still retains much of its freshness, Graetz describes paganism as the cult of Nature, while Judaism appears as the Spirit, the antithesis of Nature, and hence represents a more developed phase of historical development (again, the Hegelian overtones are evident). Pagans, according to Graetz, saw Nature in its broader meaning as an immanent force acting out of its own power. Even among the Greeks, with their sublimated notion of nature, "god remains forever idealized nature, even in its highest stage of development where it is stripped of every animal and plant form and becomes humanized."[5] The Olympian gods remain, just like ordinary mortals, subservient to the blind force of Tyche, the goddess of fortune. In such a context, there exists no moral freedom since there is no choice. Human praxis, be it good or bad, is perceived as a natural necessity, preordained by fate. In such an amoral world, there exists only tragedy, where there is no relation between crime and punishment, only the unredeemable human involvement in a fate over which no one has any control and from whose furies no one, be he man or god, can escape.

To Graetz Judaism is the exact obverse of this relation. The divine and the natural are separated, and nature becomes an *object* of divine activity; nature is even considered as being created by God *ex nihilo*. God is omnipotent and is not himself ruled by nature. It is before God that man is responsible for his actions. Judaism thus signifies man's emancipation from matter, and it is only with the emergence of Judaism that human moral responsibility becomes a possibility.

Paganism is thus an immanent religion of nature, Judaism a spiritual religion of the transcendental. Pagan art is consequently also steeped in nature, and this is expressed in its being mainly figurative art, whereas Jewish art is poetic, verbal. Pagan man *sees* the deity in natural, physical form and molds it accordingly, whereas in Judaism one *hears* God. He appears as being mediated through consciousness and spirit.

Up to this point, Graetz follows Krochmal and Hegel in seeing monotheism as the central Jewish contribution to world history. But this, to Graetz, is only the negative element in Judaism, the element of revolt and protest. For Judaism did not stop at this negative moment—monotheism as the negation of paganism—but also tried to realize positively the idea of God in historical reality by anchoring it in a concrete, historical subject. The negation of paganism is not an abstract idea floating in thin air, but it has to have an actuality on the level of historical praxis. This, then, is, to Graetz, the role of the people of Israel as a political structure whose content is defined by the monotheistic belief. According to him, "Thus the concept of an extramundane God does not hover in the ethereal region of thought, but creates for itself a living people: an adequate political constitution must serve as the living carrier of this idea."[6]

The conventional thinkers of the Jewish Enlightenment in Germany always tried to dissociate themselves from the traditional

Christian—or secularized Christian—accusation that Judaism is a theocracy. To Graetz, however, Judaism is truly theocratic in the sense that religious precepts underlie normative social behavior. Scandalizing the most cherished views of Reform Judaism, Graetz maintains that "Judaism is not a religion for the individual, but for the community, and the promises and rewards attached to the fulfillment of commandments do not refer to the individual . . . but rather are apparently intended for the entire people."[7] Judaism is not a religion of personal salvation. The idea of the immortality of the individual soul, Graetz maintains, is alien to Judaism and was introduced into postbiblical Judaism mainly under Greek influence. Judaism is characterized by its *public* nature, unlike Christianity, which views itself as a religion of personal salvation:

> Judaism does not promise any other-worldly happiness for faithfulness. Immortality is not its concern; the survival of the soul has as little place in Judaism as the dogma of transubstantiation, and who knows whether this deficiency is not precisely its strength. . . .
> Knowledge of God and social welfare, religious truth and political theory form the two components of Judaism which are destined to flow through history thoroughly mixed. The dogmatic and the social, or to put it another way, the religious and the political, constitute the twin axes around which Jewish life revolves.[8]

Judaism is then a religion intertwined with politics, and, therefore, Graetz maintains, there is a Jewish history while strictly speaking there can be no Christian history. While so many of the efforts of the first Reformers, following Moses Mendelssohn, were to deny this public nature of Judaism and thus also exculpate Judaism from the frequently voiced accusation of being a state within a state, Graetz proclaims exactly the opposite. By claiming that Judaism is inherently public and political and the Jewish people its subject, he also places Judaism squarely in the historical, not merely the religious, realm. It is, in Hegelian parlance, necessarily involved in the "Objective Spirit," possesses political and legal institutions, has a national infrastructure, and requires self-government. Judaism has both a religious and a social aspect, it is Church and State interwoven into one community. The existence of every individual Jew is premised upon the existence of a Community of Jews (*Klal Yisrael*), which views itself publicly as Jewish.

The historical subject of Judaism, then, is not only the religious consciousness of the individual Jewish person. In order to realize Judaism on the level of historical praxis, it needs concrete and

actual manifestations. Judaism is not only rules and regulations—
as it is sometimes viewed by Christianity—it is also the historical
context for the realization of these regulations, and this leads
Graetz to focus on the political and geographical aspects of Judaism, that is, the Jewish people and the Land of Israel. If the Law
is the spirit of Judaism, and the Jewish people its historical subject, it also needs a material foundation, the Land. Consequently
Graetz posits a theoretical and historical unity of the components
of Judaism, and if this idea of a triad owes much to the Christian
concept of the Trinity, the components are certainly of a very different nature.

The Torah, the nation of Israel, and the Holy Land stand, one
might say, in a mystical relationship to each other; they are insepa-
rably united by an invisible bond.[9]

Graetz thus sees Judaism not only as a national phenomenon
but also as being inextricably bound to the Land of Israel—again,
in total opposition to the prevalent views of the Reform movement, which tried to sever any relation to Palestine and to the
messianic dreams of Jewish statehood. While the Reform movement argued most forcefully that Jewish survival in the Diaspora
should be considered proof for the marginality of the political
element in Judaism and should suggest that Judaism can truly
exist outside the realm of politics, Graetz argues with equal force
that "Judaism without the firm soil of national life resembles an
inwardly hollowed-out and half-uprooted tree, which still produces
foliage at the top but is no longer capable of sprouting twigs and
branches."[10]

Graetz thus takes a unique position between Orthodoxy and
Reform. While rejecting the ahistorical and self-enclosed view of
Orthodoxy, he feels that Reform was trying to mold Judaism in the
image of the post-Christian era, whose whole imagery has been
derived from Christianity itself. According to Graetz, the theology
of Reform Judaism results in an equally ahistorical image of Judaism as that of Orthodoxy, with one significant distinction: Reform
divorced Judaism from its concrete, historical subject, the Jewish
people, and substituted for it an undifferentiated and abstract
universalism:

> You may subject Judaism to a process of refinement, extract modern
> thoughts from the fullness of its contents and trumpet forth this
> essence as the heart of Judaism with stupefying, resonant phrases
> and brilliant cliches; you may build a church and accept a creed

for this refined and idealized Judaism "in a nutshell"; nevertheless, you still will have embraced a shadow and taken the dry shell for the succulent fruit. You possess neither the Judaism taught by the Bible in unambiguous terms, nor the Judaism molded by three thousand years of history, nor, finally, Judaism as it still lives in the consciousness of the majority of its adherents.[11]

To this Graetz adds another element. Unlike other religions, Judaism is also characterized by the special emphasis it puts on the future as an essential moment of its own self-consciousness. In the Jewish tradition, the Patriarchs are perceived as living not so much in the historical context of their own period but from the very beginning of God's Covenant with Abraham they are directed toward, and motivated by, the future of their progeny. This future dimension, Graetz maintains, is also connected with the Land of Israel, and the Patriarchs, who traversed Canaan from one end to the other related to the land, not as it was then, inhabited by alien and pagan people, but as it figured in their imagination of the future. In the Egyptian Exile as well as in the wanderings of the Israelites in the desert, this future dimension was actual and vivid and part of the self-awareness of the people as it became crystallized and directed toward what was considered to be the Promised Land. Most Mosaic legislation, though promulgated according to Jewish tradition by Moses in the desert, was directed toward the future life in Canaan. Graetz also points out that prophecy, that unique intellectual phenomenon within Judaism, is also future oriented.[12]

Because of this future-oriented element in Jewish life, which remained always connected with Palestine, the Jews managed to survive in the Diaspora even after the destruction of the Temple and the disappearance of any significant remnants of the Jewish population in the Land of Israel. These future-oriented beliefs, connected as they were with the Land, were nothing new for the people of Israel but were a continuation of a previous tradition. "Against all the laws of history," the people of Israel had succeeded in the distant past to forge for itself a distinct identity in the desert, even *before* entering the Land. Similarly, after the destruction and the dispersion, it maintained its identity outside its homeland through its belief in the future redemption.

It is evident that Graetz is trying here to find an adequate answer to one of the more vexing questions faced by any writer dealing with the problems of Jewish history in the context of comparative or universal history: the continued existence of a Jewish entity even after the destruction of the Temple. With the emergence of modern nationalism, a historian like Graetz, trained in the method of modern historical research, could not overlook the fact that Jewish history bears evidence of a number of unusual features: how did the Jews succeed in maintaining their identity even after being uprooted from their ancestral land and having lost all vestiges of political power? This same question which confronted Krochmal demands an adequate answer in terms of comparative history.

A traditional Jewish thinker, wholly immersed in the self-enclosed Jewish world, would not have to look for a universally valid answer; but a writer like Graetz, trying to place Jewish history in the context of world history, could not overlook the comparative element. Hence the centrality, for Graetz, of the future in Jewish historical consciousness as the key for the survival of Jewish identity. Graetz's focusing on the future dimension as central to the self-consciousness of the Jewish people is another aspect of his polemic against the Reform movement, which tried to minimize the ultimate messianic future and the Return to Zion by translating it into a contemporary, continuous messianic mission borne by the Jews. For Graetz, on the other hand, the future dimension and the Return to Zion are inextricably bound together.

Graetz posits, then, two poles around which Jewish historical existence has always revolved: the political and the religious. He also maintains that in different periods of Jewish historical development one of these two elements was more dominant than the other. During the biblical period of the First Commonwealth, the political element was, according to Graetz, dominant: the Israelites possessed an independent kingdom (or even two kingdoms, Judea and Israel), while the depth of religious observance was still rather shallow. During the time of the Second Commonwealth, after the return from the Babylonian Exile, the religious element became more dominant: during most of this period, the Jewish community around Jerusalem did not enjoy political independence but found itself under the successive rule of the Persians, the Ptolomies, the Seleucids, and finally the Romans. At the same time, religious life was being intensified and greatly enhanced, and normative Judaism, as we know it, owed its historical crystallization to that period. When a political revolt did occur, during the Seleucids, a revolution which led to the establishment of an independent Jewish state, its roots were mainly in the religious realm.

Because of these differences between the major forces during the First and Second Commonwealth, the historical heroes of each period were of a different nature. During the First Commonwealth the heroes were military leaders, judges, and kings, whereas the historical heroes of the Second Commonwealth were pious and learned men, rabbis, teachers of the Law, and members of various religious sects—Sadducees, Pharisees, Essenes.

Yet despite the fact that during each of these two distinct periods either the political or religious element was dominant, neither was wholly separated from the other. The Davidic and Solomonic kingdom attempted to forge a national unity for all Israelites around religious symbols, and the prophets set out on their historical enterprise, which was to culminate only during the Second Commonwealth, toward the end of the first period. On the other hand, the political element appeared during the Second Commonwealth in the Hasmonean dynasty, which began as a family of high priests but eventually emerged as a full-fledged royal dynasty.

Ultimately Judaism evolved into what Graetz sees as an organic synthesis of both elements; yet this synthesis is not a given, and to Graetz it has not yet evolved into a historical praxis but is posited in the future. This is the idea of messianism, which Graetz sees as the ideal integration of the religious and the political. Since messianism is basic to the understanding of Judaism as a historical phenomenon, and since it has not yet occurred but is still projected into the future, the future dimension assumes, according to Graetz, further centrality for Judaism. Other religions define their identity mainly through past occurrences—the Crucifixion, Allah's revelation to Mohammed, et cetera. In Judaism, on the other hand, while there exist past revelations, like Abraham's Covenant and Sinai, the apotheosis is fully future oriented:

> The fusion of the religious and the political, the union of a transcendant God-idea with a political life must become, in Judaism, a reality, even though both these forces in another sphere might give rise to constant friction and struggle or even appear to be irreconcilable. The naturalness of social life with its higher and lower aspects should be borne and illuminated by the idea of God. The vision of a political life conducted within the framework of Jewish institutions remains the distant ideal of Judaism; the Messiah as envisioned by the prophets, transmitted by the tradition, and embraced by the consciousness of the Jewish people, is the capstone of Judaism.[13]

Graetz's *History of the Jews* opens with the entry of the Israelites under Joshua into Canaan. This is the starting point of Jewish history; what preceded it is merely a prolegomenon, since history is what is actual and active, and what is active is the political. For this reason Graetz focuses in his discussion on the historical books of the Bible (Joshua, Judges, Samuel, Kings) rather than on the Pentateuch: it is the historical and political which counts, not the doctrinal or dogmatic. The history of the Jewish people in its land and its messianic future are the twin aspects of Jewish existence brought into relief by Graetz's historical writings.

After his theoretical preface, Graetz's *The Structure of Jewish History* launches into a short discourse on the stages of Jewish historical development. The central ideas discussed by him there, and later greatly developed in his large *History of the Jews*, were responsible for the emergence of the new historical images that became prevalent and dominant among educated, secularized Jews in the nineteenth century. While traditional Orthodox Judaism never cared too much for the Judges, for example, these biblical persons were being revitalized by Graetz and molded by him in the image of classical, semimythological heroes. In the age of heroic romanticism, Samson, Jephthah, and Gideon as well as Theseus and Odysseus were becoming new foci for adulation and emulation. Yet none of these Judges, Graetz points out, was more than a sporadic explosion of primeval energy, and hence not one of them succeeded in establishing a dynasty.

In this schematic overview of Jewish history, David appears, according to Graetz, as the first integration, albeit an undifferentiated one, of the religious and political elements. Here is a king who was a fighter and a poet, and despite the fact that the politically unified realm forged by him did not outlive his son Solomon, David's kingdom would always remain in the national consciousness as the idealized model for that future Jewish messianic vision: the Messiah, in the Jewish tradition, will always be hailed as the Son of David. Yet all through the First Commonwealth the pagan element would still subsist in national consciousness alongside the monotheistic cult, and only during the Babylonian Exile, when the people would be uprooted from the natural element of its existence—the land—did the pagan element disappear completely. With the Return from the Exile, under Ezra and Nehemiah, Jewish faith became distilled from its political element. The Maccabean Revolt is seen by Graetz in a concrete religious context. Yet echoing nineteenth-century ideas of national liberation, Graetz presents Judah the Maccabee and his brethren as models of national liberation heroes, and the Maccabean Revolt assumes universal dimension as a rebellion against the crude materialism of Seleucid pagan society. In the conflict between the Sadducees and Pharisees Graetz again sees the confrontation between the political and the religious elements in Judaism, and with the disappearance of the Hasmonean Kingdom and the destruction of the Second Temple by the Romans, the religious, Pharisaic element obviously became once again the dominant element in Judaism.

Graetz's attitude toward Jesus is highly interesting—a difficult intellectual test for any Jewish thinker in the nineteenth century. On the one hand, Graetz describes the emergence of Jesus in the general context of the Jewish expectation for salvation, caused by the despair over the disintegration of the Hasmonean Kingdom and the political subservience to Rome. In this sense Jesus was not unique, and Graetz mentions the emergence of similar leaders at that time within the same atmosphere of religious and political ferment. Yet at the same time Graetz gives a highly original interpretation for the reasons of Jesus's rejection by most Jews in his time. To Graetz, this disappointment was caused precisely by the reasons which, to the Christians, became the cornerstone of his message. When Jesus said that his kingdom was not of this world but was intended to be the Kingdom of Heaven, he disappointed the Jewish masses. "The people were expecting a Messiah who should carry them further into Judaism rather than out of it and who, at the same time, *would rejuvenate and strengthen the decaying state*" [italics added].[14] Since the messianic belief in Judaism is the ideal expression of the synthesis of the religious and the political, the apolitical and purely spiritual nature of Jesus's message did not address itself to the concrete expectations of his generation. He obviously and explicitly rejected one of the central elements of Jewish existence—the political moment. For this Jesus was ultimately rejected by the Jews.

Like Krochmal, Graetz also takes issue with conventional Christian historiography which loses all interest in Judaism after the destruction of the Second Temple. A Christian theology, even secularized, would obviously view Judaism after Exile as marginal to world history, yet Graetz maintains that it was after Judaism was exiled from its land that some of its major developments took place. It was precisely in Exile that Judaism evinced a most profound vitality and creativity, whose high intensity was probably necessary as a compensation for the lack of an immediate, terrestrial base. Contrary to the conventional Christian view, Judaism was far from becoming petrified in Exile; it rose to new heights of self-awareness. In the Hegelian sense of the term, Graetz sees the development of Judaism in the Diaspora as the discovery of Jewish self-consciousness. Judaism in Exile was an attempt to create a theoretical edifice for preserving the communal and collective existence of the Jews.

According to Graetz, the Talmud is the instrument forged by Judaism in Exile in order to preserve its existence. Unlike both the Jewish Enlightenment and the Reform movement, which were generally ill at ease with the Talmud, Graetz welcomes it not for its content, which he occasionally criticizes rather harshly, but for its role in preserving the Jews' apartness from their surrounding world, thus ensuring their continuing survival and Return to the Land of Israel. According to Graetz, the somewhat xenophobic and ethnocentric precepts of the Talmud have to be understood in that context:

> The same function which the natural borders of Palestine—the high Lebanon in the north, the sandy deserts of the east and south, and the partial ocean border of the west—had served, namely, to cut off the Holy Land from too close contact with the polytheistic world, was now served by the protective measures of the Talmud. These talmudic injunctions turn every Jewish house, anywhere in the world, into a precisely defined Palestine. . . .[15]

For the same reasons Graetz, in his account of medieval Jewish thinkers, tends to prefer Judah Halevi over Saadia Gaon and Maimonides. Graetz greatly appreciates the enormous intellectual achievement of Maimonides in integrating Aristotelian philosophy into Judaism. At the same time he does not feel that the "rational laws" of Saadia Gaon's and Maimonides's theology are the essence of Judaism, which, according to Graetz, is much better expressed in the messianic beliefs of Judah Halevi's writings. In his *Kuzari*, written in the form of a Platonic dialogue, Judah Halevi had shown how the Exile had severed the essential links between Jewish Law, the People of Israel, and the Land of Israel. Only with the coming of the Messiah would these links be reestablished so that the divine idea could again be reflected in the Jewish people but on a higher level, having now been distilled through Exile and suffering. Of Judah Halevi, Graetz observes that his "intense longing for the Holy Land, for the cradle of Judaism where inspiration and prophecy were born, caused him to regard his birthplace as a foreign land."[16] His basic philosophical perception of Judaism, Graetz maintains, was "thoroughly nationalist" (*durch und durch nationell*).[17]

Graetz takes from Moses Mendelssohn the idea of Judaism not as "revealed religion, but rather as revealed legislation,"[18] an idea in accord with his emphasis on the political nature of Judaism. That is why Graetz calls not for a further spiritualization of Judaism (which he regards as nothing more than an attempt to make Judaism live up to basically Christian precepts of religiosity) but for a modern reaffirmation that should emphasize the social and legislative (that is, political) elements of Judaism. Such a political reformation of Judaism accords very well with the era of renascent nationalism, Graetz argues, and any attempt to belittle the messianic element in Judaism, which is also primarily political, is a vain attempt to make Judaism acceptable to the Christian or post-Christian world that lacks authenticity and inner cohesion.

The Structure of Jewish History trails off rather abruptly when Graetz reaches the nineteenth century. Perhaps it could not be otherwise in a treatise which, for all its polemical edge, is intended as an essay on the philosophy of history rather than on pragmatic politics.

Despite this, the programmatic significance of Graetz's position is enormous and revolutionary: the Jews are a people, a nation, not just a community of faith. They have a history, and Jewish national history has a meaning within the structure of world history. Judaism, moreover, has a political content as well as its religious belief system, and the messianic dimension of Judaism has clear political connotations inextricably connected with Palestine.

Though he visited the country in the 1870s and showed great interest in the first Jewish villages established there, Graetz did not explicitly call for Jewish immigration to Palestine or for its resettlement. Some years earlier he greatly encouraged Moses Hess in the publication of his *Rome and Jerusalem*. Yet Graetz's main impact and legacy was his monumental *History of the Jews*. Many Jews who became deracinated from their religious and traditional background drew their historical self-awareness as Jews from Graetz's volumes. Biblical heroes who slumbered in Jewish self-consciousness for generations were revived and underwent a far-reaching process of emancipation, secularization, and romanticization. Perhaps more than any other person Graetz contributed to the view of Jews as a nation. Today, his historical method can quite rightly be criticized as inadequate and highly slanted. Yet it educated a whole class of modern, secularized Jews to view their own history in terms relevant to a modern, secular, and highly politicized world.

CHAPTER 3

MOSES HESS: SOCIALISM AND NATIONALISM AS A CRITIQUE OF BOURGEOIS SOCIETY

IN MOSES HESS (1812–1875) TWO POWERFUL IDEOLOGICAL AND political forces—socialism and the beginning of Jewish national thought—were integrated into a unique synthesis. When he died after decades of activity in the German and international socialist movement, the inscription on his tomb, near Cologne, read: "Father of German Social Democracy." Seventy-five years later, when the State of Israel was established, its government (then under the leadership of the Labor Party) transferred his remains from Germany and reinterred them in the cemetery of the first kibbutz, near Lake Tiberias. There he lies now, among the other founders of Zionist socialism—Syrkin, Borochov, Katznelson.

The focal point which Hess thus occupied in two political movements has other aspects as well. Most of his manuscripts are at the International Institute of Social History in Amsterdam, but others are scattered among the Zionist Central Archives in Jerusalem and the Institute for Marxism-Leninism of the Central Committee of the Communist Party of the Soviet Union in Moscow. Similarly, new editions of his works have been published by the Academy of Sciences of the German Democratic Republic and by the Zionist Library in Jerusalem under the editorship of Martin Buber.

This unusual combination calls for some reference to his biography.[1] Hess was born in an Orthodox Jewish family in the Rhineland; his strongly devout father wanted him educated in the religious tradition and groomed him to take over the family business. Yet Hess was drawn into the intellectual ferment of pre-1848 German radicalism. As a young man, he joined a group of Left Hegelians, which maintained, as Engels put it in 1843, that "a *social* revolution based upon common property was the only state of mankind agreeing with their abstract principles." This group, which also included Ludwig Feuerbach, Bruno Bauer, Arnold Ruge, and Karl Marx, decided to prove, according to Engels, "either that all philosophical efforts of the German nation, from Kant to Hegel, have been useless—worse than useless; or, that they must end in Communism."[2]

Hess's specific contribution to this radical intellectual ambience was his insistence on the dimension of the future, which was developed in the Hegelian school by the Polish thinker August von Cieszkowski. Hess was greatly influenced by him, and in his writings he developed the future dimension of world history as characterized by the activist praxis directed toward social revolution.[3] He calls for a radical social revolution based on a rejection of bourgeois society as contrary to the universalist postulates of Hegelian thought.

These writings were later greatly praised by Marx, who always acknowledged his indebtedness to Hess whom he occasionally called "my communist rabbi." Both later served as coeditors of the radical *Rheinische Zeitung*, in which many of their earlier articles were published. Like Marx, Hess had to leave Germany because of his radical politics, and the two continued to work together in exile in Paris and Brussels, where a common friend of similar background, Heinrich Heine, also became very prominent in their circle. Hess helped Marx and Engels compose some of their early theoretical writings, was a member of the League of Communists, and although critical of Marx's philosophical materialism, remained very close to Marx in spite of the latter's sometimes acerbic strictures in the *Communist Manifesto* against Hess and his True Socialism. Their partnership continued well into the 1860s, when Hess acted as Marx's liaison with the nascent German working-class movement and tried, albeit not very successfully, to mediate between Marx and Lassalle.

Thus for several decades Hess's main activities took place within the revolutionary socialist movement. Together with Marx, Engels, and Lassalle he must be viewed as one of the founders of German Social Democracy—as is rightly inscribed on his tombstone.

But parallel to this work in the socialist movement with its universal message, there existed another aspect of Hess's intellectual activity, and this came to a dramatic head with the appearance in 1862 of his book *Rome and Jerusalem*. There he calls for a solution to the Jewish problem through the establishment of a Jewish socialist commonwealth in Palestine.

This duality between Hess the universalist socialist and the proto-Zionist Jewish nationalist has given rise to a number of misunderstandings. Some writers have maintained that until the appearance of *Rome and Jerusalem* Hess denied his Jewish background and was so involved in cosmopolitan socialism that the Jewish problem did not interest him until the German chauvinistic shock in the 1860s prompted him to compose his dramatic *cri du coeur*. Others say that the appearance of *Rome and Jerusalem* is a testimony to his rejection of socialism and his transition from socialism to nationalism.

Both claims are wrong. Despite the fact that as a young man Hess rejected the Orthodox and traditional religion of his parental home and viewed himself as a universalist Left Hegelian and communist, the Jewish question appears in all his early writings. The solution he proposed to the Jewish problem at that period in his life was assimilation and integration into the revolutionary universal socialist movement. This is obviously a different solution from the one he later espoused in *Rome and Jerusalem*. Yet a deep awareness of the various dimensions of the Jewish problem accompanied him throughout his life. Similarly, when Hess arrived at a national solution to the Jewish problem, he did not advocate this at the expense of his socialist commitment. On the contrary, he was convinced that the national solution in Palestine, and not his earlier proposal of assimilation, was the correct *revolutionary* and *socialist* answer to the dilemmas raised by Jewish existence. That is why the Jewish commonwealth envisaged by him in the ancestral land of the Jewish people was to be founded on a socialist basis.

Hess continued his activity in the socialist movement after the publication of *Rome and Jerusalem*, though much of his time was devoted to his quest for a solution to the Jewish national problem. The same criticism of bourgeois society which made Hess a socialist also convinced him that only a national home in Palestine could provide an adequate solution to the plight of the Jews, which was both a national and a socialist problem. Socialism and Zionism are thus integrated in Hess's thought into a comprehensive critique of modern society. The development of these ideas on the Jewish problem can be followed in Hess's various writings.

Hess's first book, published anonymously by "A Young Spinozist" in 1837, was *The Holy History of Mankind*.[4] Theoretically this work combines a Young Hegelian philosophy of history with a social *Weltanschauung* derived in part from the Saint-Simonians. The book's thesis is that human history is characterized by periods in which subject and object are alternately united and separated. In Saint-Simonian terms, history is an intermittently alternating succession of organic periods of subject-object unity and inorganic periods in which there is a breach and alienation between subject and object. After surveying, with some obvious oversimplification, the sequence of these periods in human history, Hess arrives at the threshold of the modern industrial age, which he views as a new period of alienation between subject and object. But out of the disruption (*Zerrissenheit*) of the industrial age there will arise the vision of a new, harmonious future, in which contradictions between the individual and society will have been resolved. There will emerge a new social humanism based on the abolition of private property.

Despite its universal theme, *The Holy History of Mankind* reveals the beginnings of Hess's struggle with the Jewish question. In a philosophical history of this kind Hess had to consider Judaism's contribution to history, and this he did in essentially Hegelian terms. The main contribution of the Jews was to give the world monotheism and introduce the spiritual dimension into religious consciousness. The climax of this process of "spiritualization" of the world by Judaism was embodied in the appearance of Jesus, but since Jesus's appearance—and especially since his rejection by the Jews—Judaism's contribution to history had come to an end.[5] As Hess expresses it in this book, there are two peoples in history whose past contribution to history were considerable but who have no future: the Jews, who today are a spirit without a body; and the Chinese, who are a body without a spirit.

According to Hess, Jews have a future in modern times only as individuals and not as a collective entity, and as individuals they should merge into the general universalism. That is why Hess regards Spinoza as the classic example of the modern Jew, the first to have breached the walls of Jewish exclusiveness, to have left his tribe and been excommunicated by it, and thus to become a world citizen. Such is also the path to be followed by the modern Jew (that is, by Hess himself). Hence the significance of his concluding chapter, "The New Jerusalem," which deals with the new society that is to emerge. It is, Hess emphasizes, "here, in the heart of Europe, that New Jerusalem will be built."[6] Here, in the heart of Europe, and not in Palestine.

In a parallel manuscript from the same period (1840), "Poles and Jews," Hess also deals with two peoples who had a distinguished past but a problematic present. But while the Poles, according to Hess, have a future because they never resigned themselves to the partition of Poland and the disappearance of their polity, the Jews do not have the social power necessary for attaining national expression. The Jews suffer from an absolute lack of national consciousness (*Mangel an Nationalsinn*). As an example, Hess points to the way the Jews reacted that year (1840) to the Damascus Blood Libel, the first time when the medieval blood libel against the Jews was resurrected in modern times. In spite of all the protests of Western Jewry, the upheaval caused by the Damascus affair did not lead to the emergence of a general Jewish national consciousness.

What is significant here is not only that Hess deals with Jewish subjects even during this early universalistic socialist phase, but that in these writings his attitude toward Judaism is not merely as toward a religion. *His yardstick in assessing the future of Judaism is not whether it has a future as a religion but whether it has a future as a nation.* True, the answer is negative, but it is important that even during this period of absolute negation Hess uses national and not religious criteria in evaluating Judaism. In *Rome and Jerusalem* his view of the future of Judaism as a nation is positive, and therein lies its novelty. However, his view of Judaism in national terms is derived from an earlier period in which Hess denied Jewry's capacity for regeneration. Indeed, it is interesting to note that Hess was one of the first writers in the modern era to see Judaism in national terms, even while denying it a future.

At the same time, it was in this period that Hess wrote one of the harshest statements that has ever been made by a Jew about Judaism. It is connected with Marx's essay "On the Jewish Question," which he wrote in 1843 and which appeared in 1844.[7] In the year 1845 Hess's essay "On Capital" appeared, which contains very severe pronouncements regarding the Jews and identifying Judaism with capitalism.[8] Only recently has it been shown that Hess's work preceded that of Marx. Hess wrote his essay in 1843 and sent it to Marx for publication. However, it was published a year and a half later. Hence, Hess's work was known to Marx while he wrote his essay "On the Jewish Question," and most of the images which appear in Marx's works are borrowed from Hess. More than that, Hess's work "On Capital" contains material that is much more extreme than anything used by Marx, and it is to Marx's credit that he did not include it. For example, Hess writes that the Children of Israel were originally idolaters whose principal god, Moloch, demanded blood sacrifices. Hess knew Hebrew from his childhood *heder* and used this linguistic knowledge in his essay. In the course of time, he maintains, the Jews passed from blood (*dam*) sacrifices to money (*damim*) sacrifices, this being the origin of the Jewish money cult, as money took the place of Moloch. Throughout the essay Hess calls the God of Israel "Moloch-Jehova," and it is difficult to find a parallel to such a collective blood libel in even the most virulent anti-Semitic literature. These expressions of Hess are less well known than Marx's essay "On the Jewish Question," but they are much more drastic and, ironically, served Marx as a source of information when he wrote his essay.

Still in contrast to Marx, who did not struggle, at least explicitly, over the problem of his Jewish identity (he was, after all, born to a family which had converted to Christianity), Hess's universalism was for him not merely a theoretical speculation but no doubt also represented a solution to the problem of his personal existence and his own identity. Since he tried hard from the outset to find a solution to this problem, one can understand that the failure of the Emancipation had far-reaching repercussions on his worldview.

Rome and Jerusalem, subtitled *The Last National Problem*, appeared in 1862. At the time of publication, it made little impact and was soon forgotten. Hess's socialist friends considered the work a personal idiosyncrasy and did not take it seriously; Reform rabbis criticized it violently, and Orthodox rabbis could not but approach it with a great deal of skepticism.

The Rome of the title was neither Imperial Rome nor Papal Rome but the *Roma terza* of Giuseppe Mazzini and Italian nationalism. As Hess writes in his introduction,

With the liberation of the Eternal City on the Tiber begins the liberation of the Eternal City on Mount Moriah; with the resurrection of Italy begins the resurrection of Judea. The orphaned children of Jerusalem will too be permitted in the great renaissance of the nations. . . .[9]

The autobiographical details with which the book opens reveal something of the agonies of a person discovering his own people after struggling through the purgatory of an undifferentiated universalism:

Here do I stand once more, after twenty years of estrangement, in the midst of my own people, sharing their festivities and their days of sorrow, their memories and their hopes, their spiritual struggles in their own house and with the cultures within which they live and with whom they cannot fuse organically despite two thousand years of cohabitation and effort.

A thought which I believed I had repressed forever has come to life once more: the thought of my nation, inseparable from the heritage of my ancestors, from the Holy Land and the Eternal City, where the belief in the divine unity of life and the future Brotherhood of Man was born.[10]

The main thrust of the work is its concept of Judaism as a nation and its perception of the Jewish problem as a national problem, not just a problem of equal rights and the emancipation of a religious minority. The uniqueness and novelty of Hess lie not only in the fact that the Zionist solution put forward in this work directs the Jewish people to the Land of Israel but that Hess's conceptual system views the Jews in terms of nineteenth-century national liberation movements.

It is clear that once Hess views Judaism in national terms he cannot ultimately consider Emancipation as a solution. Only if Judaism is kept within the confines of a religious sect can Emancipation solve its problems. Moreover, according to Hess's ideas, Emancipation only creates new tensions between the modern Jew and the national society surrounding him, a society which does not and cannot see him as an integral part of its national culture. Emancipation is based on the universalist doctrines of the French Revolution, but it functions in a world whose basic doctrine is the rise of national movements; hence it is ridden with insuperable internal contradictions.

Hess was consequently also more conscious of the rise of anti-Jewish nationalist racialism, particularly in Germany. Precisely because Hess's point of departure is that of the secular world, he was one of the first to recognize that during the period of Emancipation and secularization there occurred a transition from the old Christian anti-Jewishness to a new national racial anti-Jewishness—to modern anti-Semitism. In spite of the fact that these attitudes were only beginning, Hess was perceptive enough to see in 1862 the dangers of this new anti-Semitism in Germany, and his utterances on this subject are chillingly prophetic.

Viewing the Jewish problem in national terms led Hess to his criticism of German Jewry's Reform movement. His main argument is simple enough: Reform ignores the fact the Jews are a nation and sees Judaism in religious terms only. It wishes to make Judaism into a kind of Protestantism with Jewish coloring, thereby distorting the historical essence of Judaism. Hess's argument against Reform is not on the level of religious liberalization. Rather, it refers to the disruption of the Jewish people's historical consciousness caused by the Reform movement's emphasis on the experience of Christianity. A large part of *Rome and Jerusalem* is devoted to demonstrating the intrinsic futility of religious emancipation as a solution in an environment of rising national movements.[11]

Hess's own solution is to set up a Jewish socialist commonwealth in Palestine. It should be emphasized that this was to be a *socialist* commonwealth, because some of the literature on Hess, especially in communist writings, frequently presented him in the later national, Jewish phase of his public activity, as having cut himself off from the socialist past and, as it were, having changed from a socialist to a Jewish nationalist. This is incorrect. Hess's socialist assumptions remained intact, except that in *Rome and Jerusalem* he combines his support of revolutionary Mazzinian nationalism with his socialist vision.

As far as Hess is concerned, there is no solution to the Jewish problem without a Jewish proletariat rooted in the framework of a national Jewish society. Hess realizes that the Jews who would emigrate to Palestine would not come from the middle classes of Western Jewry; the Jewish bourgeoisie of Central and Western Europe would not constitute the social infrastructure of Jewish socialist society in the Land of Israel.[12] Rather, the Jewish commonwealth would provide an answer to the plight of the Jewish masses in Eastern Europe and the Muslim world.[13] Hess's awareness that these two large communities, East European and Middle Eastern Jewry, would form the basis for the Jewish state is of central importance to our understanding of the way Hess visualized the Jewish national society that would arise in the Land of Israel.

The foundations of the Jewish socialist commonwealth would be based on public ownership of the land and of the means of production, which would be organized on cooperative and collective lines. One of the interesting elements in Hess's book is his attempt, occasionally forced, to read into the history of the Jewish people quasi-socialist concepts, a trend that was to become common practice in the Zionist Labor movement later on, though Hess was the first to do so. Thus Hess sees in the traditional Jewish social ethos a protosocialist element. Christianity, according to Hess, was individualistic, and this is why it was Christian society that produced capitalism (how far Hess has come from "On Capital"!); Judaism, on the other hand, was based on the family, that is, on a unit already characterized by elements of social solidarity. Furthermore, in gentile society, both pagan and Christian, the central figure was that of the male, while in Judaism it was that of the woman and mother. Thus, if the principal characteristics extolled in gentile society are the aggressive ones, focused on the man or the father, the specifically Jewish characteristics are those of love, suffering, willingness to help, and understanding one's fellow-being, characteristics connected with the Jewish mother. In a most interesting mixture of metaphors Hess states that every "Jewish mother is a *mater dolorosa*."[14]

Hess interprets all the biblical laws connected with the Sabbath—the fallow year, the Jubilee, et cetera—in socialist terms and even designates the Mosaic code as "social democratic." Going beyond the literal meaning of the verse in *The Sayings of the Fathers*, "He who says, what is mine is mine and what is thine is thine, is a mediocre character: some say, this is a character like that of Sodom," Hess sees it as proof that the Jewish ethos has always harbored a suspicion of individualism based on private property.[15]

A comment about Hasidism in *Rome and Jerusalem* provides an interesting footnote. Hess's attitude to Hasidism is characteristic of his state of mind as a whole, for he presents it as an organic experience as opposed to the opportunistic individualism of the German Reform movement. Hess argues that even though a whole system of what he calls superstitions developed in Hasidism, the internal cohesion of the Hasidic community, the fact that it does not live an individualistic but a communal life is further evidence of the social ethos of Jewish society and may well constitute the basis for a future integration on socialist premises. Thus Hess is able to combine secular criticism of some customs of the Jewish religious tradition with a realization of its contribution to the social context of general Jewish national existence.[16]

As a whole, Hess's conception of nationalism follows Mazzini's in that it combines national particularity with a universal vision. Mazzini said that by being a member of a nation, he is also a member of the human race, and the only way of belonging to humanity is by belonging to a specific nation. Nationalism and universalism are not mutually exclusive but complement one another.

Another aspect of Hess's project for a Jewish commonwealth in Palestine concerns his awareness of the future needs of the Arab population in the area. Given his radical philosophy, Hess realizes that the whole Levant, as it was then called, would soon be in the throes of national movements that would dismember the Turkish Empire in Asia and Africa just as they had already diminished Turkish hegemony in the Balkans. Hess draws encouragement from French support, under Napoleon III, for Italian nationalism, a support which was motivated both by the liberating spirit of France's revolutionary heritage and by opportunistic considerations of France's interest as a great power. He hopes that a similar combination of spiritual and material considerations will move France not only to support Jewish independence in the Middle East but also to help the *reestablishment of Arab states in Egypt and Syria.*[17] Thus decades before the emergence of an active Arab national movement, Hess's universalist nationalism leads him to become one of the first to call for both Jewish independence and Arab national self-determination. There is considerable historical irony in the fact that one of the first modern thinkers to call for a Jewish state also had a parallel vision of the emancipation of the Arabs and the reemergence of their sovereignty.

Like many of his generation, Hess became a socialist under the impact of the Industrial Revolution, which threatened to turn society into a veritable fulfillment of a Hobbesian war of all against all. The atomistic individualism at the root of the bourgeois worldview contradicts, according to Hess and all those who have been influenced by Hegel, the basic social nature of man as a species-being (*Gattungswesen*), who needs other human beings, relates to them essentially and not only contingently, and who cannot exist except through these relations to other *zoa politika.*

What strikes Hess when he applies these considerations to the Jewish problem is that Emancipation approaches the issue in a similarly individualistic vein. It views the problem in terms of individual human beings, not in terms of the Jewish *Gattungswesen*, which is why it could posit the idea that Jews as individuals are entitled to all rights, but as an entity, they have no title to any right. Such a view necessarily creates an internal contradiction. Non-Jews view Emancipation as a vehicle for the integration of Jews into general society and their ultimate disappearance within it, while many Jews think—erroneously, Hess points out—that they can eat their cake and have it: on the one hand, enjoy all the benefits and immense richness, spiritual and material, of individualistic bourgeois society, while at the same time keeping, albeit in a modified form, their collective existence. Hess became one of the first Jewish writers to realize how fraught with dangers and internal contradictions such a position is and how much it would entangle the Jews in novel and unheard-of complications, especially in an era of social migration for the Jews from the periphery to the center of European society. A modified socialist version of this integrationist program is equally rejected by Hess because of its inherent internal contradiction. Emancipation, after all, is an individualistic project, while socialism relates to human collectivities, and if the Jewish collectivity is doomed to disappear in a rosy universalism, to which collectivity would the Jews belong? Nations, after all, are bound to continue to exist as sociocultural entities even in the socialist future as envisaged by Hess under Mazzini's influence. In the name of what principle of liberty or socialism would the Jews then be asked to forgo their own collective identity in a world where all other similar entities would be able to maintain their national existence?

The solution advocated by Hess—the creation of a Jewish commonwealth in Palestine—is thus an integral part of his general *Weltanschauung*. Far from conflicting with his socialism, it is considered by him as the realization of the emancipatory principle of socialism as applied to the specific context of Jewish existence.

CHAPTER 4

ALKALAI AND KALISCHER: BETWEEN TRADITION AND MODERNITY

ENLIGHTENMENT AND SECULARIZATION MOLDED THE CON-sciousness of first-generation emancipated Jews. It was these forces that led to the quest for a new identity, to attempts to redefine Jewish history in terms relevant to nineteenth-century nationalism. This new Jewish national consciousness, later to be called Zionism, appears thus as one of the dialectical consequences of the process of Emancipation itself. As such, it was revolutionary and radical in relation to the traditional course of Jewish history and indeed was initially rejected as heretical and dangerous by the rabbinical establishment.

Yet despite this initial enmity, there appeared even within religious Orthodoxy the first stirrings of a new trend, itself impregnated with ideas derived, albeit with great circumspection and caution, from the radicalized reality of the nineteenth century. Thus, while the majority of rabbinical writers of that time continued in the traditional, passive approach to the problem of redemption, in the writings of at least two rabbis during the first half of the century can be discerned the spiritual echoes of modern, non-Jewish nationalism, which evoke the first gropings after a more activist attitude toward traditional Jewish messianic ideas. These two, Rabbi Yehuda Hai Alkalai, a Sephardi, and Rabbi Zwi

Hirsch Kalischer, an Ashkenazi, add a praxis-oriented and slightly secular twist to the traditional messianic pious hopes and prayers.

Both these men present an extremely complex set of ideas. On the one hand, they remain squarely within Orthodoxy, and their quest for redemption is firmly rooted in the traditional messianic yearnings of Jewish religion. On the other hand, there is no doubt that the activist elements in their thought can be most clearly traced to the impact that developments in the surrounding non-Jewish communities must have had on their own ideas as well as on the general position of the Jewish population in their areas. For both Alkalai and Kalischer came from typical multiethnic border areas, where contending nationalisms were fighting each other, and the Jewish communities found themselves in the cross fire of these conflicting movements.

Yehuda Hai Alkalai (1798–1878) was born in Sarajevo, then part of the Turkish Empire, and in 1825 he was called to the rabbinate in the city of Semlin, in Serbia. The whole Balkan area was awash with emerging national conflicts—Serbs, Croats, Greeks, Bulgarians, and Rumanians were all just beginning to find their own national self-consciousness and to carve a national homeland for themselves out of the multinational Turkish and Austrian empires. During Alkalai's youth, the Greeks and the Serbs fought for their independence and achieved it. From a Jewish perspective, his area was the meeting point of Ashkenazi and Sephardi Jewry.

Rabbi Zwi Hirsch Kalischer (1795–1874) flourished at about the same time in a similar multiethnic area. He was born in Posen, the same border area that was the birthplace of Heinrich Graetz. This was the area of western Poland which came under Prussian rule after the partition of Poland and in the wake of the Napoleonic wars. The majority of the population was Polish speaking, but the German element, mostly urban, was the ruling minority group. In some cases, when Prussian officialdom tried to make the German-speaking minority look slightly larger, they added the Yiddish-speaking Jews to the statistics of the German community, since, after all, Yiddish was a Germanic tongue. Such attempts, while generally welcomed by the Jewish leadership, which looked largely to Germany as an emancipating *Kultumation*, created friction between the Jews and the Polish populace and were consequently viewed as a mixed blessing by many Jews. The several Polish attempts at insurrection put the Jewish community again and again in an ambivalent position regarding its political and linguistic-cultural identification. The Jewish community in these border areas, therefore, became highly sensitized to issues of culture, nationalism, and linguistic policies. From a Jewish point of view, the province of Posen was also an internal border area between the emancipated Jews of the German lands proper and the more traditional and Orthodox *Ost-Juden* of the old Polish Commonwealth.

Both Alkalai and Kalischer are examples of what often occurs when outside nationalist pressures begin to develop in the non-Jewish society. The delicate and complex balance between Jewish society and its surrounding world begins to disintegrate, and even the traditionalists in the Jewish community begin to look for new solutions. Hence, despite their disparate geographical and cultural backgrounds, Alkalai and Kalischer shared the same predicaments and looked for new answers because of the analogous situations of their respective communities. In the traditional Orthodox manner, both wrote in rabbinical Hebrew.[1]

In his book *Minhat Yehuda* (The Offering of Judah),[2] first published in 1845, Alkalai tries to give a terrestrial dimension to the traditional redemptive vision. Arguing on the basis of exegetical references to biblical allusions to the redemption, Alkalai maintains that the Redeemer will not appear suddenly but will be preceded by a number of preparatory processes. In parallel fashion, since the Land of Israel is at present mainly uninhabited, Alkalai maintains it would be practically impossible for all the Jews of the world suddenly to come and settle there. Somehow some preparations have to be made, Alkalai says, adding, "The Lord desires that we be redeemed in dignity; we cannot, therefore, migrate in a mass, for we should then have to live like tent-dwellers all over the fields of the Holy Land. Redemption must come slowly. The land must, by degrees, be built up and prepared." He also remarks that some Jews will initially have to remain in the Diaspora, "so that they can help the first settlers in Palestine, who will undoubtedly come from among the poor."[3]

In this careful, practical way, always bolstering his arguments with biblical and talmudic quotations, Alkalai is able to extricate the process of redemption—though not, of course, redemption itself—from its mystical one-dimensionality. The process of redemption thus ceases to be a merely divine affair and becomes a human concern. Alkalai is consequently able to avoid being accused of heretical ideas of "Pushing the End of Days" (*Dehikat ha-Ketz*), while at the same time trying to legitimize, within the tradition itself, practical attempts connected with the settlement of Palestine.

This demystification of the process of redemption is also extended by Alkalai to cover a more pragmatic attitude to the usage of the Hebrew language. Rabbinical Orthodoxy relegated Hebrew to the status of a sacral language that should not be profaned by daily use for mundane affairs. Prompted, no doubt, by the literary revival of obscure vernaculars in the wake of national reawakenings in the Balkans, Alkalai's attitude is imbued with much more practical considerations. The dispersion among the nations, Alkalai maintains, has created a situation in which the Jews no longer speak one language—a consideration which does not concern traditional thinkers:

> We are, alas, so scattered and divided today, because each Jewish community speaks a different language and has different customs. These divisions are an obstacle to the Redemption. I wish to attest to the pain I have always felt at the error of our ancestors, that they allowed our holy tongue to be so forgotten. Because of this our people was divided into seventy people; our one language was replaced by the seventy languages of the lands of exile.[4]

This lack of a national language might pose a practical problem to the Jews with the coming of the Messiah:

> If the Almighty should indeed show us his miraculous favor and gather us into our land, we should not be able to speak to each other and such a divided community could not succeed. . . . This sort of thing is not accomplished by a miracle, and it is almost impossible to imagine a true revival of our Hebrew tongue by natural means. But we must have faith that it will come. . . .[5]

Alkalai's conclusion is practical and utterly novel: everyone should be taught *spoken* Hebrew, so that through the creation of a unifying mode of communication, another preparatory facet of the Redemption should be encouraged. "There one should not despair, but try with all our might to reestablish our language and make it central; and God Almighty will inspire the teachers and the students, *the boys and the girls*, to speak Hebrew fluently [italics added]."[6]

Alkalai then presents a pragmatic program of buying land in Palestine and reviving the Hebrew language as elements of the human praxis preparatory to the divine Redemption. He also suggests that not only the rabbis but also the richer strata of Jewish society should learn Hebrew. The emergence of a new Jewish bourgeoisie, itself an outcome of Emancipation, is used by Alkalai as proof for a slow amelioration in the position of the Jews and a hint at even better things to come. These people should be a cornerstone for the organized effort to purchase land in Palestine. Alkalai also knows enough of the innovations of modern capitalism to suggest that the company be organized "on the mode of the fire insurance companies and of the rail companies."[7] Although Alkalai may have been steeped in talmudic scholarship, his suggestions are deeply imbued with the spirit of his age.

The same attitude applies to other questions of organization. Alkalai suggests the election of a Jewish constituent assembly—again, the model of other renascent national movements is obvious. But he is also aware that such an innovative move is highly unorthodox within the Jewish rabbinical tradition. Hence it is cloaked in an extremely traditionalist exegetic language, which sometimes obscures the novelty of the idea.

In order to legitimize such modern innovation, Alkalai resorts to one of the more intriguing elements in the Jewish messianic tradition. According to one version of this tradition, the appearance of the Messiah, Son of David, will be preceded by the appearance of a forerunner, a Messiah who will be called the Son of Joseph. This tradition maintains that this first Messiah (*Mashiah Ben Yosef*) will participate in the wars of Gog and Magog, will conquer the land of Israel from the infidels but will fall in the battle. Only after this will the ultimate Messiah, *Mashiah Ben David*, appear and miraculously lead the Children of Israel back to the Promised Land.

Alkalai argues that the very appearance of the Messiah Son of Joseph, whose acts will be characterized by terrestrial conquests and not by miracles, suggests in a symbolical way the necessity for a secular, practical activity preceding the appearance of the Messiah Son of David. Moreover, Alkalai maintains that one should not take the vision of a Messiah Son of Joseph as if he were a person. It is rather a *process* that in modern times would take the form of the emergence of a political leadership among the Jews that would prepare the "beginning of the redemption" (*atchalta di-geula*, in the traditional Aramaic version). The traditional vision of a "preparatory," activist Messiah is thus rendered into the language of relevant modern social development and institutions:

> The Redemption will begin with efforts by the Jews themselves; they must organize and unite, choose leaders, and leave the land of exile. Since no community can exist without a governing body, the very first new ordinance must be the appointment of the elders of each district, men of piety and wisdom, to oversee all the affairs of the community. I humbly suggest that this chosen assembly—the Assembly of the Elders—is what is meant by the promise to us of the Messiah, the Son of Joseph.
>
> These elders should be chosen by our greatest magnates, upon whose influence we all depend. The organization of an international Jewish body is in itself the first step to the Redemption, for out of this organization there will come a fully authorized Assembly of Elders, and from the Elders, the Messiah, Son of Joseph, will appear . . . .[8]

These ideas, as well as the idea to establish a Perpetual Fund (*Keren Kayemet*) to be used for the purchase of land in Palestine (again legitimized by Abraham's purchase of the Cave of Machpela from Ephron the Hittite), were not realized in Alkalai's own time, though they contain some of the seminal elements of later Zionist organizational activity.

In his old age Alkalai emigrated to Jerusalem, and this step, as well as the plethora of ideas propagated by him, single him out among his generation for his rich imaginative blend of new ideas within a traditional normative order. A national language and a representative assembly were almost heretical ideas to Orthodox Judaism, and to voice them while remaining within the fold of the tradition was an intriguing innovative effort.

Zwi Hirsch Kalischer, who officiated as a rabbi to the community of Torun in the province of Posen, presents a similar amalgam of the old and the new. The impact of non-Jewish national movements on his thinking is stated most clearly in his book *Derishat Zion* (Seeking Zion), first published in 1862 and reprinted many times during Kalischer's own lifetime:

> Why do the people of Italy and of other countries sacrifice their lives for the land of their fathers, while we, like men bereft of strength and courage, do nothing? Are we inferior to all other peoples, who have no regard for life and fortune as compared with the love of their land and nation? Let us take to heart the examples of the Italians, Poles, and Hungarians, who laid down their lives and possessions in the struggle for national independence, while we, the children of Israel, who have the most glorious and holiest of lands

as our inheritance, are spiritless and silent. We should be ashamed of ourselves![9]

Like Alkalai, Kalischer does not think that the redemption will come suddenly. Preparatory steps are necessary, and Kalischer pursues the process of demystifying the beginnings of the redemptions, as suggested by Alkalai:

> The Redemption of Israel, for which we long, is not to be imagined as a sudden miracle. The Almighty, blessed be His Name, will not suddenly descend from on high and command His people to go forth. Neither will He send the Messiah from heaven in a twinkling of an eye, to sound the great trumpet for the scattered of Israel and gather them into Jerusalem. He will not surround the Holy City with a wall of fire or cause the Holy Temple to descend from heaven.[10] The bliss and the miracles that were promised by His servants, the prophets, will certainly come to pass—everything will be fulfilled— but we will not run in terror and flight, *for the Redemption of Israel will come by slow degrees and the ray of deliverance will shine forth gradually* [italics added].[11]

Kalischer refers to some verses from Isaiah about the Redemption, where it is likened to the slow gathering of the corn from the field:

> He thus revealed that all of Israel would not return from exile at one time, but would be gathered by degrees, as the grain is slowly gathered from the beaten corn. . . . It is evident that both a first and a second ingathering are intended: the function of the first will be to pioneer the land, after which Israel will blossom forth to a most exalted degree.[12]

Kalischer even wistfully suggests that the very fact that some Jews would gather in Jerusalem by themselves, without overt divine intervention, might even hasten the providential design for the ultimate deliverance:

> When many Jews will settle [in the Land of Israel] and their prayers will increase at the holy mountain in Jerusalem—the Creator will then heed them and hasten the Day of Redemption. For all this to come about there must first be Jewish settlement in the land; without such settlement, how can the ingathering begin?[13]

Kalischer also addresses the problem of the relations with the existing, albeit small, Jewish Orthodox community in Palestine. Kalischer is aware that there is widespread unwillingness in the

Diaspora to maintain financial assistance to this community, most of it dependent on alms from abroad and known for its reluctance to be self-supporting. "There are many," Kalischer says, "who will refuse to support the poor of the Holy Land, saying: 'Why should we support people who choose idleness, who are lazy and not interested in working, and who prefer to depend upon the Jews of the Diaspora to support them?'"[14] This, Kalischer maintains, is a false argument. The Jewish community in Palestine is at present too small to provide for itself. Once mass immigration to Palestine starts, the foundation for a self-supporting economic structure would be established, and then the Old Yishuv could be productively integrated into this new society. The establishment of an agricultural Jewish community in Palestine would make it possible for Jews to observe again the religious commandments related to working the soil (*mitzvot ha-teluyot ba-aretz*). "As we bring redemption to the land in this-worldly way, the ray of heavenly deliverance will gradually appear,"[15] Kalischer adds, bringing out again the dialectical relationship between human praxis and providential design.

Kalischer also spells out some of the details of his envisaged project for resettling Palestine. In a way similar to Alkalai's proposals, he suggests following the traditional Jewish manner of raising money through communal offerings and establishing a fund for land purchase. This fund should be financed mainly by the rich Jewish families like the Rothschilds, the Montefiores, the Foulds, and the Albert Kahns. These magnates should also explore the possibility of ensuring a charter from the Sultan incorporating the Jewish settlement trust. The model of settlement itself envisaged by Kalischer resembles the structures of later Jewish efforts in its combination of public and cooperative initiative with private agriculture:

> Let there assemble Jewish people from Russia, Poland and Germany, who will receive wages from the Company [the Jewish Land Company financing immigration and land purchase], so that they can learn agriculture under the supervision of instructors provided by the Company. Anyone who will himself be already acquainted with agriculture, will be given a plot of land for a set period of time and will be able to cultivate it free of charge until the moment when it will become productive; once the land will begin to produce, he will pay the Company according to a set assessment; and if he will need credits before then, the Company will guarantee it, so that he and his family will not go hungry.[16]

Kalischer also proposes establishing an agricultural school in Palestine. This idea was pursued by the Alliance Israelite Universelle, which founded the Mikveh Israel agricultural school near Jaffa in 1870. This school later became instrumental in the development of Jewish agriculture in Palestine.

Among nineteenth-century rabbis, Alkalai and Kalischer are unusual phenomena. Their very singularity brings out how deep was the impact of the modernization processes on the conceptual world of traditional Judaism. Emancipated Jews needed a redefinition of their identity in the wake of secularization and the emergence of nationalism. For the traditionalists, like Alkalai and Kalischer, problems of identity did not arise, since their identity continued to be determined within the confines of Orthodox, normative Judaism. But even they sensed the need to respond to the new challenges of their surrounding societies. Thus they introduce in their writings specific terms directly derived from modern nationalist movements, a demystification of the redemptive process with a focusing on the natural aspects of the messianic process. All these are another aspect of the impact of the revolutionary situation of the nineteenth century on Jewish consciousness in the post-Emancipation era.

This ability of the traditional structures to absorb novel and modern ideas attests to a potential for adaptation to be found in traditional Judaism. While Alkalai and Kalischer remained lone figures within the rabbinical establishment of the nineteenth century, it was this adaptive potential which, a few generations later, enabled wide sectors of the Orthodox community to adopt Zionism despite the initial negative response Zionist activists encountered among the traditionalists. This development avoided a breach between the Zionist movement and Jewish Orthodoxy. However, it occurred much later, when the national Jewish idea had become crystallized and had already emerged as a historical force due to the intellectual and spiritual activity of people whose own experiences had been molded by the quest for identity under conditions of secularization and a break with religious tradition.

CHAPTER 5

SMOLENSKIN: FROM ENLIGHTENMENT TO NATIONALISM

MOST JEWS IN THE NINETEENTH CENTURY LIVED WITHIN the confines of the czarist empire, which comprised not only Russia proper but also Central and Eastern Poland, the Ukraine, Bessarabia, Lithuania, and the other Baltic countries. While Jews in the West at this time experienced Emancipation and the granting of equal rights, those who lived under czarist rule were confronted with an autocratic and authoritarian regime officially committed to an anti-Jewish policy limiting the right of residence for Jews to the traditional Pale of Settlement and excluding them from the professions and the public service. Just as nineteenth-century Russia did not experience a radical process of liberalization, so the impact of French revolutionary ideas did not impinge on the position of the Jews there. Despite this generally bleak picture, some attempts at partial liberalization were made in the second half of the century: schools and universities were opened on a limited scale to select Jewish students, and processes of Enlightenment, parallel to those already operating in the West, gradually developed within the Jewish community in Russia.

These developments suffered a traumatic setback in 1881, when widespread pogroms, of almost unprecedented scope and intensity, swept across Russia, mainly in the southern districts where the

Jewish population was densest. The complicity of the authorities in these disturbances, as well as a reversal of some of the limited liberalizations which ensued in their wakes, threatened to end even the gradual amelioration of the Jews' position.

Peretz Smolenskin (1842–1885), Hebrew author, scholar, and editor, is perhaps one of the archetypical members of that generation, whose hopes were kindled and then extinguished after 1881. Born in the Pale of Settlement, a student at the famous Shklov *yeshiva*, Smolenskin experienced the typical tribulations of his age and later wrote an autobiographical novel about them. After leaving the *yeshiva* he earned a living as an itinerant house teacher and eventually settled in Odessa.

Odessa, one of the most unusual cities in Russia, played a leading role in the development of the Hebrew Enlightenment in the czarist empire. It was a new city, built by the czars as a Russian outpost in the southern areas captured from the Turkish Empire at the end of the eighteenth century. In their attempt to develop and russify the region, the authorities allowed Jews to settle in Odessa while the premier cities of Russia proper—St. Petersburg and Moscow—remained closed to them. In this modern and pioneering context, free from the stifling atmosphere of traditional populations and their rivalries, Odessa developed as a relatively open and liberal city. The non-Jewish population was relatively well educated and tolerant, and the Jews who settled there were mainly forward-looking businessmen and entrepreneurs, professionals and members of the intelligentsia, more or less emancipated from the traditional Orthodoxy of the Pale of Settlement. Thus Odessa became not only the most liberal, Western-oriented city but also the capital of Hebrew letters and Jewish Enlightenment in Russia. Here the first modern Hebrew school was established, which was modeled on Western European ideas and tried to emancipate Jewish education from rabbinical and talmudic traditions. Here flourished—and collapsed—numerous journals, in Russian and in Hebrew, advocating Emancipation and Enlightenment for the Jews. Here groups of writers, poets, and *maskilim* (the enlightened ones) were formed, freed from the persecution of religious traditions, dreaming about the promise of a liberalized Russia, in which emancipated, enlightened, and russified Jews could participate in building a new, multinational and multireligious Russian homeland, free from both czarist autocracy and religious bigotry, be it Christian or Jewish. And indeed, the reforms of the 1860s under Czar Alexander II gave sustenance to these dreams. The serfs were emancipated; a new, relatively enlightened bureaucracy slowly opened Russian society to Western ideas; Jews were gradually allowed into schools, universities, and the professions.

After living for a few years in this atmosphere in Odessa, Smolenskin moved to Vienna where he stayed for the rest of his life. From Vienna he edited his journal *Hashahar* (The Dawn), and there he wrote most of his books and articles, mainly addressed to the Russian *maskilim*.

For Smolenskin's generation, the 1881 disturbances were a cruel shock. Almost overnight, religious bigotry and intolerance, bureaucratic harassment and official connivance in the pogroms seemed to obliterate twenty years of slow progress. For thousands of Jews who managed in the 1860s and 1870s to enter, through schools and universities, the ranks of the Russian intelligentsia, the pogroms vividly demonstrated how fragile and shallow all this development was. Beneath the thin veneer of relative tolerance an abyss of deep hatred continued to exist. The fact that not only Orthodox Jews but emancipated and enlightened Jews as well fell victims to the pogroms seemed to undermine a central precept of the *maskilim*, namely, that only the strangeness of the Orthodox Jew made him a target for fear and hatred. The victims of the pogroms were religious and secularized Jews alike, the pious as well as the agnostics; and when official reaction was to reimpose some of the old restrictions—especially those relating to residence permits and access to secondary and higher education—it became more and more clear that the Enlightenment slogan—"Educate yourselves!"—was a hollow symbol.

This was also the beginning of massive Jewish emigration from Russia. From 1882 to 1914 almost three million Jews emigrated from czarist Russia to the West—to North America, England, South Africa, Argentina. Parallel to this demographic and sociological change in the structure of the Jewish Diaspora, a much deeper intellectual transformation was having an impact on members of the Russian Jewish Enlightenment. Just as twenty years earlier Moses Hess became conscious of the groundswell of modern, nationalist anti-Semitism in Germany, thus casting doubt on the ability of liberalism to solve the Jewish question, so the events of 1881 posed, for the Russian *maskilim*, a question about the adequacy of the liberal and humanist dream in the Russian context. The Jewish masses reacted in 1881 in the traditional Jewish fashion—emigration. The intellectuals went through an agonizing reappraisal. No one symbolizes this transition better than Peretz Smolenskin.

The enormity of the impact of 1881 on Smolenskin's thoughts can best be gauged by following his development in the years preceding this cataclysmic event. In a series of essays called "It Is Time to Plant" (1875–77) the general contours of Smolenskin's ideas about Jewish identity and the need for Enlightenment are explained. According to Smolenskin, Emancipation from religious Orthodoxy proves that Jewish identity cannot be based any longer on mere religious observance. In pre-Enlightenment days, religion and its institutions—the religious community, the heder and yeshiva, the shtetl—could be conceived as the focus of Jewish solidarity ("fraternity," in Smolenskin's flowery Hebrew, echoing, of course, the third component of the French revolutionary triad). But the emergence of secularized, modern Jews, unattached to the religious tradition, poses to these individuals a novel problem. Despite their Russian education, they have difficulty identifying as members of the Russian nation, as most Russians are still uneducated, deeply imbued with religious intolerance and xenophobia and, unlike Western nations, totally closed to the acceptance of foreigners into their midst. These enlightened Jews are trying to keep their Jewish identity, act within Jewish public and cultural contexts. Out of their predicament, an old truth comes forth and gains new relevance and meaning: the Jews are a nation, and a national identity unites them. In Smolenskin's language,

> For four thousand years we have been brothers and children of one people. . . . Such unity can come only from a fraternal feeling, from a national sentiment which makes everyone born a Jew declare: I am a son of this people. . . . *No matter what his sins against religion, every Jew belongs to his people so long as he does not betray it*—this is the principle which we must succeed in establishing.[1]

Yet Smolenskin is aware that the Jewish people is different from other peoples in some of its crucial historical dimensions. According to him, its unifying principle is not material—territory—but spiritual—an intellectual and ethical heritage. Just as territory protects other peoples, the spiritual heritage protects the people of Israel. The intellectual impact of Krochmal and Graetz is clearly discernible here. Consequently, Smolenskin argues, the Jews could be loyal subjects and citizens in their countries of residence and at the same time unified through their spiritual solidarity. The Jews are thus a universal nation, the only truly universal nation, because its principle of solidarity is spiritual and not material:

> Yes, we are a people. We have been a people from our beginnings until today. We have never ceased being a people, even after our kingdom was destroyed and we were exiled from our land. . . . But we are not today a people like all others, just as we were not a people like all the others when we dwelt in our land. The foundation of our unity was never the soil of the Holy Land and we did not lose the basis of our nationality when we were exiled. We have always been a spiritual nation, one whose Torah was the foundation of its statehood. . . . We are a people because in spirit and thought we regard ourselves bound to one another by ties of fraternity. Our unity has been conserved in a different way, through forms different from those of all other peoples, but does this make us any the less a people?
>
> In practical reality every Jew is a citizen of the land in which he dwells, and it is his duty to be a good citizen, who accepts all the obligations of citizenship like all other nationals of the country. The land in which we dwell is our country. We once had a land of our own, but it was not the tie that united us. Our Torah is our native land which makes us a people, a nation only in the spiritual sense, but in the normal business of life we are like all other men.[2]

The deep ambiguities of the Jewish Enlightenment movement are clearly visible in this statement. On the one hand, there is a clear insistence that the Jews have the attributes of a nation; on the other hand, there is an equally strong affirmation that they are citizens of the countries of their residence and should be considered as such. Hence the distance Smolenskin takes vis-à-vis Palestine: not the Land but the Spirit is the focus of Jewish identity. At the same time Smolenskin opposes the attempts of the German Jewish Reform movement to limit the existence of Judaism to its purely religious dimension. Like Graetz and Hess who preceded him, Smolenskin sees in such an attempt an emasculation of the actual historical contribution of Judaism.[3]

The events of 1881 had a major impact on Smolenskin's thinking, and in an essay published in the same year, "Let Us Search Our Ways," he expresses his frustration at what happened and calls for new ways to solve the Jewish problem in Russia. Smolenskin first recounts the deep horror and brutality experienced by tens of thousands of Jewish families and asks whether the pogroms really represent a change of attitude toward the Jewish population.

Answering in the negative, he accuses the leaders of Russian Jewry, especially the intellectuals among them, for having lulled their brethren. "If anyone had told the Jews of Russia of the impending danger even a month before it came, he would have been mocked as a madman. Nonetheless *any intelligent person could have foreseen that it would not be long in coming* [italics added]."[4] According to Smolenskin, for twenty years prior to the disturbances, Russian newspapers and intellectual journals were full of violent anti-Semitic writings opposing even the limited liberalization for the Jews that the government tried to introduce. Russian writing in the decade before the pogroms was full of every possible accusation against the Jews—religious, moral, social, or otherwise—yet the Jews preferred to overlook the depth of this enmity against them because they had been so deeply involved in their meliorative dreams of Enlightenment:

> During all this time the Jewish philanthropists in Russia were preoccupied with *Haskala*, in imitation of the German Jews. They, too, were foolish enough to believe that the way of Enlightenment would bring them success and honor. If only they would reach a high level of Enlightenment, the Gentiles would accept them with respect and brotherly love, and troublemakers would no longer attack them.[5]

Yet while they were immersed in these attempts at education and self-betterment, the Jews became oblivious to the sociological and intellectual processes through which society at large was going. Smolenskin's contention is that the process of Enlightenment among the Jews *intensified*, rather than minimized, the frictions between Jews and non-Jews, as additional strata in non-Jewish society saw the educated Jews entering the professions and the middle class as serious competitors and contenders for their own positions. It would be an illusion to imagine that education per se can be a solution to social animosities and that non-Jewish intellectuals would welcome Jewish intellectuals into their own midst. Consequently, only one outlet is open to the Jews:

> At present our enemies in Russia are venting their rage by demanding that the Jews leave the country. This horrifies our brethren even more than all the disasters that have befallen us. . . . [But] why should we not emigrate [and thus] reduce the number of Jews in the countries where they are hated. . . .[6]

Smolenskin is convinced of the necessity for emigration from those countries where the very existence of a dense Jewish population is creating the conditions for friction with the majority population. But in his view, such an emigration should not be undertaken on an individual basis, each person looking only for salvation for himself or his family. Fraternity, that is, solidarity, is a crucial ingredient of Jewish identity for Smolenskin. Consequently the emigration process should be a collective one, a process incorporating national solidarity. America could be a target of individual emigration, but anyone looking for a focus of mass emigration based on solidarity and social responsibility would have to look elsewhere. "If the wave of emigration is to direct itself to one place, surely no other country in the world is conceivable except Eretz Israel."[7] Smolenskin is aware that until recently the idea of going to Palestine has been viewed with horror mixed with ridicule by all except those "who wished to be buried there." Yet the last years have proven that agricultural settlements can be established there and more and more Jews might be convinced that the country is livable, not only a ritual burial ground.

Smolenskin thus turns from his initial rejection of the Land of Israel as the national focus of the Jewish people to viewing it as a national haven. The land to which he now refers is, however, no longer the celestial City of God as it had figured ideally in Jewish prayer and hope, but the Terrestrial City, the real Palestine of nineteenth-century travelers and explorers. This pragmatic attitude to the real Palestine is typical of the radical change signified in Smolenskin's novel attitude. It is national consciousness which leads Smolenskin to look for the collective solution to the problems of the Jewish people in the Land of Israel, but this land is no longer a mere ideal postulate or a spiritual entity; its attributes are immediately translated into pragmatic questions about absorptive capacity and industrial potential—a secular, this-world approach well attuned to the spirit of the Enlightenment itself:

Many experts—non-Jews—have investigated this land and distinguished English explorers have been sent to travel in the country and study it [the British Palestine Exploration Society was established in 1865]. They have established that the land is very good and that, if cultivated with skill and diligence, it could support fourteen million people. Even if we assume that there is room for only half that number, Eretz Israel can nonetheless contain all those who might wish to take refuge there. Not all Jews will go there—

only those who are destitute or persecuted will look for a place to which to emigrate. It would be enough if only one million of our brethren would go, for it would be a relief both to them and to those remaining in the lands of the dispersion.[8]

The transformation of the image of Palestine from the Holy Land of dreams, visions, or edifying tales to a land of potential immigration could not have been more far-reaching. For six reasons Palestine is preferable, according to Smolenskin, to any other country as a target for Jewish immigration:

1. The Orthodox religious community, "those who cherish the memories of their ancestors," will identify more easily with emigration to the Land of Israel than with the necessity of moving to another, even more distant Diaspora, like the United States or South America.
2. Palestine is nearer than the other alternatives to the present countries of Jewish residence, so it would be easier to keep family contacts with those who remained behind.
3. Emigration to Palestine could be organized and well ordered, so that the newcomers would not be exposed to the alienation and social fragmentation characterizing immigrant communities in the New World.
4. Even the small, religious Jewish community already living "in idleness" in the Land of Israel and dependent on alms (the Old Yishuv) could be made productive and "thousands will therefore be saved from all the evils which such idleness creates."
5. Palestine has a potential for commercial development besides its agricultural possibilities, and it could become "the center of commerce linking Europe with Asia and Africa."
6. The country also has an industrial potential (for some quaint reasons Smolenskin mentions "factories for glass").[9]

Much as these arguments are not all of the same order, and some of them may appear questionable, it is the pragmatic rather than the religious elements which stand out here in Smolenskin's preference for Palestine over America, even though he includes the religious attachment of *some* of the more religious Jews as another *pragmatic* consideration which might facilitate developing a positive attitude to the land. Smolenskin thus envisages a population that would "make a living from farming, commerce and industry," and in this way a Jewish community with wide social and economic distribution could be established in Palestine, so that not all the Jews would be concentrated in the commercial middle classes. In all other countries of immigration, where there already exists a considerable non-Jewish population, Jewish immigrants would tend, because of the pressures of the market and their own traditional skills, to gravitate toward their old middle-class roles. The creation of a new society in the Land of Israel would force them to disperse over the whole socioeconomic spectrum.

Here, for the first time in modern Jewish thinking, the prognosis and the hope is clearly expressed that the Jewish collective process of emigration should be not merely a geographical but also a sociological transformation. Anyone looking for personal salvation—preferring America, for example—does not envisage a radical change in the map of Jewish social occupations; those, on the other hand, who look for a process of emigration whose aims and context would be national, expect and demand a change in the socioeconomic structures of the Jewish people. This aspect appears time and again in the Zionist vision and finds its institutional expression within the socialist wing of the Zionist movement with its plethora of transformative institutions—kibbutzim, moshavim, cooperative and collective industries—all aimed at creating a real context for this radical social change and ensuring its durability. But the beginnings of these trends can be discerned in the writings of Smolenskin and others of his generation. The transition from a humanist Enlightenment to nationalism and from emigration as a salvage operation to a program for national renaissance also implied radical thinking about the economic and occupational structures of the new society.

CHAPTER 6

LILIENBLUM: THE CRISIS OF JEWISH ENLIGHTENMENT IN RUSSIA

LIKE SMOLENSKIN, MOSHE LEIB LILIENBLUM WAS A FIRST-generation Russian *maskil.* Like him, he was severely shocked by the 1881 pogroms, which raised serious doubts about the validity of the historical and theoretical prognosis offered by the Jewish Enlightenment movement in Russia.

Moshe Leib Lilienblum (1843–1910) was born in Lithuania, the center of Jewish learning in the Russian Empire. After a traditional, religious education, he quarreled with the rabbinical establishment and found his way to the *Haskala.* In 1869 he moved to Odessa and in its liberal atmosphere became acquainted with the ideas of the Russian positivists and was also drawn toward socialist thought. In his early writings he called for far-reaching reforms in Jewish religious observances and a radical transformation in the social habits of the Jewish population. Only through such an adjustment to modernity, Lilienblum argued, could the gap between the Jewish and the non-Jewish population be overcome and the Jews accepted as equals. He viewed the spread of education among Jews and Gentiles alike as the best guarantee for tolerance and mutual understanding. If Jews and Christians both would emancipate themselves from their traditional religious prejudices about each other, they would be able to coexist peacefully in an atmosphere of understanding and reciprocal respect.

The 1881 pogroms did not spare Odessa. Even there, in this modern, largely educated and secularized city, where Jews and non-Jews had lived for decades in an atmosphere of relative enlightenment, wild disturbances occurred. To people like Lilienblum, who saw the roots of anti-Semitism in religious prejudice and lack of education, this came as a cruel shock. Educated Odessa did not behave basically very differently from the most backward village in the Pale of Settlement.

In a series of articles called "The Way of Return," published in Hebrew immediately after the disturbances, Lilienblum tries to come to grips with the harmonistic vision of the *maskilim*. His conclusions suggest that the solution does not lie anymore in an integrationist solution but in a novel and radical direction—the creation of a Jewish national self-consciousness. "I became convinced that it was not a lack of high culture that was the cause of our tragedy—for aliens we are and aliens we shall remain even if we become full to the brim with culture . . ."[1]

The 1881 disturbances have proved, Lilienblum maintains, that not only the uneducated, illiterate mobs participated in the mass killings and lootings, as the *maskilim* tried to maintain in their conventional wisdom, but among those involved in the disturbances were also educated groups. Even proletarians, in whose emancipatory potential Lilienblum had firmly believed before 1881, had taken part in the pogroms. Lilienblum also points out that not only the traditional, Orthodox Jews, whose habits and external appearance differed from those of the majority culture, were attacked and victimized, but emancipated, enlightened Jews as well. Cultural integration and linguistic assimilation were no guarantee against murder or mutilation. Consequently Lilienblum does not accept the view, strongly urged after 1881 by other *maskilim*, like Yehuda Leib Gordon, that the Jewish response to the pogroms should be more education and more integration. While Gordon argued that even more radical reforms in Jewish religious practice would further eliminate the social differences between Jew and Gentile, Lilienblum feels that from the point of view of the non-Jewish masses, there is no basic difference between the Orthodox, caftan-wearing traditional Jews and the modern, secularized ones.

In another article written in the wake of the pogroms, "Let Us Not Confuse the Issues" (1882), Lilienblum agrees with other *maskilim* that further religious reforms should be undertaken by the Jewish religious establishment. This, however, is not the problem. Since 1881, he says, the issue is not the extent of religious reforms or liturgical modernization but a problem of sheer survival. Because of the acute crisis threatening the very existence of the Jewish population in Russia, Lilienblum calls upon the various groups and factions within the Jewish community—mainly the Orthodox and the *maskilim*—to overcome their differences and join in a concerted public action to confront the existential dangers faced by the community as a whole. The aim of such combined action would be emigration to Palestine:

> Let all special questions, whether religious or economic in nature, take second place to the general question, to the sole and simple aim that Israel be "saved by the Lord with an everlasting salvation." Unite and join forces; let us gather our dispersed from eastern Europe and go up to our land with rejoicing; whoever is on the side of God and His people, let him say: I am for Zion.[2]

It is this shift from integration through education in Russia toward a national solution in Palestine that would make Lilienblum in a few years one of the central figures of the Hovevei Zion (Lovers of Zion) movement. This became the first organization involved with creating the conditions for Jewish settlement in Palestine. By focusing on the central existential problems Lilienblum is able to cut through secondary issues and reach some theoretical conclusions regarding the nature of Jewish existence. Against the Reformers and Orthodox, who wanted to create or maintain one normative structure of Judaism, Lilienblum argues that historical Judaism was never uniform or unitary but has always been pluralistic. The criterion for future Jewish existence does not hinge on the theoretical question whether Jews would follow the Orthodox or Reform liturgy, or whether they would be religious or secular. Under stress—the 1881 disturbances proved—no distinction is made between the religious and the secularists. History shows the Jewish people have always been very deeply divided along doctrinal and theoretical lines, but on a practical basis Jews always shared the same fate, regardless of their differences and sometimes petty squabbles. This pluralism within a common identity should also be maintained when Jews return to Palestine, and care should be taken not to create in the new community a uniformity which excludes other groups within the Jewish people. Lilienblum thus presents a very impressive statement that the unity of Jewish identity should encompass a plurality of differences and crosscurrents. Later Zionist activity very much followed this pluralistic view of a nondoctrinaire and liberal interpretation of Jewish existence, and despite the flowery language—in typical *Haskala* style—the message is clear:

> The nation as a whole is dearer to us all than all the divisions over rigid Orthodoxy or liberalism in religious observances. . . . Any one of Jewish seed who does not forsake his people is a Jew in every sense of the word. It has been well said that just as people do not have identical faces, so they are not of one mind. There is no logic in any desire for all the future Jewish settlers in the ancestral land to belong to the exact same sect. Let each man there follow the dictates of his conscience. . . . But let no man oppress his fellow. *Within our autonomous political life everything will find its place.* . . .
>
> Let the Orthodox know that *we are all holy,* every one of us— unbelievers and Orthodox alike, we have been laying down our lives. . . .
>
> There is no doubt that if the liberals will practice restraint, our Orthodox brethren will be tolerant, and there will be peace among the Jews at this critical moment. . . . What reason cannot achieve, time will . . . [3]

Another dimension of Lilienblum's change of mind after 1881 is his novel assessment of anti-Semitism. Before 1881, and even in the immediate wake of the disturbances, Lilienblum views anti-Semitism as a carryover from the past, eventually due to disappear when Enlightenment and integration would drive away prejudices and misconceptions. In "The Way of Return," written during the weeks of the pogroms, Lilienblum still talks in an undifferentiated way about "Jew haters" being responsible for the disturbances, and he optimistically adds, "But why do they labour in vain to bring back their beloved Middle Ages, for the age *will never* return [italics added]."[4]

By 1883, however, Lilienblum is far less sure that anti-Jewish feelings are a thing of the past. By this time he has become acquainted with the new, racial anti-Semitic literature of Central Europe and thus has begun to realize that the Jews face a modern phenomenon, not a mere repetition of the residual old religious prejudices. Moreover, Lilienblum realizes that the emergence of modern racial, secular anti-Semitism is deeply linked with the rise of modern nationalism. If traditional, religiously inspired anti-Jewish feelings have become weakened through Emancipation and secularization, the Jews are being confronted now with an anti-Semitic movement arising from the wave of the future—modern national liberation movements. Lilienblum thus becomes one of the first to see the dialectical relationship between the emergence of modern nationalism and a new kind of anti-Jewish sentiment, politically expressed and organized:

> Civilization, which could virtually deliver us from those persecutions which have a religious basis, can do nothing at all for us against the persecutions with a nationalistic basis. . . . No civilization in the world has the power to demand that an alien be accepted by a strange family as if he were a natural-born child of that family. . . .
>
> Furthermore, not only can civilization and progress do nothing to eradicate anti-Semitic views, but indirectly they even help them along. . . .
>
> It is evident that the over-all trend toward nationalism is not a regression, despite the assertions of the students of Roman cosmopolitanism; it represents progress which must ultimately do away with war and direct humanity, with all its nations, to the way of true unity. But this true civilization, i.e. *the drive for national self-determination, is the very soil in which anti-Semitism flourishes*—as nettles flourish in a green field, for there is no rose without thorns and no good without evil. Anti-Semitism is the shadow of our new and fine contemporary civilization; it will no more do away with anti-Semitism than the light will destroy the shadows it casts. That is why anti-Semitism is making such great strides.
>
> We remember how, three years ago, when Marr came out with his anti-Semitic doctrine,[5] we all jeered at him, made fun of his schemes, dubbed them an "anachronism" and said that they were about three centuries behind their times. But hardly four years have passed and the anti-Semitic trend has already swept almost all of Europe. It has shaken the world with petitions, riots, arson, congresses, speeches in parliaments, and so on. What will happen next? [italics added].[6]

Lilienblum, moreover, is aware of the multiple pressures becoming apparent in modern societies. Cosmopolitan ideas vie with an emergent nationalism; the rise of capitalism is being followed very quickly by the emergence of a militant socialist movement. All these create a situation in which every group, recognizing some Jews in the group opposing it, tends to identify its social or national enemy with the Jews in general. Each social stratum, each ideology, begins to view its enemy as the Jews. In popular mythology, the Jew thus becomes the enemy of everyone. In a passage

whose full impact could be sensed fully only decades later, Lilienblum writes,

> The opponents of nationalism see us as uncompromising
> nationalists, with a nationalist God and a nationalist Torah; the
> nationalists see us as cosmopolitans, whose homeland is wherever
> we happen to be well off. Religious Gentiles say that we are devoid
> of any faith, and the freethinkers among them say that we are
> Orthodox and believe in all kinds of nonsense; the liberals say
> that we are conservative and the conservatives call us liberal. Some
> bureaucrats and writers see us as the root of anarchy, insurrection
> and revolt; and the anarchists say we are capitalists, the bearers of
> the biblical civilization, which is, in their view, based on slavery and
> parasitism. Officialdom accuses us of circumventing the laws of the
> land—that is, of course, the laws directed specifically against us. . . .
> Musicians like Richard Wagner charge us with destroying the beauty
> and purity of music. Even our merits are turned into shortcomings:
> "Few Jews are murderers," they say, "because the Jews are cowards."
> This, however, does not prevent them from accusing us of murdering
> Christian children.[7]

These are modern dilemmas, and the conventional wisdom of
the *Haskala*, Lilienblum argues, has no adequate answers to them.

Lilienblum had been close to some of the socialist ideas then
prevalent in Russia. He consequently acknowledges that "there is,
as yet, one community, the proletariat, which knows no children
nor aliens—only workers."[8] Yet he warns against a naive reliance
on a proletarian victory, since the Jews could be very easily turned
into "the scapegoat . . . and a lightning rod" for the fury of the
underprivileged. What will appear to all of mankind as universal
liberation might turn—because of the specific social and national
context in which it will be realized—into a holocaust for the Jewish
population.

Lilienblum sees three choices for the Jews: (1) the continuation
of the status quo, which would entail "to be oppressed forever, to
be gypsies, to face the prospect of various pogroms and not be
safe even against a major holocaust"; (2) ultimate integration and
assimilation by the adoption of Christianity and the disappearance
of any remaining residue of Jewish identity, so that in a few generations "descendants of ours who no longer retain any trace of their
Jewish origin will be entirely assimilated among the Aryans"; and
(3) a national renaissance "in the land of [our] forefathers, where
the next few generations may attain, to the fullest extent, a normal
national life."[9]

Lilienblum chooses the third alternative. The first, he argues, means asking for a holocaust, and the second may be a solution for individuals but cannot be a public policy adopted by the community. He then puts forward a number of operative ideas, which foreshadow to a large extent the nature of Zionist activity as it would develop a few decades later. He calls for the establishment of a Jewish National Fund to finance the purchase of land in Palestine and the establishment of agricultural settlements there. This fund would be based on small contributions ("a kopek a week") as well as an allocation from all Jewish social functions. "It is also possible to earmark given percentages of the sums donated in the synagogues, at weddings, at funerals of the rich, et cetera. Perhaps, too, a Jewish lottery can be set up, so that there will be no more need for talk about the sale of shares in stock companies and the like." All these funds, collected through the already existing Jewish communal infrastructure, should be aimed at "buying many large holdings in Eretz Israel from the Turkish government."[10]

Lilienblum is aware that the Jewish upper classes, which have been integrated with some success into European society, will not make up the bulk of Jewish emigration to Palestine. Like Moses Hess before him and Leo Pinsker a few years later, Lilienblum sees in the more impoverished Jewish masses the basis for the new society in Palestine. This is consistent with the populist tendencies running through Lilienblum's writings, influenced as he was by the Russian Populist movement. This also causes Lilienblum to reinterpret some dramatic moments in Jewish history, like the Maccabean wars, in a populist vein. Graetz also had turned the Maccabean insurrection into a national war of liberation, after it had slumbered in Jewish popular consciousness for centuries as a homely festival of lights, Hanukkah, surrounded by stories of miracles and denuded of its concrete historical significance. To this national reinterpretation of the Maccabean Revolt against the Hellenistic Syrians, Lilienblum adds a populist radical strain. After warning nineteenth-century Jews not to rely on "our plutocrats in Paris, Berlin and St. Petersburg. . . . Do not expect them to take the lead," Lilienblum says,

> when Antiochus condemned the Jewish people to death, its salvation did not come from Jerusalem, but from the Hasmonean village of Modin. The wealthy assimilationists of that capital, together with the proud Sadducees, submitted shamefully to the insolence of the Greek hangmen. It took the true sons of the people, the unbelievably

courageous Hasmonean priests, to rescue Israel, and only afterward did Jerusalem, too, join with them.[11]

In contemporary Europe, just as in historical Judea, redemption and liberation will come from the popular masses, not from the assimilated elites.

Though Lilienblum's thinking is diffuse and highly unstructured, it does focus on a number of aspects characterizing the transformation of Jewish Enlightenment in Russia—the *Haskala*—after 1881. The debate about religious reform has become irrelevant and obsolete in the face of the existential danger now faced by the whole community, secular as well as Orthodox. Lilienblum realizes that 1881 was not the last echo of the Middle Ages but may have signaled the wave of the future—the explosion of modern, racial, and social anti-Semitism. Lilienblum's analysis makes him aware of the complex social and nationalist forces giving rise to the tensions leading to this new kind of anti-Semitism, and the conventional wisdom of the *Haskala*, with its harmonistic and progressivist beliefs in education and Enlightenment, becomes more and more irrelevant. He also understands that the position of the Jews in the modern world will not be determined solely by their objective status but also by the subjective modes through which this status will be perceived by the social and national forces of contemporary society. Integration and assimilation thus fail to provide an adequate answer to this novel dilemma and force Lilienblum's transition from *Haskala* to a quest for a national solution to the Jewish problem as now defined in the modern world.

CHAPTER 7

PINSKER: FROM EMANCIPATION TO AUTOEMANCIPATION

THE IMPACT OF THE 1881 MASSACRES ON JEWISH PUBLIC OPINion can perhaps best be gauged by the appearance of one of the seminal essays in modern Jewish thought, which became a milestone in the evolution of modern Jewish nationalism. In 1882 a Russian Jewish doctor, Leo Pinsker, published anonymously a pamphlet in German called *Autoemancipation,* whose very title was at once innovative, polemical, and revolutionary.[1] For a generation that saw Emancipation as the key word for the solution of the Jewish problem in the modern age, the idea of *auto*emancipation became a challenge to the conventional wisdom of the age.

Like many other educated Russian Jews of his generation, Leo Pinsker (1821–1891) grew up in Odessa, a typical product of its culture. His father was a distinguished Hebrew scholar, an authority on the Karaites, who taught at the Hebrew school in Odessa, the first such institution in Russia. Leo Pinsker studied medicine at Moscow University and then returned to Odessa. During the Crimean War he volunteered to serve as a field doctor with the Russian army and was awarded a decoration from the czar for his services, certainly a very unusual honor for a Jewish person in Russia at that time. In short—his was the story of an enlightened, educated Jewish intellectual who succeeded in being integrated into Russian society and for many years advocated a similar path for the younger Jewish generation of his country.

As for many others of his age, 1881 was a cruel shock to him, and his pamphlet is an attempt to confront the failure of the dream of Emancipation through education and integration. The events of 1881 suggested to Pinsker that it is not the prejudices of the uneducated or those carried over from medieval times that are at the root of the Jewish question. Rather it is the structural problems of contemporary society. Such problems require a radical solution, and a mere call for tolerance and universal loving kindness would not suffice. The bond to Palestine is initially secondary in Pinsker's thought and does not trouble him or motivate him. What motivates him is the plight of the Jews in the nineteenth century. At first Pinsker is utterly equanimous to the question whether the solution should be found in Palestine or in America, but his essay is the clearest and most outspoken call in his generation for a solution of the Jewish problem in the spirit of national self-determination.

Like Moses Hess before him, Pinsker sees the dilemmas facing the Jews in nineteenth-century Europe not just from the point of view of the Jews themselves. He relates their plight to some basic processes through which European society as a whole is passing, and out of the principles of European society and its ideas he seeks a solution to the Jewish problem.

Pinsker's criticism of the wisdom of the conventional call for Emancipation is double-edged—pragmatic and theoretical. Pragmatically, 1881 proved that Emancipation as such is not a viable solution; theoretically, Emancipation proceeds from an assumption that the Jews are a passive object of historical development. One has to liberate *them*, one has to award *them* rights, one has to treat *them* on the basis of equality and tolerance. The historical subject in these actions is always the non-Jewish majority culture; the Jews themselves remain a passive element. According to Pinsker, in the modern world, based on the principles of self-determination and liberty, such a solution is out of tune with the rest of the world and hence cannot work. Through the idea of autoemancipation, or self-determination, Pinsker tries to reintegrate the Jews into the historical process, to make them once again an active factor in history, conscious of themselves and their historical activity. To Pinsker, what Exile ultimately meant was to deprive the Jews of their active role in history. It turned them into mere objects, and freedom cannot be a gift offered on a platter by the non-Jews. Hence the motto of the essay, "If I am not for myself, who will be for me?" and the pamphlet's closing sentence, "Help yourselves, and God will help you!"[2]

Autoemancipation is written in the style of a manifesto. It is a brief, terse, and linguistically aggressive essay, sometimes short on historical depth and conceptual rigor but very effective in its impact. In this respect it is truly reminiscent of the *Communist Manifesto*, which is also characterized by a combination of simplistic formulation and aggressive language, broad generalizations, and verbal power. The analogy can be stretched even further; both have pithy and uncompromising closing sentences and a radical unwillingness to entertain even the slightest doubt about the correctness of the method applied or to listen to alternative solutions, which might be less radical and perhaps (at that time) more realizable. This oversimplification, encapsulated in the effective slogans formulated by the essay, can easily charm great masses, and this gave both to the *Communist Manifesto* as well as to *Autoemancipation* their enormous historical impact in their respective contexts.

The massacres and pogroms of 1881 prove to Pinsker that the Jewish problem cannot wait any longer for a messianic or utopian solution—be it the traditional belief in the coming of the Messiah or the secularized version of a liberal brotherhood of all men—when all friction between persons and peoples would disappear under the victorious aegis of Liberty, Equality, and Fraternity. What contemporary Jews need, because of the immediate perils to their lives, is a realistic and pragmatic solution, a solution that has to start from the premise of the Jews as a nation, a people, not a mere religious community. Therefore a solution based, as conventional Emancipation has been, on integration into the non-Jewish nations of Europe, is not adequate.

However, at the same time that Pinsker asserts that the Jews are a nation like all other nations, he points out that their status as a nation has been accompanied by an anomaly which distorted the relationship between them and the rest of the world: lack of sovereignty. On the one hand, most nations treat the Jews as members of an alien nation; on the other hand, they do not grant them the rights usually quite readily granted to members of other nations for the simple reason that the element of reciprocity is lacking. The Jews are thus a nation and viewed as such by others, but they lack the effective attributes of a nation. Therefore they

are relegated to the limbo of marginal existence, to the hazy bor-
derland between reality and fantasy, where things appear different
from what they really are. This abnormal situation creates traumas
and fears:

> The Jews lack most of those attributes which are the hall-mark
> of a nation. They lack that characteristic national life which is
> inconceivable without a common language, common customs,
> and a common land. The Jewish people have no fatherland of
> their own, though many motherlands; they have no rallying point,
> no center of gravity, no government of their own, no accredited
> representatives. They are everywhere as guests, and are nowhere *at
> home*. The nations *never* have to deal with a Jewish *nation* but always
> with mere *Jews*.[3]

Emancipation has been the attempt to solve the Jewish problem
on an individual basis, so that each individual Jewish person could
partake, on an equal basis and according to his abilities, in the general good. But Emancipation is not a social, collective solution to
the problems of the Jewish nation. For this reason Emancipation is
not, ultimately speaking, really accepted by the non-Jewish world.
Because the Jewish nation did not possess the effective external
attributes of a nation, it is conceived as a specter, a ghost, haunting
the land of the living.

Entering this psychological field, Pinsker ushers in perhaps
the least convincing of his arguments: hatred of the Jews lies in a
mental illness called *Judeophobia*, the fear of Jews. Because he was a
doctor, such quasi-clinical explanations obviously appealed to Pinsker's mind, but the terminology is, of course, begging the question. By saying that Judeophobia is the cause of Jew-hatred, Pinsker
really says that non-Jews fear Jews because they are afflicted by a
malady whose main symptom is a fear of Jews. Such an explanation
is simplistic and lacks an adequate historical dimension, since it
fails to explain why attitudes to Jews have, after all, changed from
place to place and from time to time, and for all the continuity
in certain aspects of anti-Semitism, there have always been cultural, geographical, and temporal differences in the outbreak of
anti-Jewish sentiments.

This is an aspect which Pinsker neglects in the generalized picture he paints. Late-nineteenth-century fashionable psychological theories clearly echo in Pinsker's description of Judeophobia,
and methodologically, the same weaknesses which accompanied

similar explanations of psychopathology in his time can also very easily discerned in Pinsker's approach:

> Along with a number of other subconscious and superstitious ideas, instincts, and idiosyncracies, Judeophobia also has become quite naturalized among all the peoples of the earth with whom the Jews had intercourse. Judeophobia is a form of demonopathy [fear of demons], with the distinction that the Jewish ghost has become known to the whole race of mankind. . . .
>
> Judeophobia is a psychic aberration. As a psychic aberration it is hereditary, and as a disease transmitted for two thousand years it is incurable. . . . [4]

Unsatisfactory and simplistic as Pinsker's quasi-medical diagnosis may be, it does try to address itself to the exceptional conditions of Jewish existence. If the Jews are a nation and they continue to exist as a nation despite the lack of the effective attributes of national life, this is an obvious anomaly, and an explanation has to be found. Krochmal and Graetz tried to explain this deviation from the norms of universal historical development by rearranging the conventional norms of universal history itself. Pinsker lacks this philosophical dimension of history, and he therefore limits himself to stating what he conceives as an anomaly and attempting to suggest a clinical diagnosis for it. Pinsker's diagnosis may appear irrelevant, but his cure is radical. If the nations of the world see the Jew as a soul without a body, a shadowless Ahasver, an eternal Wandering Jew, lacking real, corporeal existence, the cure surely has to be radical. If the Jews are hated because they have no homeland, normalization will become possible only if they acquire one. Were this to happen, then the nations of the world would view the Jews as normal human beings and would consequently lose their inordinate fear of them. No concrete, real attribute of the Jews causes Judeophobia; it is the abnormality of the Jews being somewhere between a national existence and a lack of a real foundation for that existence. For the Jews to appear like any other people they need a homeland, Pinsker argues: then everybody will relate to them as normal people and Judeophobia will wither away.

In discussing the demonological aspect of Judeophobia Pinsker maintains that some concrete accusations against the Jews do not make sense because the Jews are often accused of traits which contradict each other. Only a demonological view of the Jews can sustain such contradictory accusations. "To sum up what has been said: for the living, the Jew is a dead man, for the natives an alien and a vagrant, for property-holders a beggar, for the poor an exploiter and a millionaire, for patriots a man without an country, for all classes a hated rival."[5]

Emancipation cannot fundamentally change this. The Jew is still conceived as a foreigner who has to be naturalized. This stigma will not disappear as long as the Jews do not emancipate themselves and determine their own existence. He who needs others to liberate *him* will never be free until he liberates *himself*. Likewise, Jewish unfreedom will continue as long as individual Jews have to concentrate all their energy on individual survival, for what the Jews lost in the struggle for individual survival was their own collective identity:

> Single-handed each separate individual had to waste his genius and his energy for a little oxygen and a morsel of bread, moistened with tears. In this hopeless struggle we did not succumb. We waged the most glorious of all partisan struggles with all the peoples of the earth. . . . But the war we have waged . . . has not been for a fatherland, but for the wretched maintenance of millions of "Jew peddlers." . . .[6]

The history of the Jewish people in the Diaspora is the history of the relative success of these myriads of individual solutions to the Jewish plight. The point, however, is to find a solution for the community, a collective answer. For this reason Pinsker is not satisfied with those who view emigration to America as an adequate solution to the Jewish problem in Eastern Europe. This would be another quest for a new Diaspora, which, perhaps, would solve the problem of the plight of the individual emigrants for a shorter or a longer period but would not solve the national plight.

In this context Pinsker mentions, in true Enlightenment fashion, his criticism of the religious Jewish tradition. To him, religious Orthodoxy as well as the traditional messianic beliefs have contributed to the basically passive Jewish response to the abnormal lives Jews were leading in the Diaspora. Religion helped to internalize the Diaspora and legitimize it, because religion taught the Jews "that we must bear patiently a punishment inflicted upon us by God"; the belief in the Messiah, "in the intervention of a higher power to bring about our political resurrection . . . caused us to abandon every care for our national liberty, for our unity and independence. . . . Thus we sank lower and lower."[7]

With Enlightenment and Emancipation Pinsker sees the first stirrings among the Jews and a break with the passivity and quietism characterizing the religious tradition. Pinsker does not initially advocate a solution leading to Palestine, but he notes with satisfaction the "irresistible movement" among some Russian and Rumanian Jews to emigrate to the Land of Israel. Pinsker points out the "lamentable outcome" of this movement, but it is for him a symptom of the deep transformation in Jewish self-consciousness from a passive to an active attitude. The attempts to organize emigration to Palestine from Russia and Rumania testify "to the correct instinct of the people, to whom it became manifest that they need a home. The severe tests which they have endured have now produced a reaction which points to something other than fatalistic submission to punishment inflicted by the hand of God."[8]

Emancipation, for all its shortcomings and basic failures, has nonetheless pointed the right way: activism. In the concrete historical context of the nineteenth century, the Jewish problem assumes a new and revolutionary connotation. It can no longer be isolated from a universal problem that has already become focal to the political and cultural preoccupations of the modern era: nationalism. The Jewish problem has ceased to be a specific and particularistic issue:

> The *general* history of the present day seems called to be *our* ally. In a few decades we have seen rising into new life nations which at an earlier time would not have dared to dream of a resurrection. The dawn already appears amid the darkness of traditional statesmanship. The governments are ready to incline their ears—first, to be sure, in those cases in which they cannot do otherwise—to the louder and louder voices of national self-consciousness.[9]

The ideas of this new age have not been lost on the Jews, who are now breaking out of their historical isolation and beginning to relate to humanity at large. In a language consciously modeled on that of Giuseppe Mazzini, Pinsker writes, "The great ideas of the eighteenth century have not passed by our people without leaving a trace. We feel not only as Jews; we feel as men. As men, we, too would fain live and be a nation like others."[10]

For the first time, Pinsker argues, the universal and the particular meet in the course of Jewish history: a national solution to the Jewish problem is no longer a particularistic Jewish idiosyncrasy but addresses itself to the universal values of modern world history.

The Jewish claim to nationhood can no longer be denied on the basis of universal ideas.

It is to this modern reality that Pinsker turns in the formulation of his practical plans in the second part of the *Autoemancipation*. His plan relates both to problems of leadership as well as to a detailed sketch of institution building. Pinsker likes to compare the modern plight of the Jews to the traumatic Exodus from Egypt, mainly because the Exodus was carried out as a collective enterprise, not as a mere running away of individual slaves. At the present time, Pinsker argues, the Jewish people does not possess a leadership figure compared to Moses. But there exists an infrastructure of leadership in the many Jewish voluntary associations and organizations, and these should form the basis for convening a National Congress and setting up a National Directorate. Such a body should include "men of finance, of science, and of affairs, statesmen and publicists." Pinsker obviously takes his example from the nationalist and liberal context of constituent assemblies involved in the national and political transformations of the nineteenth century. Eventually, this structure emerged with the convening of the first Zionist Congress by Herzl.[11]

Such a national leadership, comprising the spiritual, political, and economic forces of the Jewish people, should then create the tools to realize the territorial base for the Jewish commonwealth. Just as in the case of Lilienblum, here were the beginnings of the ideas later to be utilized in the Zionist Organization. The National Congress would elect a permanent National Directorate that would have to decide between Palestine and America. It would mobilize, through fund raising among the wealthier Jews, capital for the creation of a joint-stock company to buy a tract of land, as large and as sparsely populated as possible. The land would then be divided into small plots for agriculture and industry. These plots would not be sold but only leased to individuals, and the income, after defraying initial capital expenses, would accrue to a National Fund which would finance the immigration and settlement of those Jews who could not assume these costs through their own means. The land would, however, remain in perpetuity in the hands of the National Fund.[12]

Pinsker clearly sees that the emigration involved would not necessarily comprise all the Jewish communities in the world. Western Jewry, living comfortably in relative security and liberty, would probably remain where it is.[13] Yet in looking for a tract of land suitable for Jewish settlement, Pinsker is thinking in terms of mass immigration; the area has to be "sufficient to allow the settlement of several millions."[14] This immigration would come from countries with a dense Jewish population, for Pinsker maintains that there always is "a certain point of saturation beyond which the number of the Jews may not increase if they are not to be exposed to the dangers of persecution." He singles out Russia, Rumania, and Morocco as the three main reservoirs of surplus Jewish population for mass immigration to Palestine.[15] This was again a striking forecast of the eventual structure of Israel.

For Pinsker, these processes of forming a national leadership will be a test for the Jewish potential for self-emancipation. Leadership formation is itself part of the process of liberation. Autoemancipation is not only a desired goal, but based as it is on self-realization, it is also a conscious continuous social process, and its main test is in its own self-realization. A people creating for itself the structures for its emancipation is already on the road to freedom and self-determination—a parallel, probably unknown to Pinsker yet nonetheless significant, to Marx's views about the self-emancipation of the proletariat through consciousness-forming praxis.

Pinsker's point of departure is not Palestine; his premise is the Jewish people. Given his intellectual background, Pinsker's choice of the exact location of the future homeland is a question of pragmatism, not programmatic determination. He saw the beginnings of Jewish settlement in Palestine as an indicator of the novel, activist elements in the contemporary Jewish context. But it is the act itself—trying to find a solution based on self-realization—which counts for him, not its location. Yet Pinsker returns to this question several times in his *Autoemancipation*, and it remains for him an open question.

Pinsker starts by saying that the question of the location of the future homeland should not be a priori determined by the historical link to the Land of Israel:

> If we would have a secure home, so that we may give up our endless life of wandering and rehabilitate our nation in our own eyes and in the eyes of the world, we must above all not dream of restoring ancient Judea. We must not attach ourselves to the place where our political life was once violently interrupted and destroyed. The goal of our present endeavors must be not the "Holy Land" but a land of our own. . . .[16]

But immediately he adds,

> Perhaps the Holy Land will again become ours. If so, all the better, but *first of all*, we must determine—and this is the crucial point—what country is accessible to us, and at the same time adapted to offer the Jews of all lands who must leave their homes a secure and unquestioned refuge, capable of being made productive.[17]

Ultimately a decision will have to be made between Palestine and America, but what is important to Pinsker is that a decision be made, so that there would be *one* national goal and not conflicting orientations. The Jews should not get involved in a public effort for two parallel emigration processes. Which would eventually be chosen depends, according to Pinsker, on the economic absorptive capacities and the political considerations involved in each of the proposed alternatives. In both cases, the possibilities of a political future have to be taken into account. If the area selected is in America, it should eventually form a Territory within the United States federal system, if "in Asiatic Turkey . . . it should be a sovereign Pashalik [Province] recognized by the Porte and the other Powers as neutral. It would certainly be an important duty of the Directorate to secure the assent of the Porte, and probably of the other European cabinets to this plan."[18] Herzl's idea of securing a charter from the sultan is clearly foreshadowed here.

Yet the question whether the homeland should be in Palestine or America remains open in the pamphlet. Pinsker's later public activity and his association with Hovevei Zion and the convening of the Kattowitz Conference in 1884, which laid the groundwork for the first Zionist Congress, eventually moved him in the direction of the Palestinian solution. The novelty of Pinsker's thought remained, however, in the revolutionary radicalism of his first pamphlet. Emancipation granted by others cannot truly free a people, since they remain an object at the mercy of alien historical forces. Only autoemancipation would bring the Jews back into history. The solution to the Jewish problem should be found in a national manner, Pinsker argues, and education and philanthropy cannot solve it. This was the shift in the search for self-identity which characterized so many Jewish *maskilim* in Russia in the wake of 1881, and Pinsker's polemical essay is perhaps the most eloquent—if not always the most profound—expression of that shift.

CHAPTER 8

BEN YEHUDA: LANGUAGE AND NATION

ELIEZER BEN YEHUDA (1858–1922), WHOSE ORIGINAL NAME was Perlman, is known mainly in connection with the revival of Hebrew as a spoken, everyday language. He was among the first to advocate that Hebrew has to be used as the language of daily intercourse and not, as maintained by most of the *maskilim*, merely as the cultural, intellectual medium of the Jewish people. For decades he prepared the first modern dictionary of the Hebrew language, which became the foundation of modern Hebrew lexicography, and in his studies he enriched the Hebrew language through the introduction of hundreds of new terms intended to enable the modern Hebrew speaker to confront the realities of the contemporary world. Yet there is much more than this in his own life story. As a student in Lithuanian *yeshivot*, later as a medical student in Paris, and then as an emigrant to Palestine in 1881, he had a rather unique intellectual development, which was another variant of the multifaceted growth of the Jewish Enlightenment in Russia into an ingredient of the Jewish national movement aimed at Palestine.[1]

During his student days, Ben Yehuda had been connected with the Russian Populist movement, and for a time he was quite close to those in the Russian revolutionary intelligentsia who were ready to advocate terrorism for the furtherance of radical aims. At the same time he was close to Peretz Smolenskin in whose journal

Hashahar he published most of his early articles. At that time he also adopted his *nom de plume*, Ben Yehuda (Son of Judah) and inaugurated the trend which became dominant later among Zionists who immigrated to Palestine to change their non-Hebrew surnames into Hebrew ones.

Ben Yehuda's own emigration to Palestine in 1881 was by itself a radical step, unique in his time. None of the Hebrew Russian *maskilim* found their way to Palestine even after the 1881–82 disturbances; Ben Yehuda, however, had gone to live in Jerusalem even before the outbreak of the anti-Jewish riots in southern Russia. The ideological reasons for his emigration as well as his practical moves in carrying out their implication are characterized by rare cultural and intellectual insights. Ben Yehuda's arguments relate to a radical criticism of the crisis of the Russian Jewish *Haskala*, and his ideas are novel in their context and implications.

An open letter written by Ben Yehuda at the end of 1880 to the editor of *Hashahar* sets forth his ideas in their most concise form. It relates to a polemical exchange which broke out at that time between Peretz Smolenskin, the editor of *Hashahar*, and a number of German Jewish intellectuals regarding the usage of the Hebrew language. Some writers connected with the German Jewish Reform movement contended that since Reform views Judaism merely in terms of a religious community and not as a national entity, the preservation of Hebrew in religious Jewish worship is anachronistic and should be discarded. Consequently, the Reform movement wanted to replace Hebrew with German in the religious liturgy. Smolenskin, on the other hand, argued that there exists a historical uniqueness in Jewish national existence as a universal, spiritual people even without a unifying territorial concentration. Consequently, the Hebrew language should be maintained as the spiritual bond uniting the various Jewish communities all over the world. While the Gentiles are united by material elements like territory and political force, the Jewish nation should be united by the spiritual links. And the Hebrew language is one of these.[2]

Ben Yehuda generally supports Smolenskin's position, but he transcends this debate by asking another question: why is it that the Hebrew literary attempts of the *Haskala* were not successful in producing truly masterful aesthetic and artistic achievements? Ben Yehuda points out that over a period of a few decades, the *Haskala* movement was able to bring about a true renaissance in Jewish intellectual life in Eastern Europe. Essays, novels, plays, and poems were being written profusely in Hebrew, and the Hebrew language had turned into the spiritual medium of communication of an ever-growing Hebrew-reading public which has been graduating in increasing numbers from the new Hebrew, secular schools fostered by the *maskilim*. Nonetheless, Ben Yehuda shares the widely held view that literary greatness has not yet been achieved, and he tries to find the reasons for the mediocre, derivative, highly pedantic and stilted style of the *Haskala* literature.

In his letter to Smolenskin, Ben Yehuda's answer is fairly simple: true literature can emerge only in a social environment speaking the language in which that literature in being written. *Haskala* literature in Russia is artificial, alienated from the sources of true artistic creativity—life itself. The authors who write in Hebrew do not use Hebrew in their daily life; and in their writings they describe in Hebrew a society which does not speak Hebrew but speaks Yiddish or Russian or Polish. How can an aesthetically sensitive literature develop on the basis of such a hiatus between life and imagination? A Hebrew literature, Ben Yehuda argues, can develop only in a society which speaks Hebrew, with a Jewish majority which will relate to Hebrew as its living language of daily intercourse:

> We will be able to revive the Hebrew tongue only in a country in which the number of Hebrew inhabitants exceeds the number of gentiles. There, let us increase the number of Jews in our desolate land; let the remnants of our people return to the land of their fathers; *let us revive the nation and its tongue will be revived, too!*[3]

The revival of the Hebrew language cannot, then, be limited to a mere intellectual attempt to develop it as a purely spiritual medium of intellectuals. Such an intellectual revival, which has been the program of the *maskilim,* is doomed to condemn Hebrew to a jejune, imitative fate, to turn it into another sort of medieval Latin. Anyone interested in the revival of the Hebrew language must therefore aim at the creation of a Jewish territorial concentration in the Land of Israel. The cultural-linguistic romanticism of nineteenth-century nationalism is clearly audible in Ben Yehuda's impassioned cry to Smolenskin, "But, sir, we cannot revive [Hebrew] with translations; we must make it the tongue of our children, on the soil on which it once blossomed and bore ripe fruit!"[4]

It has sometimes been argued that Ben Yehuda's attempt to revive the Hebrew language as a spoken medium was a result and consequence of his immigration to Palestine and his awareness of the emergence of a new Jewish community there. In reality it was the other way round: Ben Yehuda emigrated to Palestine from his conviction that only with the creation of a Jewish society in the ancestral land of the Jews is there a chance for the emergence of an artistically significant Hebrew literature and a Hebrew cultural renaissance. For Ben Yehuda, the program of immigration to Palestine and turning Hebrew into a spoken medium, not a mere intellectual *jeu d'esprit*, was the solution to a dilemma faced by the *Haskala* movement in Russia. His insistence that the revival of Hebrew cannot be limited to the intellectual elite but has to express concrete, popular processes that would make Hebrew the language of the whole people is by itself an interesting attempt to apply to the Jewish context ideas originating in Russian Populist thought, with which Ben Yehuda has been connected. The Russian Populists maintained that the social revolution could not succeed if it remained a spiritual effort of the intelligentsia alone; they called for the intellectuals to "go down to the people," live with them, share their sufferings, and educate them toward revolutionary consciousness and action. This also applies to the Hebrew *Haskala*: if it remains ensconced within the confines of a narrow intellectual elite, priding itself on its linguistic prowess and biblical scholarship, it will ultimately be condemned to archaism and irrelevance. According to Ben Yehuda, the Hebrew language has to be brought to the people; it has to be made into the medium of daily commerce and intercourse, become a mass language, the language in which the mother talks to her children and the husband to his wife. The revival of the Hebrew language must be taken out of fashionable salons into the streets. This is Ben Yehuda's unique translation of the Russian Populist tradition to the reality of the linguistic-cultural transformation which the Jewish public was undergoing at that time.

For Ben Yehuda, no national culture—and no national language—is possible without the concrete, social infrastructure of national life. Concepts like that of a People of the Spirit, so prevalent in the Hebrew *Haskala* before 1881, are to him based on abstraction and, hence, precarious and doomed to failure. Just as linguistic renaissance and national political revival have gone hand in hand among other nations in the nineteenth century, so they will among the Jews:

> It is senseless to cry out: "Let us cherish the Hebrew language, lest we perish!" The Hebrew language can only live if we revive the nation

and return it to its fatherland. In the last analysis, this is the only way to achieve our lasting redemption; short of such a solution we are lost, lost for ever! . . . The Jewish *religion* will no doubt be able to endure even in alien lands; it will adjust its forms to the spirit of the place and the age, and its destiny will parallel that of all religions. But the *nation?* The nation cannot live except on its own soil; only on this soil can it revive and bear magnificent fruit, as in the days of old.[5]

Ben Yehuda's emigration to Palestine, his attempt to teach his wife and children to speak Hebrew at home, his bitter fight against the fundamentalist Jewish religious establishment in Jerusalem, which viewed all this as utter sacrilege, were all the logical outcome of his conviction that sees the linguistic revival of Hebrew in the context of a national revolutionary transformation which needs a wide, popular basis and cannot be merely an elitist, intellectual game.

This "going down to the people," making Hebrew into the language of fishmongers and street urchins, became the *second* linguistic revolution to overtake the Hebrew language in the nineteenth century. The first was turning it from a rabbinical and liturgical language into the secular language of the intellectual discourse of the *Haskala*. This second revolution was greatly enhanced by Ben Yehuda's work and by the ideological underpinning he gave it through both his writings and his emigration to Palestine and his public struggles in Jerusalem. His revolutionary synthesis of the Jewish people, the Hebrew language, and the Land of Israel became a crucial ingredient in the development of Jewish national thought and practice.

CHAPTER 9

HERZL: THE BREAKTHROUGH

A S THE CONVENER OF THE FIRST ZIONIST CONGRESS IN BASLE in 1897 and the founder of the World Zionist Organization, Theodor Herzl has become identified more than any other person with the emergence of political Zionism. His life (1860–1904) has acquired legendary proportions, his portrait has become one of the trademarks of Zionism, and the symbolism attached to his personality has become one of the powerful elements of the Zionist creed. His life has consequently become a subject of study, discussion, and analysis more than that of the other founders of Zionism.[1]

This, however, is not the subject of discussion here, nor will the obvious, and by now quite familiar, facts relating to his activity be restated. Our discussion will be limited mostly to one issue, raising a fundamental query about Herzl.

Anyone reading Herzl's writings—mainly *The Jewish State* (1896) and *Altneuland* (*Old-New Land*) (1902)—will find a plethora of ideas about the dilemmas of Jewish existence in the modern world as well as some very practical suggestions toward their solution. Yet few of these ideas are novel or original. Herzl's acute analysis of the roots of anti-Semitism in the post-Emancipation era was preceded by the even more analytical writings on this subject by Hess, Lilienblum, and Pinsker; Herzl's ideas about the establishment of Jewish national institutions to further the aims of Zionism

were preceded by similar ideas—and institutions—dating back
to Kalischer, Smolenskin, and the founders of the Hovevei Zion
movement. And Jewish settlements had been established in Palestine decades before Herzl, and for all their limited scope and
mixed success, they had become a focus of attraction and admiration for numerous Jewish organizations in various countries.

What, then, were the novelty and historical significance of Herzl's activity? They lie neither in the originality of his thoughts
nor in his organizational skills, which were rather limited, but in
something quite different. Herzl was the first one to achieve a
breakthrough for Zionism in Jewish and world public opinion. He
turned the quest for a national solution to the plight of the Jewish
people from an issue debated at great length and with profound
erudition in provincial Hebrew periodicals read by a handful of
Jewish intellectuals in the remote corners of the Russian Pale of
Settlement into a subject for world public opinion. From a marginal phenomenon of Jewish life he painted the Zionist solution
on the canvas of world politics—and it has never left it since.

Herzl had no financial resources and no political power to back
him up. The Jewish establishment, both financial and rabbinical,
viewed him, in most cases, with suspicion if not outright horror.
His appearance in the arena of world public opinion was achieved
through his own almost maniacal heroic struggle, and in the
course of this activity Herzl sometimes showed signs of irresponsi-
ble, if not slightly dangerous, egotism. What helped Herzl in this
leap into the public limelight was his profession and personality:
he was a journalist—brilliant, sometimes superficial—hungry for
publicity and adept at public relations.

In this Herzl was a true child of his milieu. His intellectual
eclecticism, the lack of real spiritual depth usually characterizing
his writing with all its brilliance, his Viennese feuilletonistic bon
mots—all these traits, which seem to point toward the basically
lightweight part of his nature, were the elements which helped
him in his one-track endeavor. More careful and less superficial
people would have feared to tread where he did. But from the
moment Herzl came to his conclusion about the necessity for a
national solution to the Jewish problem, he correctly realized that
such a momentous and revolutionary task could not be achieved
through silent labor at the edge of world politics. Articles in
obscure Jewish publications would not mobilize the massive forces
needed for such a tremendous transformative effort, ideological

disputations between a few scores of semiemployed Jewish intellectuals in unheard-of tracts would never get the message across. Only a daring breakthrough, which might have something of adventurism in it, would succeed in bringing it into the center of the world's attention.

Therefore, his writing was sometimes pompous, bombastic, and theatrical—especially in *The Jewish State*—and his solutions look not only as if their author has discovered them for himself for the first time but also as if he had been the first one to pose the very questions. Thus his attempt to solicit the help of Jewish financial magnates, like Edmund de Rothschild and Maurice de Hirsch, was done with all the prophetic *chutzpah* of a beggar claiming to speak for the whole Jewish people. All his rather dramatic approaches to the Pope, to Emperor Wilhelm II, to the Sultan, to the Archduke of Baden, to the British Colonial Secretary were motivated by his profound understanding that the efforts of a small and persecuted people could become successful only if they were thrust directly, without mediation, with unrelenting simplemindedness, straight into the commanding heights of world power and international opinion. He, Theodor Herzl, a well-known but penniless journalist, would negotiate with the Sultan about granting a charter to the Jews for Palestine; he, the assimilated Jew, would find paths to the heart of the Pope; he, whose only weapon was his pen, would convince the Kaiser, Her Majesty's Government, the Russian Imperial Minister of the Interior, all the high and mighty.

None of these efforts proved successful. The Sultan was not convinced that an alliance with the Jews was the wisest policy open to him; the British government backed off even from the outlandish idea of allocating parts of East Africa for Jewish settlement; Emperor Wilhelm II probably did not exactly realize the implications of what Herzl was asking for; even Rothschild and Hirsch remained unconvinced and did not open their coffers. Nevertheless, Herzl could point to his achievements: through lobbying and impressing courtiers, bribing his way through the maze of the Ottoman court, calling on Wilhelm II when he visited Jerusalem, cooling his feet in the antechambers of the High Porte, besieging and pestering the shakers and movers of world politics— eventually, despite his failures, Herzl did reach all those rulers, talk to them or their immediate entourages, propose to them his ideas and plans. In that he succeeded more than anyone before him, and in doing all this he always appeared as if speaking as a plenipotentiary for a mighty Jewish empire—while behind him he had no movement and practically no organization, no money and no influence, and a pawnbroker's shop was sometimes his only financial support.

All this was the virtuoso performance of a master of public relations, of a person becoming aware of the new powers-that-be of the twentieth century—public opinion, mass communication, gimmicks whose main significance is the impact they leave behind, not necessarily their substance. All this explains the overdramatization of events, the insistence on talking only to the people at the very top (Pope, Emperor, Sultan); it explains the theatrics of so much of Herzl's appearances—the top hat, the correct coattails, the white gloves, the ceremonial opening of the first Zionist Congress. All these externals were sometimes viewed critically by Herzl's contemporaries and collaborators. Some rightly sensed in them overcompensation for internal psychological deficiencies, perhaps even the ravings of a slightly unstable soul; some accepted them as idiosyncrasies which proved their point when Herzl managed to reach the pinnacles toward which he aimed; others found it more difficult to reconcile themselves to the flamboyancy of his style (no wonder that Disraeli was Herzl's favorite statesman). But foe and friend alike had to admit that since Herzl's meteoric appearance, Zionism had begun to move in another sphere; from a parochial concern of some Jewish intellectuals *it* became an issue of world politics and transcended the mere organizational fact of the founding of the Zionist movement.

With this breakthrough Herzl forged the weapon that later was to become the mainstay of Zionism as the struggle of a weak people, which initially had no legions and no political power to support its claim against the overpowering strength of politics and history: public opinion. This was Zionism's only weapon when it set out to wrest a homeland for the Jewish people from the clutches of world history. The Balfour Declaration of 1917, the United Nations Resolution of 1947 calling for the establishment of a Jewish state in a part of Mandated Palestine, and other landmarks on the way to the Jewish state have been achieved not through Jewish economic or political power but through the ability of the Zionist movement to enlist again and again the intellectual and spiritual resources of a highly literate and vocal people, adept at polemics, loquacious and oriented toward public debate. These were the weapons wielded by a weak, persecuted, and small nation in its struggle against extremely uneven odds. Herzl was the first one to realize their potential and forge them into a public force. Zionism and the State of Israel rely to a large extent on them until this very day.

Consequently in discussing Herzl's writings it is necessary to balance the very limited originality of his ideas with the immense impact left by them when they became—for the first time in Zionist thought—virtual best sellers.

One common misconception is that only in *The Jewish State* did Herzl for the first time address the Jewish question and that only the Dreyfus affair alerted him dramatically to the emergence of a virulent kind of anti-Semitism and convinced him that Emancipation had backfired. In his own generation, Herzl was a typical product of this Emancipation: born in Budapest to the family of a well-to-do merchant, he moved as a child to Vienna, graduated in law, and became one of the most popular and widely read journalists and columnists of the liberal Vienna *Neue Freie Presse*. He tried his hand, albeit not very successfully, as a playwright, and it is in his plays that his first doubts about Emancipation were being voiced. Most of his plays, addressed to the Viennese Jewish theater-going bourgeoisie, deal with the problems of the modern, emancipated Jewish intellectual. One of his more successful plays, *The New Ghetto* (1894), expresses the feelings of frustration and having arrived at a dead end, so typical among many of these successful, emancipated middle-class Jews. When one of the heroes of the play insists on escaping this new limbo, another of the protagonists, Rabbi Friedheimer, tells him,

> And I tell you we cannot do it! When there was a real ghetto, we were not allowed to leave it without permission, on pain of severe punishment. Now the walls and barriers have become invisible. . . . Yet we are still rigidly confined to a moral ghetto. Woe to him who would desert![2]

In France, where he served from 1891 as the Paris correspondent of the *Neue Freie Presse*, Herzl became even more sensitive to this ambiguity in the status of the modern Jew. If Viennese popular anti-Semitism could at least partially be explained by the residues of traditional religious feelings against the Jews in a basically traditional society, it was in Paris that Herzl learned of the new populist power of anti-Semitism, nurtured by the contradictions of a modern, highly secularized, and parliamentary society. Many of Herzl's dispatches from Paris during this period deal with the emergence of social anti-Semitism in France.[3] Herzl follows with deep apprehension the public debate that begins to focus on the growing salience of Jews in economic, intellectual, and parliamentary life in France. Discussions about economic crises and financial scandals, intellectual debates and parliamentary fireworks were becoming helplessly muddled, sidetracked, and disfigured by focusing on the Jewish identity of some of the protagonists. Herzl sees in this a new problem which is caused by Emancipation itself and cannot, therefore, be remedied by it. The paradox is evident to Herzl that precisely in the country which first granted Emancipation to the Jews—republican France, the heir to the Great Revolution—a new and ominous Jewish problem is emerging, originating in the tensions and stresses of modern society itself. The Dreyfus affair was correctly understood by Herzl as only the dramatic expression of a much more fundamental malaise.

The emergence of this modern anti-Semitism in the country that stood for universalism and human fraternity and where the Jewish population was minuscule made Herzl realize the irony of the liberal conventional wisdom that Emancipation and equal rights will solve the Jewish problem. Not only is Emancipation unable to solve the problem, the problem in its new dimensions is itself *caused* by Emancipation and the emergence of the modern, secular Jew. In *The Jewish State* Herzl says,

> In the principal countries where anti-Semitism prevails, it does so as a result of the Emancipation of the Jews. When civilised nations awoke to the inhumanity of discriminatory legislation and enfranchised us, our enfranchisement came too late. It was no longer possible legally to remove our disabilities in our old homes. For we had, curiously enough, developed while in the Ghetto into a bourgeois people, and we stepped out of it only to enter into fierce competition with the middle classes. Hence, our Emancipation set us suddenly within the middle-class circle, where we have a double pressure to sustain, from within and from without. The Christian bourgeoisie would not be unwilling to cast us as a sacrifice to socialism, though that would not greatly improve matters. . . .[4]

In *Altneuland* Herzl gives a poignant view, which Lilienblum and Pinsker had also expressed, of how modern life places so many Jews in the middle of numerous social and economic cross fires:

> The persecutions were social and economic. Jewish merchants were boycotted, Jewish workingmen starved out, Jewish professional men

proscribed—not to mention the subtle moral suffering to which a sensitive Jew was exposed at the turn of the century. Jew-hatred employed its newest as well as its oldest devices. The blood libel was revived; and at the same time, the Jews were accused of poisoning the press, as in the Middle Ages they had been accused of poisoning the wells. As workingmen, the Jews were hated by their Christian fellows for undercutting the wage standards. As business men, they were dubbed profiteers. Whether Jews were rich or poor or middle-class, they were hated just the same. They were criticized for enriching themselves, and they were criticized for spending money. They were neither to produce nor to consume. They were forced out of government posts. The law courts were prejudiced against them. They were humiliated everywhere in civil life. It became clear that, in the circumstances, they must either become the deadly enemies of a society that was so unjust to them, or to seek out a refuge for themselves.[5]

According to Herzl, these processes would intensify, and he sees no guarantees or built-in mechanisms to curtail or reverse these developments in the future. The painful conclusion is that the Jews have ultimately only one way open to them—out.[6]

Once Herzl has reached this radical conclusion, all his activity is geared to realizing this end, and his career as a journalist becomes inextricably interwoven with his new endeavors at a novel Jewish diplomatic effort. This is a well-known and oft-told story; therefore, the discussion here will be limited to the nature of the future Jewish society as envisioned by Herzl in his two programmatic books, *The Jewish State* and *Altneuland*.

In their form, the two books are as different from each other as possible. *The Jewish State* is written as a combination of political manifesto and legal brief. It summarizes the problems of Jewish existence in modern society and then sets forth, sometimes in exaggerated legal detail, the structure of the Jewish organizations for creating a Jewish society in a new land. The question whether this new society will be in Palestine or Argentina (as was earlier suggested by some of Baron Hirsch's philanthropic efforts) is left open, though Herzl appears to tilt toward a solution based on the historical homeland of the Jewish people. *Altneuland* is a utopian novel, the sort of book which in *The Jewish State* Herzl says he is not about to write, because there is "nothing to prove that it can be set in motion."[7] *Alteneuland*, written in 1902, is a description of a Jewish Palestine as Herzl projects it into the year 1923. Despite its didactic form, which it has in common with most utopian novels, and its rather obvious plot, the book is written with a rich imagination that is nonetheless deeply rooted in the realities of the Jewish situation and the conditions of Palestine. Compared to the realities of Israel as it emerged later, it certainly is an interesting yardstick by which to measure the Zionist dream. Its vision, on the other hand, should be viewed within the general context of utopian literature as a genre. There is no doubt that much of its fascination lies in the vivid and moving description of a revived Land of Israel. No longer does Herzl have doubts about the venue of the new homeland. It becomes clear to him that the revival of the Jewish people is possible only in its ancestral land.[8]

There is, however, a common pattern to both books. In both volumes Herzl not only describes a society that would be a refuge to the Jews but also builds it up as a model of social justice, based on the socialist utopian literature of the nineteenth century.

This is to a large extent quite paradoxical, since Herzl is himself almost an archetypical bourgeois, liberal thinker, and there is nothing of the political extremist in his makeup. His political philosophy generally tends even toward the conservative. In *The Jewish State* he says, for example, that his ideal form of government would be an "aristocratic republic" and cites Venice as a model.[9] There is a similar reference in *Altneuland*.

Despite his moderate, if not conservative, politics, Herzl ultimately realizes that the revolution involved in the establishment of a Jewish state would be inevitably connected with a radical transformation of the Jewish social structure. Furthermore, since Herzl realizes that the Jews are virtually all middle-class people, creating a Jewish national society would also involve transforming the Jews from a class into a people, bringing them out of the old-new ghetto into an overall social structure, in which all occupations would be filled by Jews. Herzl—ironically—even mentions that while the Jews would occupy the industrial, scientific, and agricultural positions in the New Society, most of the merchants in his Haifa of 1923 are Greeks and Armenians.[10] Such a transformation of the social structure of the Jewish people, Herzl realizes, cannot be achieved through the market mechanisms of a laissez-faire society.

Thus the element of public ownership of land appears in *The Jewish State*: land will be owned collectively, and there will be no private property in land and natural resources. Individual farmers will lease their plots from the National Fund. In *Altneuland* Herzl elaborates on this and suggests that the old Mosaic principle of the Jubilee Year should be institutionalized into the landowning patterns of the New Society and no private ownership of land ever allowed in the country. This principle was later followed by the Jewish National Fund, which became owner of all the land purchased by the Zionist Organization.

In *The Jewish State* Herzl envisages the massive settlement of Palestine through the establishment of public housing estates for workers and through the evolution of a wide network of social welfare institutions designed to structure the New Society along welfare state lines. As the pinnacle of these social achievements Herzl views the seven-hour working day as well as the provision of public work in lieu of public assistance.[11] So central is the seven-hour day to Herzl that he also expresses the idea in the flag that he proposed for the Jewish state. "I would suggest a white flag, with seven golden stars. The white field symbolises our pure new life; the stars are the seven golden hours of our working day. For we shall march into the Promised Land carrying the badge of labour."[12]

In *Altneuland* this social element appears in an even stronger form. The social structure of the country is called *gemeinschaftlich* and mutualistic, a term directly derived from French utopian socialism. The foundation of the economy is thus cooperative, but the individual shall not be deprived of the ability to give vent to his individual initiative:

> Our method provides the mean between individualism and collectivism. The individual is not deprived of the stimulus and pleasures of private property, while at the same time, he is able, through union with his fellows, to resist capitalist domination. The plague, yes, the curse of the poor has been removed—they no longer earn less as producers and pay more as consumers than the rich.[13]

One of the dramatic high points in the narrative of *Altneuland* is the town meeting of the villagers in the new cooperative village Neudorf (New Village) in the Galilee. This town meeting is used by Herzl for a long didactic discourse delivered by the main hero of the novel, David Littwak, about the principles of social organization of the New Society. Here Littwak delineates the genealogy of the Jewish cooperative society in Palestine:

> Don't imagine I am jesting when I say that Neudorf was built not in Palestine, but elsewhere. It was built in England, in America, in France and in Germany. It was evolved out of experiments of both practical men and dreamers who were to serve you as object lessons, though you did not know it.[14]

Littwak goes on to enumerate these forerunners of the Jewish cooperative commonwealth in Palestine: the French utopian socialist Charles Fourier, the founder of the phalanstère system; the French utopian communist Etienne Cabet, author of *Voyage en Icarie*; Theodor Hertzka, the author of *Freiland*; Edward Bellamy, "who outlined a noble communistic society in *Looking Backward*"; and the Rochdale pioneers. Summing up this heritage, Littwak says to the members of the Neudorf,

> When you go to the consumers' co-operative societies and buy goods of the best quality and at the lowest prices, you have the pioneers of Rochdale to thank for it. And if your Neudorf is a prosperous producers' co-operative you owe it to the poor martyrs of Rahaline in Ireland. . . .
> The New Society rests squarely on ideas which are the common stock of the whole civilized world.[15]

It is clear that the political, revolutionary socialism of the militant working class is not Herzl's paradigm but the utopian, humanitarian, and reformist brand that would later be called, in the Zionist socialist context, "constructivist." What is significant is that the founder of modern political Zionism, who was himself a liberal if not a moderate conservative politician, describes the future Jewish commonwealth as based on socialistic, cooperative lines. He saw the New Israel as realizing the social vision of nineteenth-century European utopian socialism. Herzl is aware that the conditions of the New Society in Palestine, starting from scratch, were especially favorable for the establishment of such a mutualistic society, because of "our advantage of being free from inherited burdens; we did not have to ruin anyone in order to ease the lot of the masses." Such a society can also serve, according to Herzl, as a model for a parallel social transformation in Europe.

These socialistic elements in Herzl's description of the future Jewish society in Palestine are accompanied by a number of other arrangements conspicuously novel in the context of Herzl's own period. Herzl clearly transcends the limits of his own bourgeois-liberal horizon in many of the innovations he attributes to his utopian society. Thus, for example, at a time when no European country had yet granted the franchise to women, Herzl postulates the political structure of the New Society on universal suffrage, and women's full participation in the political life of the community is described in much detail.[16] At a time when practically every European country still restricted even manhood suffrage through all kinds of property qualifications, this certainly suggests a breadth of vision far beyond Herzl's generalized preference for an "aristocratic republic."

Among the other radical and revolutionary institutions of the New Society, all directly derived from utopian socialist literature, is Herzl's insistence that schooling be free and universal from kindergarten to university—also quite novel in terms of 1902. At the same time, all members of society "men and women alike, are obligated to give two years to the service of the community."[17] This national service is not for military purposes. The young people, usually between the ages of eighteen and twenty, devote these two years to carrying out the social services offered by society to its members: hospitals, infirmaries, orphan asylums, vacation camps, homes for the aged. All these and other social welfare institutions are thus staffed by people doing their national service. Thus all inhabitants are insured against sickness and old age, and no person is threatened by poverty and sickness. Herzl is aware that his own nineteenth-century society could have established these institutions; "the old society was rich enough at the beginning of this [the twentieth] century, but it suffered from ineffable confusion. It was like a crowded treasure house where you could not find a spoon when you needed one."[18]

Urban planning is also central to the development of the New Society. The new towns of Palestine are all very carefully planned and thus would not evolve chaotically as clusters of urban sprawl. Their growth would not be determined by land speculation. There would be an electrified system of mass transport, mainly overhead railways, in all cities; express trains and super highways would connect the cities to each other, and hydroelectric plants, utilizing the difference in elevation between the Mediterranean Sea and the Dead Sea, through channels, would ensure cheap electricity, et cetera. In short, Herzl's *Altneuland* has all the elements of a utopian society in which mutualistic socialism is wedded to technological progress and centralized planning.

In *Altneuland* Herzl also discusses the future relations between Jews and Arabs in the New Society. Herzl is extremely aware that the country is already populated, albeit sparsely, by Arabs, and his solution, which may look today, in retrospect, as slightly naive and simplistic, is nonetheless motivated by the universalistic, humanistic ethos of the whole novel. All Arab inhabitants who wish to join the New Society as equal members and citizens are free to do so. A central figure in the novel, Reschid Bey, is the romanticized archetypical Oriental of nineteenth-century European literature: deeply rooted in the values of his Arab and Muslim society, yet at the same time combining the courtesy and tolerance of the Orient with the scientific education and broadmindedness of the Occident. Reschid Bey and his like are equal members in the society, and on several occasions he explicitly says that the Arabs of Palestine have greatly benefited from Jewish immigration.[19] Herzl, however, points out that the rapid Westernization of Palestine by the Jews was to be tempered by a tolerance toward the need to preserve the cultural traits of Arab society. Thus a pluralism in social behavior would develop. While Arab women have an equal right to elect and be elected for public office, most of them, in deference to Muslim custom, might prefer to stay within the confines of the traditional Oriental home, which is their prerogative.

It is of some significance that the main public debate which agitates Herzl's New Society for 1923 deals with the relationship between Jews and Arabs and with the question of tolerance. During the time in which the novel is set, an election campaign to the Representative Assembly takes place in the country. An extremist party, led by a rabbi, Dr. Geyer, advocates limiting citizenship rights and membership in the New Society to Jews only;[20] the moderate party, led by David Littwak, maintains that non-Jews living in the country should continue to have equal rights. It is superfluous to add that the Sons of Light triumph over the Sons of Darkness: Littwak's party soundly defeats Geyer and his henchmen, and tolerance and equal rights prevail. What is of some interest is Herzl's foresight in recognizing intolerance and national-religious fanaticism as one of the issues which would plague the social achievements of the New Society in the Land of Israel. In this, as much as in his more positive prognostications, Herzl's projections were surprisingly accurate about the kind of society to be established by the Zionist effort.

With all his tolerance and universalistic humanitarianism, characteristic of his Central European outlook and his impeccable vision of civil rights as related to the Palestinian Arabs, Herzl obviously overlooked the potential of a *national* movement emerging among the Arab population, not least as a response to Jewish immigration and the attempts of Zionism to transform the country into a Jewish national home. There is no doubt that for Herzl the problem was limited to ensuring the human, civil rights of the Arabs as *individuals*. The issue of an *Arab* national movement never crossed his mind. This is, obviously, a serious flaw, except in the context of the time in which Herzl was writing. There hardly existed at that time any political national movement among the Arab population in Palestine. Perhaps people like Herzl should have been aware of the potential for the rise of such a movement, but to ask Herzl, seeking a solution to the Jewish national problem, to envisage the emergence of such a movement in Palestine at a time when neither the ruling Ottomans nor the Western powers nor even the Arab population itself were aware of its imminence, would be, historically speaking, asking perhaps too much.

In any attempt to assess Herzl's contribution to the development of Zionist thought two points stand out. First, he was incredibly successful in bringing ideas that had been germinating for a long time to the attention of world public opinion and into the general consciousness of the age. Second, for a thinker who was himself far from socialism or radical revolutionary thought, he envisaged the social utopian elements in Zionist reconstruction and accurately predicted how the Zionist effort eventually came to be realized in the concrete organization of the new Jewish community in Palestine.

CHAPTER 10

NORDAU: THE JEWS AND THE CRISIS OF WESTERN CIVILIZATION

L IKE HERZL, MAX NORDAU (1849–1923) REACHED ZIONISM after a brilliant career as an essayist and journalist, one of the most fashionable writers of the German fin de siècle. He wrote for various German papers, and his books—*The Conventional Lies of Civilization, Paradoxes*, and *Degeneration*—translated into many languages, earned him a prominent place in the world of German letters. Like Herzl, he was born in Budapest, and like many of its middle-class Jews, he viewed himself as belonging to the German cultural sphere. For many years he lived in Paris, as a correspondent for the prestigious German-language Budapest paper, *Pester Lloyd*; and, like Herzl, in Paris he witnessed Dreyfus's degradation and imprisonment. But unlike Herzl, Nordau came from a religious yet enlightened Jewish home. His father, Gabriel Südfeld, was an ordained rabbi and Hebrew author (in 1831 he published a Hebrew grammar in Prague). When he was quite young, however, Nordau cut himself off from this parental background, changed his name from Südfeld, with its obvious Jewish connotation, into the much more Germanic and even Nordic-sounding *Nordau*, and, as he wrote in an autobiographical sketch, "when I reached the age of fifteen I left the Jewish way of life and the study of the Torah. . . .

Judaism remained as a mere memory, and since then I have always felt as a German, and as a German only."[1]

Nevertheless, it was the penetrating critique of contemporary European civilization, as expressed in his essays, which brought Nordau to also reassess Emancipation and its impact on Jewish life. With his entry into the Zionist movement under the influence of his close friend Herzl, this critique found its way into numerous articles and speeches. Nowhere have these thoughts been better expressed than in Nordau's great programmatic speech inaugurating the first Zionist Congress in Basle in 1897.

"The Western Jew has bread, but man does not live on bread alone."[2] With this poignant statement Nordau launched into one of the most penetrating analyses of the state of Western Jewry. The question bothering Nordau was the same one that had bothered Herzl as well as Pinsker and Lilienblum. Why is it that in the era of Emancipation and liberalism, there has arisen a new kind of political Jew-hatred, an anti-Jewishness no longer derived from the old religious prejudices but grounded in the new liberal atmosphere, which was supposed to cure the traditional hatred of the Jews?

According to Nordau, Emancipation has basically been a failure—not of implementation but on a much deeper and more fundamental level. It is a twofold failure: an external one, from the point of the *view* of the relationship of non-Jewish society toward the Jews; an internal one, from the point of view of the Jews' own relation to themselves in the wake of Emancipation.

In discussing the external failure Nordau explains that Emancipation came about under conditions deeply imbued with ambiguity and illusion. The Jews thought that the various nations granted them equality of rights and emancipation because of their conscience and feelings. But it appears that the reasons for Emancipation have been far more abstract and quite isolated from the concrete context of the general feeling about the Jews. In the following, much of Nordau's critique of his contemporary Europe can be seen:

> The Emancipation of the Jews was not the consequence of the conviction that grave injury had been done to a race, that it had been treated most terribly, and that it was time to atone for the injustice of a thousand years; it was solely the result of the geometrical mode of thought of French rationalism of the eighteenth century. This rationalism was constructed by the aid of pure logic, without taking into account living sentiments, and tried to apply its principles with

the axiomatic certainty of mathematical action; and it insisted upon trying to introduce these creations of pure intellect into the world of reality. The Emancipation of the Jews was an automatic application of the rationalistic method. The philosophy of Rousseau and the Encyclopedists had led to the Declaration of Human Rights. Out of this Declaration, the strict logic of the men of the Great Revolution deduced Jewish Emancipation. They formulated a regular equation: Every man is born with certain rights; the Jews are human beings, consequently the Jews are born to own the rights of man. In this manner, the Emancipation of the Jews was pronounced, not through a fraternal feeling for the Jews, but because logic demanded it. Popular sentiment rebelled, but the philosophy of the Revolution decreed that principles must be higher than sentiments. The men of 1792 emancipated us only for the sake of principle.[3]

In other words, the roots of Emancipation were not in the concrete sociocultural context of real, historical life but in an abstract idea; and just as other abstract ideas of French eighteenth-century rationalism remained null and void or became distorted when attempts were made to implement them in conditions which bore no resemblance to their origins and causes, so Jewish Emancipation became a hollow reality.

This abstract element of a generalized rationalism repeated itself in other countries, which embraced the principles of the French Revolution and through it the principle of Emancipation of the Jews:

As the French Revolution gave to the world the metric system and the decimal system, so it also created a kind of normal spiritual system which other countries, either willingly or unwillingly, accepted as the normal measure for their state of culture. A country which claimed to be at the height of culture had to possess several institutions created or developed by the Great Revolution; as, for instance, representation of the people, freedom of the press, a jury system, separation of powers, etc. Jewish Emancipation was also one of these indispensable articles of a highly cultured state; just as a piano must not be absent from the drawing-room of a respectable family even if not a single member of the family can play it. In this manner Jews were emancipated in Europe not from an inner necessity, but in imitation of a political fashion; not because the people had decided from their hearts to stretch out a brotherly hand to the Jews, but because leading spirits had accepted a certain cultured idea which required that Jewish Emancipation should figure also in the statute book.[4]

Formally, it could be written into all statute books, but this formal Emancipation contrasted sharply with popular social consciousness. Thus there arose a tension between the formal, external norms of Emancipation and the real, concrete feeling toward the Jews in society.

According to Nordau, there has been one exception, which throws this development into sharp relief: in England, Nordau says, Emancipation grew gradually out of the organic development of social and political life there, just as the general English constitutional development grew out of internal concrete developments and not out of abstract ideas or their adoption. "In England, Emancipation is a truth. It is not only written into the law, it is living. It had already been completed in the heart before legislation expressly confirmed it."[5] Emancipation of the Jews in England conforms to real, social consciousness, and therefore one hardly finds any traces of anti-Semitism there. Anti-Semitism on the Continent, in France, Austria, Germany, or Eastern Europe, on the other hand, *is* the outcome of the tension and the gap between the egalitarian postulate of abstract legislation and the unwillingness of concrete popular consciousness to accept the Jews as equal citizens.

Yet there is a further aspect of failure, a frailty, which helped to distort the inner authenticity of Jewish life. This concept Nordau explains in his speech to the first Zionist Congress when he embarks on a lavish praise of the ghetto, which seems highly incongruous for a person of his background. Coming from such an archetypical representative of the liberal, Westernized Jewish intelligentsia, which tended to look with distaste if not utter disgust at ghetto life, the Pale of Settlement, and the *shtetl*, this is really quite surprising. But Nordau succeeded in giving back to the ghetto its balanced historical place, above and beyond the criticism of the Enlightenment, which saw it merely as the spiritual and physical prison of Jewish life in the Middle Ages.

The ghetto also enabled the Jews psychologically to overcome medieval persecutions and Christian bigotry. In the ghetto, Nordau says,

> the Jew had his own world; it was to him the sure refuge which had for him the spiritual and moral value of a homeland. Here were the associates by whom one wished to be valued, and also could be valued, here was the public opinion whose acknowledgment was the aim of the Jew's ambition. To be held in low esteem by that public opinion was the punishment for unworthiness. Here all specific Jewish qualities were esteemed. . . . What did it matter that outside

the ghetto was despised that which within it was praised? The opinion of the outside world had no influence, because it was the opinion of ignorant enemies. One tried to please one's co-religionists, and their applause was the worthy contentment of one's life. So did the ghetto Jews live, in a moral respect, a real full life. Their external situation was insecure, often seriously endangered. But internally they achieved a complete development of their specific qualities. They were harmonious human beings, who were not in want of the elements of normal social life.[6]

The impact of such an analysis on the members of the first Congress can only be imagined. This was a complete reversal in the conventional Jewish liberal thinking about the ghetto. Undoubtedly, elements of idealization and romanticism, reminiscent of the then prevalent Germanic romantic adulation of the Middle Ages, were attached to this unconventional portrait of the ghetto. But beyond this, it implied a novel, post-Emancipation reading of history. Such an innovative reinterpretation of ghetto life could only come from a person who has gone through Emancipation and found it wanting—and this is its dialectical significance. Thus the circle has been closed.

This reinterpretation of the elements of solidarity and community life immanent in the ghetto leads Nordau to reassess the impact of Emancipation on the totality of Jewish life. If the ghetto represented the internal wholeness and authenticity of Jewish life, its disappearance signalled the emptying of all meaning for Jewish life.

This is what happened, according to Nordau, wherever the message of Emancipation arrived. Equality before the law guaranteed to the Jews that they would become equal citizens in their countries of residence, and "the Jews hastened in a wave of intoxication, as it were, to burn their boats. They now had another home; they no longer needed a ghetto. . . . And within one or two generations the Jew was allowed to believe that he was only German, French, Italian, and so forth."[7]

In an essay called "The History of The Israelites" (1901), Nordau goes even further. Here he maintains that until the French Revolution, the Jews preserved their national identity despite persecutions and hardships. It was precisely liberal Emancipation which put an end to Jewish national identity. "Have you forgotten the French Revolution? This is that great historical occurrence, which brought about the wonder of turning the Jewish people into a 'religious community.' It was the Revolution which granted human and civil rights. Jews, overnight, ceased to be members of a four-thousand-year-old nation. . . ."[8]

In his speech at the first Zionist Congress, Nordau explained that Emancipation was nothing but a thin veneer covering a much more complex social reality. Therefore, it rather quickly became evident that non-Jewish society was not yet ready to accept the Jews as equal members. The emergence of modern, racial anti-Semitism is now confronting the emancipated and educated Jew, and it, rather than the formalism of equal rights, expresses the authentic feelings of so many of the non-Jews vis-à-vis the Jewish question. Faced with this dilemma, the educated, Western Jew finds himself in a much greater quandary than that of the traditional Orthodox denizen of the ghetto. The ghetto inhabitant had to face a totally hostile world. But the Jewish community served as a collective bastion, and the individual ghetto Jew faced this world with his brethren, sustained by their solidarity and by a belief in his faith. Enlightenment and Emancipation put an end to this Jewish public life in the form of the *kehilla*. Equal rights meant the disappearance of the public nature of the Jewish community, and Emancipation meant atomization and alienation—for this, after all, is the nature of the modern world based as it is on deracinated individualism:

> Such is the existing liberation of the emancipated Jew in Western Europe. He has given up his specifically Jewish character; but the peoples let him feel that he has not acquired their special characteristics. He has lost the home of the ghetto; but the land of his birth is denied to him. His countrymen repel him when he wishes to associate with them. He has no ground under his feet and he has no community to which he belongs as a full member . . . With his Jewish countrymen he has lost touch: necessarily he feels that the world hates him and he sees no place he can find warmth when he seeks for it. This is the moral Jewish misery which is more bitter than the physical, because it befalls men who are differently situated, prouder and possess the finer feelings. . . .[9]

These attempts to ascribe to himself a new identity fail the modern Jew: the "New Marrano," as Nordau calls the modern, emancipated Jew, cannot become what he attempts to be, a member of a non-Jewish nation, since modern anti-Semitism, with its racial elements, refuses to see in conversion to Christianity a true change in the Jewish nature of the person undergoing this conversion. In the old world of religious prejudices, a Jew could opt out of his community by becoming a Christian; racist theories now block this way out, and the emancipated Jew finds himself trapped in his enforced identity. He cannot cease being Jewish.

This, to Nordau, is the true failure of Emancipation, which cannot be the answer to the dilemmas of the Jews in the modern world. On the contrary, Emancipation and secularization only heighten these dilemmas both by confronting the Jew with modern problems, which he now has to face in isolation from his brethren and by making it impossible for him to solve these problems in the world of nationalism and racial theories.

The Jews themselves, Nordau claims, are well aware how precarious is Emancipation. In an article, "The Jewish People among the Nations of the World" (1901), Nordau points out that for all the equal rights granted to them, the Jews are still traumatized by the memory of the ghetto. Until this very day, he says, they fear lest their rights will be challenged and they will be pushed back into the ghetto:

> For this reason they evince a much more vociferous patriotism than their Christian colleagues, and thus a further distortion takes place: namely, that the emancipated Jew proclaims his German or Hungarian nationalism much more noisily than his Christian neighbor, and this at the expense of his solidarity with his Jewish brethren in other countries. The Jews' patriotism has something sick about it; it is much tenser and more demonstrative than that of the Christians, who possess a nonartificial and natural patriotism.[10]

Thus a double distortion occurs; the modern Jew has lost his old identity, yet the new identity does not sit well with him.

Zionism is, to Nordau, the re-creation of a collective, communal Jewish identity, its rediscovery in terms relevant to the modern age. It is a return to Jewish identity from the atomized anomie of Emancipation—a return necessitated by the impact of liberalism and nationalism. In an article, "On Zionism" (1902), Nordau sharply distinguishes Zionism from the traditional, religious Jewish messianic yearnings. "Zionism rejects all mysticism, does not believe in a Return to Zion through miracles and wonderous happenings, but sets out to create it through its own efforts."[11] Zionism, according to Nordau, grew out of the pressures and social forces of the modern age, and its solution to the Jewish question is a modern one, within the context of contemporary nationalism:

> The idea of nationalism has taught all the nations to acknowledge their own worth, to view their specific qualities and values, and it

implanted in them the strong desire for self-rule. This idea could not just by-pass the educated Jews without leaving any impact on them. It instructed them to think about themselves, to feel themselves as what they have forgotten that they were—as a nation unto themselves, looking for a normal national future for their own people.[12]

The Jewish national idea is thus an integral part of universal history in its national phase, and Nordau is well aware of the far-reaching revolutionary consequences of such a restorative transformation of Jewish life:

> The Zionists know that they have taken upon themselves a task of unprecedented difficulty. Never has it been attempted to uproot, peacefully and in a short time, millions of people from different countries and integrate them into a new country; never has it been attempted to transform millions of feeble, unskilled proletarians into peasants and shepherds, to link to the plow and Mother Earth shopkeepers and peddlars, brokers and seminarists, all of them city-dwellers alienated from nature. It will be necessary to acquaint Jews from different countries with each other, to educate them in practice toward national unity and to overcome the enormous drawbacks stemming from the difference in language, culture, modes of thinking, prejudices and deviations grafted from alien nations, which all of [these immigrants] will bring from their old homeland.[13]

The social consequences of this transformation also are discussed in Nordau's article "The Jewish People among the Nations of the World." He maintains that it is not true that Jews have a special ability or inclination for business life, but this is a trait which became associated with the Jews during their years in the Diaspora, when they were uprooted from immediate productive labor. History shows, Nordau argues, that when the Jews were settled in their own country, most of them were peasants, shepherds, warriors, and priests; one hardly finds traders among them, and those in the Orient who engaged with great success in trade were not the Jews but their neighbors, the Phoenicians. Moreover, the Jews were not influenced by the example of the Phoenicians but "hated trade and did not envy their neighbors, who became enormously wealthy due to their business proficiency. . . . Nothing could have been more popular among the Jews than that New Testament story about the expulsion of the money-changers from the Temple. . . ."[14]

Nordau goes even further and suggests that for all the centuries in which Jews have engaged in trade in the Diaspora, they have not developed one novel idea in this sphere, which again proves that this was basically not the Jews' special inclination. He attempts to show that hardly any Jews are found in the development of modern economy, that "the mortgage and the promissory note were invented by the Lombards and the Goths in the Middle Ages, that double bookkeeping was the contribution of the Christian Italians, the first insurance companies were instituted in England, and neither Gresham nor Lloyd was Jewish; and it was the French who established the joint-stock companies."[15] In other words, it was the Gentiles, not the Jews, who were inventive and innovative in business.

Nordau supports his view that Jews are not particularly interested in business by pointing to the Jewish tendency not to see in economic activity the pinnacle of social success but to view it as a mere ladder for educational opportunities for the next generation. Education, not economic success, is for the Jews the true mark of achievement, and this craving after educational mobility is, to Nordau, solid proof of the basic inferiority that Jews attach to their own mercantile activity. "It is evident that the sons of Jewish merchants who become rich have no other ambition that to turn away from their parents' occupations, though they know only too well that from the point of view of pecuniary success, there is no more lucrative occupation than business."[16]

Nordau does, however, think that there is a specific Jewish talent—for politics, not for business. He is aware that this is a highly unorthodox view, and therefore he enumerates in this article in great detail the salience of Jews in parliamentary life in many countries—France, Hungary, Germany, Austria, England, and even New Zealand. This is an interesting catalog of achievement, accompanied by a tragic note, since Nordau realizes that "the Jewish people [do not] benefit from their statesmen, who sooner or later became integrated into the alien nation; but to their homeland they bring enormous benefits."[17]

According to Nordau, Jews possess a unique combination of characteristics which are especially useful for political life, particularly in parliamentary and democratic countries. "Their talkativeness, their stamina, their perceptual talent, their ability to work out compromises between contending parties," and that "combination of idealistic vision and realistic shrewdness and judgement," are, says Nordau, a "unique synthesis, unequalled in any other nation." This practical idealism, derived from Jewish legacy, is evident also in those Jews who cut themselves off from their heritage, and it is this legacy which gives them their political versatility, whose underlying element is the ability to realize principles.[18]

This unusual account by Nordau is, obviously, suffused with apologetic elements, as is Nordau's basic intention of trying to minimize the significance of Jewish prominence in business and to turn the tables, so to speak, on the Gentiles. Yet, Nordau's insistence that "the natural abilities of the Jew turn him toward the realm of politics" serves as a further legitimization and a strengthened argument for the political dimension of Nordau's Zionism. To Nordau Emancipation was the emasculation of the quasi-political nature of the ghetto and the *kehilla* and the transformation of Judaism from a collective, political entity to an aggregate of individuals whose aim is their mere individual, bourgeois survival and prosperity. According to this version, Zionism is consequently the reintroduction of the political dimension into Judaism, a dimension preserved even in the Diaspora through Jewish communal life and paradoxically destroyed by Emancipation. This restoration of the political dimension to Judaism is also the heightening of the element of political activity in Jewish history, which Nordau sees as a characteristic Jewish quality. Viewed this way, this also means a return to authenticity.

Intellectually, this may also be seen as a translation of Graetz's historical analysis about the political dimension in Judaism into the language of operational, historical praxis. Nordau, accordingly, becomes one of the most outspoken advocates of the *political* aims of Zionism. He is not content with trying to achieve a territorial concentration of Jews in Palestine; he always maintains that Zionism should explicitly demand the establishment of a Jewish state as one of its clearly defined goals. Nordau believes that the establishment of a Jewish state will be not only an instrumentally important achievement but also addresses itself to some essential moments in Judaism.

Thus, when Herzl contemplated the idea of negotiating with the British government on turning Uganda into a country for Jewish settlement, Nordau remained basically unconvinced. To him, Uganda could never become a Jewish state. In an impassioned letter to Herzl he writes:

Uganda is not a station on the way to Palestine, nor can it be a land for a Jewish state; because it is not a country for settlement, but merely for exploitation. Hence it cannot serve as a schooling ground for the education and emergence of a political nation. Even if it were to possess a flag and self-government, Uganda would not become a nucleus for a national-political structure; at best it could serve as a club, with its own coat of arms and self-governing rules— just like any other club and joint-stock company.[19]

In light of Nordau's advocacy of the political aims of Zionism, it is not surprising that in a speech in London in 1900 he also compared the Maccabean Revolt to the struggle of the Boers in southern Africa against British imperialism.[20] At that time, the resistance of the Boer republics to British colonialism was viewed by most European liberal opinion as the heroic struggle of a small people against an enormous and rapacious empire. This attempt by Nordau to equate the Maccabean Revolt with the first anti-imperialistic struggle of the twentieth century is another aspect of his innovative and revolutionary Zionist ideology, which had begun to reread Jewish history in the light of modern world history.

CHAPTER 11

AHAD HA'AM: THE SPIRITUAL DIMENSIONS OF THE JEWISH STATE

ASHER GINSBERG, WHO WROTE UNDER THE PSEUDONYM OF Ahad Ha'am (One of the People), was one of the more prolific writers of the turn-of-the-century Hebrew renaissance in Russia. He was responsible more than any other writer for the creation of modern Hebrew prose, which he helped emancipate from the stilted quasi-biblical imitative language of the *Haskala*, and his impact on Hebrew letters has been rivaled only by that of Chaim Nachman Bialik. He was the first to introduce positivist elements into Hebrew publicist writing, which was still highly influenced by the emotional flourishes of neoromanticism. However, the discussion in this chapter will be limited to his contribution to the debate about the nature of Zionism, in which his so-called spiritual Zionism became identified as an antithesis to Herzl's political Zionism.

His biography (1856–1927) is that of the *Haskala*: a Hasidic family background, studies in a *yeshiva*, external studies in a Russian high school, and then an unsuccessful attempt to enter a university. After many family vicissitudes, Asher Ginsberg settled in Odessa, where he, like many other young Jews of his generation, came under the emancipating influence of the relatively secular atmosphere of that city, and through the writings of the Russian positivist Dimitri Pisarev, he became acquainted with the thoughts of John Stuart Mill.

Ahad Ha'am's first essay, "Wrong Way" (1889), predetermined to a large extent his unique role within the Hovevei Zion movement.[1] On the one hand, he became one of the movement's most articulate spokesmen; on the other hand, he appears sometimes as the severest critic of many of its public manifestations. These traits would also characterize his activity within the Zionist movement, which he joined at its first Congress, but from whose daily activities he remained always somewhat aloof.

Two essays, "The Jewish State and the Jewish Problem" (1897) and "Flesh and Spirit" (1904), are perhaps most central to the way in which his views developed on the modern Jewish national movement.

"The Jewish State and the Jewish Problem" was written immediately after Ahad Ha'am returned from the first Zionist Congress (which was also the only Zionist Congress he ever attended). It was, to a certain degree, intended to counteract the uncritical euphoria which grasped many Jewish circles in the wake of the almost royal pomp and circumstance of the Basle Congress. True to his positivist and rationalist approach, Ahad Ha'am tries to sum up the message of the congress and dispassionately discuss the challenges facing the newly born Zionist movement.

Ahad Ha'am's point of departure is Nordau's opening programmatic speech, which so impressed the delegates. He sums up Nordau's message by stating that it justly stresses the double nature of the Jewish problem in the contemporary world. For East European Jewry, the problem is mainly that of economic misery, whereas in the West the Jews find themselves in moral agony when faced with the failure of Emancipation to give an adequate answer to the quest for Jewish identity in the modern world. Both communities thus turn to the Zionist solution—the establishment of a Jewish state in Palestine.

At this point Ahad Ha'am, with his sober realism, raises a number of questions.

Let us suppose, Ahad Ha'am argues, that the Zionist movement has reached its goal. A Jewish state has been established in Palestine, and it absorbs wave upon wave of Jewish immigration. Will the Jewish problem thus be solved within a generation or two? Could all the Jews in the world—then numbering around ten million—immigrate immediately to the Land of Israel and thus overcome their misery, be it economic or spiritual? Will the establishment of a Jewish state really be a solution to the problem of all Jews?

Suppose, Ahad Ha'am argues, that the establishment of a Jewish state does not mean an immediate and total Ingathering of the Exiles but will initially mean only "the settlement of a small part of our people in Palestine; then how will it solve the material problem of the Jewish masses in the lands of the Diaspora?"[2] Ahad Ha'am suggests that the economic problem will be massively solved only for a part of the people, those who will emigrate to the Jewish state. But for those who would remain in the Diaspora during the first stages of the process (which may last for a few generations), economic problems would not and could not be solved by the very establishment of a Jewish state; their economic and social fate would still hinge on the conditions in their countries of residence. Since the Jewish state would not be able to solve the *economic* problem of those Jewish masses who would remain—even temporarily— outside its confines, its only contribution toward solving some aspect of their problems would have to be in the *spiritual* and *cultural* spheres. Therefore the cardinal problem to be faced by Zionism is not merely how to establish a Jewish state, but, granted that a Jewish state will eventually come about, it is imperative for Zionism to ask itself now how it will help solve the spiritual agonies and dilemmas of the vast majority of the Jewish people who will continue to reside for the foreseeable future *outside* the Land of Israel.

For someone considered to be among the most intellectual, visionary Zionist thinkers, Ahad Ha'am, nonetheless, succeeded in articulating the practical problems that would be faced by Zionism once the State of Israel has been established. While many so-called practical Zionists saw only the immediate future involving the settlement of immigrants and pioneers in Palestine and the establishment of an independent state, Ahad Ha'am identified and defined problems that would become the most crucial existential issues for Israel after its establishment. Hence the contemporary relevance of many of his observations is far more challenging than the vision of those for whom Zionism came to a close on May 15, 1948.

Ahad Ha'am agrees with Nordau that the problem for Jews in Western Europe is basically different from that of the Jews in the East European Pale of Settlement. Yet, Ahad Ha'am argues, Zionism can, through its very existence, solve the Western problem more readily than the Eastern one. The Jew in the West, who is already separated from Jewish culture yet is alienated from the society in which he lives and acts, will find in the very existence of a Jewish state a solution to the problems of his national identity. It may compensate him for his lack of integration into the national culture of his surrounding society. In an observation remarkably relevant more than fifty years later to the meaning of the existence of Israel for many Jews in the West, Ahad Ha'am says,

> If a Jewish state were re-established [in Palestine], a state arranged and organised exactly after the pattern of other states, then he [the Western Jew] could live a full, complete life among his own people, and find at home all that he now sees outside, dangled before his eyes, but out of reach. Of course, not all the Jews will be able to take wing and go to their state; but the very existence of the Jewish state will raise the prestige of those who remain in exile, and their fellow citizens will no more despise them and keep them at arm's length as though they were ignoble slaves, dependent entirely on the hospitality of others. As [the Western Jew] contemplates this fascinating vision, it suddenly dawns on his inner consciousness that even now, before the Jewish state is established, the mere idea of it gives him almost complete relief. He has an opportunity for organised work, for political excitement; he finds a suitable field of activity without having to become subservient to non-Jews; and he feels that thanks to this ideal he stands once more spiritually erect, and has regained human dignity, without overmuch trouble and without external aid. So he devotes himself to the ideal with all the ardour of which he is capable; he gives rein to his fancy, and lets it soar as it will, up above reality and the limitations of human power. For it is not the attainment of the ideal that he needs: its pursuit alone is sufficient to cure him of his moral sickness, which is the consciousness of inferiority; and the higher and more distant the ideal, the greater its power of exaltation . . .[3]

In Eastern Europe, on the other hand, the situation is radically different. Among the *Ost Juden* (East European Jews), the agony is collective, not individual, and what is cast in doubt here is not the Jewish identity of individual Jews but the existence of a whole community. For what has happened in Eastern Europe, according to Ahad Ha'am, is not only that Jews have left the ghetto but that *Judaism* as such has left it. Traditional ghetto life enabled Judaism to maintain itself within the confines of a closed society, and thus a balance was achieved between Jewish and non-Jewish society based, as it were, on separateness and apartness. But modern cultural development, which engulfed all the peoples of Eastern Europe, has destroyed this Jewish apartness without, at the same time, allowing the great Jewish masses to identify as a community with the emerging national cultures. "In our times culture wears in each country the garb of the national spirit, and the stranger who would woo her must sink his individuality and become absorbed in the dominant spirit."[4] In the West it is liberalism that poses a challenge to Jewish existence; in the East, it is nationalism.

This challenge moves East European Jewry to forge for itself a new focus of identity. Given Ahad Ha'am's positivism, he is adamant that this new focus cannot be a return to the traditional religious symbolism of the Jewish past, nor can it be refocused on the apartness of the closed society of the ghetto. It is this new focus which East European Jewry is looking for in the new society to be established in Palestine:

> So it seeks to return to its historic center, in order to live there a life of natural development, to bring its powers into play in every department of human culture, to develop and perfect those national possessions which it has acquired up to now, and thus to contribute to the common stock of humanity, in the future as in the past, a great national culture, the fruit of the unhampered activity of a people living according to its own spirit. For this purpose Judaism needs at present but little. It needs not an independent state but only the creation in its native land of conditions favourable to its development: a good-sized settlement of Jews working without hindrance in every branch of culture, from agriculture and handicrafts to science and literature. This Jewish settlement, which will be a gradual growth, will become in course of time the center of the nation, wherein its spirit will find pure expression and develop in all its aspects up to the highest degree of perfection of which it is capable. Then from this center the spirit of Judaism will go forth to the great circumference, to all the communities of the Diaspora, and will breathe new life into them and preserve their unity; and when our national culture in Palestine has attained that level, we may be confident that it will produce men in the country who will be able, on a favorable opportunity, to establish a state which will be truly a *Jewish* state, and not merely a state of Jews.[5]

Echoes of Herder and Hegel are clearly audible in Ahad Ha'am's statement that the creation of a body politic is the apex of the cultural and spiritual forces of a people: a state is not created out of thin air or through the fiat of a mere diplomatic coup. Such a state will prove to be an ephemeral phenomenon, for the sociocultural infrastructure is a necessary condition for political life. Hence Ahad Ha'am's opposition to Herzl's diplomatic efforts to secure a Jewish state through a charter or a similar device. Such a state, Ahad Ha'am argues, will lack a solid foundation, will be without culture, without roots, and it may prove to be less than viable. Indeed, the cultural shallowness and spiritual one-dimensionality of Herzl's political structure as described in *The Jewish State* are striking.

Herzl's state, Ahad Ha'am argues, may perhaps be a State of Jews (*Judenstaat*—as Herzl's pamphlet was indeed called); but it will not be a Jewish State (*Jüdischer Staat*), and it is a *Jewish* state that Ahad Ha'am would like to see established. Since a large proportion of the Jewish people will remain for a long period outside the state after it is established—and it may also take some time for such a state to be created—it is imperative that the new Land of Israel should become a focus for identification for all Jewish people. Because of the nationalist context of modern cultural development in Europe, a renaissance of Jewish culture in the Diaspora is no longer possible. Therefore, for the continued existence of a national Jewish identity *outside* of Palestine, a Jewish community *in* Palestine is necessary, which will radiate its culture to the Diaspora and facilitate this modern Jewish existence. Otherwise, any Jewish person who does not go to Palestine will lose his Jewish identity sooner or later. A political Zionism, focusing exclusively on the establishment of a Jewish state, overlooks this cultural dimension, which is vital for Jewish continued existence.

According to Ahad Ha'am, the traditional strength of Judaism lay in the fact that the prophets taught the value of not only material but also spiritual force. A Jewish state devoid of spiritual Jewish values relevant to Jewish life in the Diaspora will lose the allegiance of Jews living outside it. Therefore, Ahad Ha'am is critical of Herzl's vision of a Jewish state in which everyone will speak either German or French or Russian, according to his country of origin, and in which Italian opera and German theater will flourish. A state "of Germans or Frenchmen of the Jewish race" is not a viable state, Ahad Ha'am argues, for

> a political ideal which does not rest on the national culture is apt to seduce us from our loyalty to spiritual greatness, and to beget in us a tendency to find the path of glory in the attainment of material power and political dominion, thus breaking the thread that unites us with the past, and undermining our historical basis.[6]

This is a challenge faced not only by Jewish nationalism. According to Ahad Ha'am it is a dilemma common to all European national movements. The national spirit, the *Volksgeist*, of all European national movements expresses itself in the spiritual, cultural, and material manifestations of a nation as well as in its political state.

The lack of such a spiritual dimension will be doubly pernicious in the case of a Jewish state. It may turn political power into an end in itself, which would sever the bonds with Jews abroad. Ahad Ha'am is afraid of a hollow and sterile étatism which turns the means—the state—into the essence of national existence. In an intriguing historical illustration, Ahad Ha'am uses the state of Herod the Great as an example of a state devoid of spiritual and cultural content:

> History teaches us that in the days of the Herodian house Palestine was indeed a Jewish state, but the national culture was despised and persecuted, and the ruling house did everything in its power to implant Roman culture in the country, and frittered away the national resources in the building of heathen temples and amphitheatres and so forth. Such a Jewish state would spell death and utter degradation for our people. We will never achieve sufficient political power to deserve respect while we shall miss the living moral force within. Such a puny state, being "tossed about like a ball between its powerful neighbours, and maintaining its existence only by diplomatic shifts and continual truckling to the favored by fortune," would not be able to give us a feeling of national glory; and the national culture, in which we might have sought and found our glory, would not be implanted in our state and would not be the principle of its life. So we would really be then—much more than we are now—"a small and insignificant nation" enslaved *in spirit* to "the favoured of fortune" turning an envious and covetous eye on the armed force of "our neighbours"; and our existence as a sovereign state would not add a glorious chapter to our national history.[7]

Ahad Ha'am also maintains that it would be illusory to imagine that the Jewish state may have a third choice—that of being "the Switzerland of the Middle East," as Lilienblum would have had it. Such an alternative, Ahad Ha'am coolly observes, is unfortunately out of the question—and here again, his chilling realism is remarkable when compared to the self-intoxicating rhetoric which flowed so freely in the writings of other Zionists of this—and later—periods:

> A comparison between Palestine and small countries like Switzerland overlooks the geographical position of Palestine and its religious importance for all nations. These two facts will make it quite impossible for its "powerful neighbors" . . . to leave it alone

altogether; and when it has become a Jewish state they will still keep an eye on it, and each Power will try to influence its policy in a direction favourable to itself, just as we see happening in the case of other weak states (like Turkey) in which the great European nations have "interests."[8]

The geographical area of the Land of Israel has always been in the center of world politics, Ahad Ha'am warns, and it will always remain so. The Zionist movement would do well to have no illusions about this or about being able to achieve its aim without confronting strong and powerful interests involved with that area.

Political independence will not take "the Jewish problem" off the agenda of world politics. Because of both history and geography, the Jewish people and the Land of Israel cannot disappear into the happy limbo of small inconsequential nations. Therefore Ahad Ha'am insisted on confronting these problems from the very outset. A purely political Jewish state—a Jewish Serbia or a Jewish Montenegro, to use pre–World War I parlance—would not be able to provide adequate answers to these questions.

Ahad Ha'am's views on the necessity of a spiritual content for Jewish existence is not merely a tactical or instrumental requirement; it relates to his fundamental understanding of Jewish history, which was deeply influenced by Krochmal and Graetz. In his essay "Flesh and Spirit" these views are presented within a historical perspective, which sees in Judaism two elements, the material and the spiritual. At the time of the First Commonwealth, these two elements—which may also be called the political and the ideal—were still interwoven, and they became differentiated only during the period of the Second Commonwealth. Ahad Ha'am sees the historical conflicts between the Sadducees and the Pharisees as focusing around these two aspects of Jewish life. The Sadducees saw the very existence of the Jewish state as the essence of national life; the Pharisees saw the spiritual content as the mainstay of Jewish existence and were ready for far-reaching compromises with the Romans, as long as such compromises did not endanger national existence as articulated in the ability to develop the spiritual content of Judaism. The Pharisees, according to Ahad Ha'am, were the true synthesis of the spiritual with the material, and hence their dialectical defense of political power was viewed as a necessary tool but not as an end in itself:

> Unlike the Essenes, the Pharisees did not run away from life, and did not want to demolish the state. On the contrary, they stood at

their post in the very thick of life's battle, and tried with all their might to save the state from moral decay, and to mould it according to the spirit of Judaism. They knew full well that spirit without flesh is but an unsubstantial shade, and that the spirit of Judaism could not develop and attain its end without a political body, in which it could find concrete expression. For this reason the Pharisees were always fighting a twofold battle: on the one hand, they opposed the political materialists from within, for whom the state was only a body without an essential spirit; and, on the other side, they fought together with these opponents against the enemy without, in order to save the state from destruction.[9]

The destruction of the Second Temple by the Romans put the Pharisees' view to the supreme test, for it proved Judaism's ability to continue to exist even without the material infrastructure of a body politic. This was the Pharisees' finest historical hour: for had the Sadducean-cum-Zealot view prevailed, that is, that the state is an end in itself, then the Jewish people would have ultimately disappeared once its independence had been destroyed, its country occupied, its Temple burned, and most of the Jewish population driven into Exile by the Romans. The Jewish fate would in such a case be analogous to the fate of all the other nations conquered by Rome. Jewish history, however, took a different turn:

> The political materialists, for whom the existence of the state was everything, had nothing to live for after the political catastrophe [of the destruction of the Temple by the Romans]; and so they fought desperately, and did not budge until they fell dead among the ruins that they loved. But the Pharisees remembered, even in that awful moment, that the political body had a claim on their affections only because of the national spirit which found expression in it, and needed its help. Hence they never entertained the strange idea that the destruction of the state involved the death of the people, and that life was no longer worth living. On the contrary: now they felt it absolutely necessary to find some temporary means of preserving the nation and its spirit even without a state, until such time as God should have mercy on His people and restore it to its land and freedom. So the bond was broken: the political Zealots remained sword in hand on the walls of Jerusalem, while the Pharisees took the scroll of the Law and went to Jabneh.[10]

Jabneh, the new center for Jewish learning, thus became a new, quasi-political focus for Jewish existence, despite the lack of political independence:

> And the work of the Pharisees bore fruit. They succeeded in creating a national body which hung in midair, without any foundation on

the solid earth, and in this body the Hebrew national spirit had its abode and lived its life for two thousand years. The organization of the ghetto, whose foundations were laid in the generations that followed the destruction of Jerusalem, is a thing marvelous and quite unique. It was based on the idea that the aim of life is the perfection of the spirit, but that the spirit needs a body to serve as its instrument. The Pharisees thought at that time that, until the nation could again find an abode for its spirit in a single complete and free political body, the gap must be filled artificially by the concentration of that spirit in a number of small and scattered social bodies, all formed in its image, all living one form of life, and all united, despite their local separateness, by a common recognition of their original unity and their striving after a single aim and perfect union in the future.[11]

According to Ahad Ha'am, the synthesis of the material and the spiritual also must guide the Jewish future after a Jewish state is established, since the ghetto has disappeared, and thus the material infrastructure for Jewish life in the Diaspora has been destroyed. To establish now a political homeland on what Ahad Ha'am would call a "materialist" or "Sadducean" basis—that is, without a spiritual content—is, according to him, counter both to Jewish and to universal historical development. For, to Ahad Ha'am, following the Hegelian school, a state is not an end in itself but merely the necessary foundation for the spiritual expression of the national spirit, the *Volksgeist*.

Ahad Ha'am's critical appraisal of Zionism's problems in Palestine is never more apparent than in the essay "Truth from the Land of Israel," written in 1891 after his initial visit to the new Jewish settlements in Palestine. Ahad Ha'am's journey was undertaken on behalf of Hovevei Zion, and the essay is deeply imbued with his immediate and exhilarating impressions of the first attempts to create Jewish villages in the country. But Ahad Ha'am, unlike other visitors, does not idealize a rather complex situation. He deplores, for example, the widespread speculation in land, which had already appeared at that early stage, and calls upon Hovevei Zion to stop this phenomenon immediately, before it leaves an indelible mark on the social and economic fabric of the new society.

His realism is deeply rooted in an understanding of the historical context within which the Jewish national movement sought its political and intellectual aims and in his agonizing realization of the dilemmas to be faced by Zionism because of the existence of an Arab population in the Jewish homeland.

What distinguishes Ahad Ha'am's essay is his awareness of the necessity to confront the Arab problem in Palestine, and he says some extremely unpleasant things about the attitudes of some of the first settlers toward the Arab population. It has frequently been claimed that Zionism overlooked the very existence of Arabs in what it considered to be the Jewish homeland. Historically, this is an utterly false claim. For Moses Hess the emergence of a Jewish commonwealth in Palestine goes hand in hand with the renaissance of Arab nationalism and the reestablishment of independent Arab states in Syria and Egypt. Herzl presented a humanitarian, although perhaps slightly naive, proposal to integrate the Arab population into the universalistic humanist values of his *Altneuland.*

Ahad Ha'am goes even further. His essay was written before Herzl's novel, but not only is he aware that a massive Arab *population* exists in the Land of Israel but also very clearly postulates the potential for the emergence of an Arab Palestinian *national movement.* Writing in 1891, at a time when there had hardly risen any manifestations of Arab nationalism in Palestine, Ahad Ha'am's perception of the problem to be faced by Zionism in the future clearly attests to a great sensitivity shown by Zionist thinkers to the tragic dimensions involved in a possible clash between the two national movements.

At the outset, Ahad Ha'am argues in "Truth from the Land of Israel," one should not harbor the illusion that Palestine is an empty country:

> We tend to believe abroad that Palestine is nowadays almost completely deserted, a noncultivated wilderness, and anyone can come there and buy as much land as his heart desires. But in reality this is not the case. It is difficult to find anywhere in the country Arab land which lies fallow; the only areas which are not cultivated are sand dunes or stony mountains, which can be only planted with trees, and even this only after much labor and capital would be invested in clearance and preparation.[12]

Another illusion that Ahad Ha'am suggests has to be overcome is the feeling that the Turkish government does not care or know what is going on in Palestine and that "for a little money we could do there whatever we want," mainly through the protection of the European consuls. Ahad Ha'am admits that "*bakshish* is a great power in Turkey," but he also suggests that "we should know that the dignitaries of state are at the same time great patriots, believing in their religion and their government, and in questions dealing with these issues will carry out their duty honestly, and no bribe could sway them."[13] He also maintains that too much reliance on the European consuls could backfire.

As in other matters, Ahad Ha'am demands a realistic attitude toward the Arab population in the country. An attitude of superiority toward the Arabs and their culture will only exacerbate relations between the two communities. Only by truly recognizing the reality of the situation will Zionism be able to develop the tools needed to deal effectively with the questions confronting it:

> We tend to believe abroad that all Arabs are desert barbarians, an asinine people who does not see or understand what is going on around them. This is a cardinal mistake. The Arab, like all Semites, has a sharp mind and is full of cunning. . . . The Arabs, and especially the city dwellers, understand very well what we want and what we do in the country; but they behave as if they do not notice it because at present they do not see any danger for themselves or their future in what we are doing and are therefore trying to turn to their benefit these new guests [coming into the country]. . . .
>
> But when the day will come in which the life of our people in the Land of Israel will develop to such a degree that they will push aside the local population by little or by much, then it will not easily give up its place.[14]

Ahad Ha'am also warns against violent or humiliating behavior toward the Arab population. In his essay he refers to Jewish settlers who found themselves entangled in typical squabbles with Arab villagers over field boundaries or water rights and in some cases used violent means to settle the disputes. Some of the Jewish settlers contended that "the only language that the Arabs understand is that of force." Ahad Ha'am wrote this almost ninety years ago, and his foresight in spotting one of the tragic dimensions that was to develop during the emergence of the Zionist movement is most impressive:

> One thing we certainly should have learned from our past and present history, and that is not to create anger among the local population against us. . . . We have to treat the local population with love and respect, justly and rightly. And what do our brethren in the Land of Israel do? Exactly the opposite! Slaves they were in their country of exile, and suddenly they find themselves in a boundless and anarchic freedom, as is always the case with a slave that has become king; and they behave toward the Arabs with hostility and cruelty, infringe upon their boundaries, hit them shamefully without

reason, and even brag about it. Our brethren are right when they say that the Arab honours only those who show valour and fortitude; but this is the case only when he feels that the other side has justice on his side. It is very different in a case when [the Arab] thinks that his opponent's actions are iniquitous and unlawful; in that case he may keep his anger to himself for a long time, but it will dwell in his heart and in the long run he will prove himself to be vengeful and full of retribution.[15]

Ahad Ha'am always underlined the spiritual, moral, and cultural elements in Jewish nationalism, but he was also able to pinpoint at a very early stage some of the more perplexing practical problems that were to vex the development of the Zionist movement in years to come. He was a political philosopher and as such he confronted practical problems with a moral and theoretical dimension. It is this vision that made Ahad Ha'am's description of the problems facing Israel today so accurate.

CHAPTER 12

SYRKIN: NATIONALISM AND CLASS CONFLICT

IN THE WRITINGS OF MOSES HESS APPEARED THE CONFLUENCE of a vision of social redemption and Jewish nationalism. This was derived from the fact that a critique of the problematical status of Jews in modern society could be very easily combined with a general critique of modern society itself. In his own generation, Hess was a lonely voice; with the emergence of modern political Zionism, however, socialist Zionism became one of the main currents within the movement, the hegemonic force in the Jewish community in Palestine, which ultimately dominated the politics of Israel until the parliamentary elections of 1977. But the first systematic attempts to formulate Zionism within a socialist context are almost as old as political Zionism itself.

Nachman Syrkin (1867–1924) was born in southern Russia, and after the usual years of wandering typical of the first-generation Russian Jewish intellectual, he reached Germany, studied economics in Berlin, became involved in the German Social Democratic movement at the turn of the century, and participated in the first Zionist Congress.[1] His brochure *The Jewish Problem and the Socialist Jewish State*, which appeared in 1898, two years after Herzl's *The Jewish State*, stands out as an extremely perceptive enquiry into the dilemmas of Jewish life under the impact of modernization, emancipation, national conflicts, and class warfare. Without being a doctrinaire Marxist, Syrkin tries to integrate his understanding of the Jewish problem into an overall socialist philosophy of world history. In a few instances—as, for example, in his identification of the social origins of modern anti-Semitism—his innovative analysis is relevant to some of the later manifestations of the radical right. If Herzl and Nordau focused on the cultural and spiritual agonies of modern Jewish existence, Syrkin added the socioeconomic dimension to this radical critique of Jewish integration into modern society. Among socialist Zionists, the wide range of Syrkin's horizons is quite outstanding: he does not have the somewhat dogmatic parochialism frequently evident in the writings of other socialist Zionists whose political impact was sometimes more immediately felt than that of Syrkin himself.

Syrkin begins with an attempt to identify the constant and changing variables in the relationships between Jews and the non-Jewish world surrounding them. These relationships abound with constant frictions and tensions between Jews and non-Jews. However, Syrkin feels that this enmity cannot be attributed to just one constant factor—as Pinsker did in his static view of the Jews as the perpetual victims of an abstract and unchanging Judeophobia. An enquiry into the sources of the strain between Jews and non-Jews should not be limited to the special position of the Jews as a community without a homeland. The specific developments through which both Jews and non-Jews have gone through the ages also need to be examined.

The very existence of the Jews in Exile, in a Diaspora, is a unique phenomenon, which Syrkin attributes to a deep streak of nonconformism characteristic of Jewish life vis-à-vis majority cultures. After the destruction of the Temple, the Jews were not ready to accept the majority culture in which they found themselves, and this nonconformism evoked hostility and persecution. This world was culturally a blend of the disintegrating Graeco-Roman civilization and of the spirit of Christianity which had originated in Palestine. The Jews brought with them spiritual attitudes which made them react inimically and negatively to both of these fundamental strains. The uncompromising subjectivism of the Jews of Palestine, which found expression in the monotheistic faith, in the quest for the absolute, and in the moral life, met utterly opposed spiritual outlooks and a fundamentally different culture in the Graeco-Roman world.[2]

The emergence of Christianity out of Judaism created further tension and alienation. According to Syrkin, normative rabbinical Judaism found two elements in Christianity particularly unacceptable. Judaism has always fought, through the institution of prophecy, against terrestrial power; hence it viewed with utter disdain the compromise Christianity reached with the Roman Empire under Constantine, elevating Christianity to the status of the religion of the Empire, yet, according to Judaism, depriving the Christian religion of its moral soul and spiritual autonomy. Furthermore, the elevation of "the Rabbi from Nazareth," as Syrkin calls Jesus, to the status of the Son of God, generated deep repugnance within normative Judaism, which saw this deification of a human being as the height of arrogance:

> In the view of Jewry the Nazarene was not the Son of God, but only an errant son. The worship of the Christian deity was, to Judaism, merely a miserable form of idolatry. The cross, the holy icons, and the church were all regarded as idolatrous symbols; and the false position assigned to Jesus in Christianity so repelled Jewry that it could not even acknowledge the ethical content of this religion.[3]

Christianity was thus ultimately viewed by Judaism as a form of idolatry, despite its monotheistic origins, and such a view naturally created a deep animosity between Jews and Christians in the medieval world. Hence the period of Christian hegemony in Europe was characterized by the *religious* dimension of the tension between Jews and non-Jews. While Jews merely despised Christians, the Christians, due to their majority status, were able to combine their hatred of Judaism with physical means of persecution and coercion of the Jewish minority. This persecution, this "feeling that all mankind was its enemy, which was the basic mood of the Jews in the Middle Ages, could have turned them into a worthless, gypsy community," Syrkin remarks. Instead, it sustained the Jews in their ideological and intellectual nonconformity, and because of the ethical content of historical Judaism and its prophetic tradition, it turned the Jews in their own consciousness into a people suffering for the sins of all mankind. Jews as individuals could sometimes be inordinately rich and exploitative, yet "out of the sensitivity born of suffering, [the Jew of the Middle Ages] prayed to his God for the very mankind which cast him out. . . . Shylock alone is not a complete representation of the medieval Jew; to see him in the most sublime, we must also include the nobility symbolized by Nathan the Wise."[4]

Syrkin then proceeds to analyze the changes in the status of the Jews in Europe in the wake of the French Revolution and the social, political, and religious upheavals inaugurated by it. Following the traditional socialist understanding of the French Revolution, Syrkin sees in its principles an expression of the interests of the emerging bourgeoisie, aiming at ensuring for itself, through political means, a maximum of economic and social laissez-faire. The Declaration of the Rights of Man and Citizen is the theoretical expression of the class interest of the bourgeoisie, and formal self-determination, including the right to freedom of conscience and of religion, is a corollary of the means to ensure the realization of these interests. In this context, Syrkin argues that the Jews found themselves for the first time since their Exile considered equal in their political and civil rights in all the countries espousing the principles of the French Revolution. A side product of the victory of the bourgeoisie was religious emancipation, enabling Jews to integrate into all spheres of economic, social, and political life.

Like Nordau before him, Syrkin points out that this enormous achievement of the Jews has not been reached on the basis of their real social strength or as an outcome of their own political power. Emancipation was a by-product of the victory of a general principle and for this reason never possessed a real political power. For a socialist like Syrkin, any political achievement not based on real social and economic power is by its very nature precarious, and this explains the intrinsic weakness and half-heartedness characteristic of Emancipation itself. In numerous cases, Emancipation was accepted by many social groups against their inner conviction, and the first social upheaval could spell its doom, since it did not derive from a real social and economic base.

Yet this ambivalent position of the Jews in modern bourgeois society is viewed by Syrkin as part of a much more fundamental ambivalence inherent in bourgeois society. This society is based on the principles of liberty and self-determination; yet, there has never existed a society in which human interdependence has been deeper and more universal. This dependence of one human being on another, immanent in capitalist society, causes new tensions when one of the partners is Jewish.

The predominance of Jews in the economic and commercial life of a bourgeois society creates in the popular mind the identification of capitalism with Judaism itself. It is here that Syrkin becomes aware of the novel aspect of modern, social, anti-Semitism. A radical critique of bourgeois society now goes hand in hand with a new kind of Jew-hatred that sees the Jews and their economic activity as responsible for the social miseries of modern society. As a socialist, Syrkin was very sensitive to the anti-Semitic currents that sometimes accompanied the socialist movement in France and in the German-speaking countries. The attitude of many French socialists and the anti-Semitism among the working class in France during the Dreyfus affair as well as the emergence of such populist anti-Semitic leaders as Karl Lueger, the mayor of Vienna, were very much on his mind when trying to confront this phenomenon, at times conveniently overlooked by many liberal and socialist observers.

Syrkin's analysis of the origins of populist anti-Semitism, whose roots are not religious but socioeconomic, is one of the first attempts to comprehend what was to become a dominant force in European politics only many decades later with the emergence of nazism. Fascism in all its varieties was to become one of the most vexing problems for socialist thought, which did not foresee the emergence of such a phenomenon and found itself at a loss to comprehend and explain its origins. By all the canons of socialism, Marxist and non-Marxist alike, something like fascism should never had happened. Traditional liberalism, too, was at a loss to explain it. In any case, Syrkin's early attempt to look into the social origins of anti-Semitism, with its later analogies to some aspects of fascism and nazism, therefore, transcends his contribution to the development of Zionist thought.

Syrkin points out that anti-Semitism in bourgeois society does not express itself with equal force in all social classes and cannot, therefore, be attributed to a generic or universal trend of Jew-hatred in modern society. Anti-Semitic attitudes are more prevalent in certain social groups and classes; in others they are virtually nonexistent. Anti-Semitism appears to be on the ascent among those whose power in the class struggles of modern society seems to be declining. To Syrkin anti-Semitism is the social protest of the *déclassés*:

> It reaches its highest peak in the declining classes: in the *middle class*, which is in the process of being destroyed by the capitalists, and within the decaying *peasant* class, which is being strangled by the landowners. In modern society, these classes are the most

backward and morally decayed. They are on the verge of bankruptcy and are desparately battling to maintain their vanished positions. They belong to the propertied class, but their property consists of debts. They are owners, but they do not possess that which even the common workers have—labour power. They stand between the capitalist class and the proletariat and live in constant fear of falling into the latter. The more wretched their positions become, the fiercer their internal conflicts, the more they are driven to become vampires who suck the blood of the working class. As time passes, the middle classes sink deeper and deeper into this infernal abyss. Unlike the proletariat, they are without culture or the desire for it, without character or ideal, without self-consciousness or desire for freedom. Despite their steady economic decline, the middle classes still hold on to the tail of the ruling classes; their eyes are focused above, though their bodies are sinking into the deep; they help maintain an order whose victims they are. . . .[5]

These classes, whose position is undermined by the very development of capitalist society, see only the economic activity of the Jewish businessmen; they choose not to see that "along with the gentile capitalist, the Jewish capitalist . . . delivered heavy blows to the petit-bourgeoisie."[6] Yet these classes do not develop a coherent social critique:

They pretend to be revolutionary, but their struggle is egotistical and far removed from any principle. . . . Since the lower middle classes were the most vulgar elements of society, their anti-Semitism, too, was of the most vulgar type. . . . Only egotism, the lust for Jewish money, the desire to undermine the Jewish competitor and expel him from the land—these were the sole reasons for their anti-Semitism.[7]

A few decades later these anti-Semitic traits became dominant in nazism and the semifascist movements in several East European countries.

Syrkin was one of the first to identify, even at that early stage, this combination of crude anticapitalism and vulgar anti-Semitism in its lower-middle-class context. Lacking an adequate sociological terminology to express this phenomenon, Syrkin calls them the "Catilinian classes" after Lucius Sergius Catilina, of Ciceronian fame, that impoverished member of the senatorial class who tried to organize a conspiracy in the waning years of the Roman Republic, deriving his social support from the increasing number of *declassé* elements of Roman society:

Anti-Semitism of the middle class is a revolutionary movement of a low, Catilinian type, the revolt of class against class and against the existing order not for the sake of higher human principles but for egotistic interests; though they clothe themselves in an ideological mantle, the debased nature of their intentions is completely apparent. The Catilinian nature of this anti-Semitism is best reflected in its leadership. The dregs of bourgeois and proletarian society, who have lost every vestige of truth and self-respect, and creatures of the semi-underworld who can be moved only by the lowest of passions, raise the banner of anti-Semitism and become its torchbearers. No party, therefore, has as many leaders whose reputation is as shady as does the party of anti-Semitism.[8]

Unlike other fellow socialists, Syrkin has no illusions about the future. Against the somewhat naive optimism of much of socialist and liberal thought, Syrkin expects an increase in social anti-Semitism with the development of further crises in the fabric of modern society. From a marginal phenomenon of the social demimonde, anti-Semitism may become the political weapon of the social establishment in its fight for survival:

> In spite of the moral degradation of the leaders of anti-Semitism, in spite of the disgust which the average intelligent person has for this movement, it is constantly growing. The more the various classes of society are disrupted, the more unstable life becomes, the greater the danger to the middle class and the fear of the proletarian revolution, directed against the Jews, capitalism, the monarchy, and the state—the higher the wave of anti-Semitism will rise. The classes fighting each other will unite in their common attack on the Jew. The dominant elements of capitalist society, i.e., the men of great wealth, the monarchy, the church, and the state, seek to use the religious and racial struggle as a substitute for the class struggle.[9]

This is a prophetic insight into the somewhat disparate elements which later combined in catapulting the Nazis into power.

Anti-Semitism is, according to Syrkin, endemic to bourgeois society, not because the bourgeoisie is anti-Semitic according to its principles (on the contrary) but because the internal tensions of capitalist society necessarily create the conditions which exacerbate relations between non-Jews and Jews. The materialist foundations of Syrkin's socialism make him skeptical about the naive beliefs of the prophets of Emancipation who saw in liberal-bourgeois society the context for the realization of equality and freedom for the Jews. Those who believed in Emancipation judged liberal society by its principles; Syrkin judges it by the internal mechanisms of its socioeconomic structure. To him, "anti-Semitism is a result of the unequal distribution of power in society. As long as society is based on might, and as long as the Jew is weak, anti-Semitism will exist."[10]

And the Jews will be weak in every society, whatever its social structure, as long as they do not possess a real, material base for their social existence—a state and political power.

This conclusion leads Syrkin to discuss the relationship between the socialist movement and Jewish nationalism, which is basically a new problem, since the complexities of the relations between socialism and Zionism could not have emerged prior to the organization of Zionism as a political movement. As such, Zionism posed a challenge to the traditional claim of the socialist movement that it could solve the Jewish problem through its revolutionary transformation of society. Syrkin's treatment of the problem *is* one of the earliest ones, but here, as in other instances of his thought, his ideas predate many issues which would gain prominence only later.

Like classical liberalism, the socialist movement viewed Judaism merely as a religion, not as a community based on ethnic and cultural ties. Hence, it viewed the future of Judaism on a par with that of Christianity: in a truly liberated socialist society, all religion would whither away. Consequently, no specific treatment was needed regarding the Jewish problem, and anti-Semitism itself was viewed as just one more of the prejudices of a society based on exploitation. Many of the socialist thinkers who were themselves of Jewish origin shared this view, and this concept can be seen as another of the many internal contradictions into which emancipated Jews wandered in the nineteenth century.

Before proposing his own synthesis of socialism and Zionism, Syrkin takes issue with those of his Jewish socialist contemporaries who saw in an undifferentiated, cosmopolitan socialism a panacea destined to overcome the Jewish problem in all its ramifications. Many of these Jewish socialists come from upper-class Jewish bourgeois families and, according to him, share the dilemmas of the assimilationist Jewish bourgeoisie:

> The Jewish socialists of Western Europe, who sprang from the assimilationist Jewish bourgeoisie, unfortunately inherited the tradition of assimilation and displayed the same lack of self-respect and spiritual poverty, except that the moral degradation of the socialist brand of assimilation was more sharply apparent. . . .[11]

All this, according to Syrkin, is just another by-product of Emancipation not having been achieved on the basis of real political power of the Jews. If in the past Jews could view themselves as members of a great, albeit oppressed nation, once Emancipation was achieved through external circumstances, Judaism had to discard its national element in order to justify equal rights on another moral basis.

The Jewish socialists, who followed the same line of argument, committed, however, according to Syrkin, two sins by overlooking the specific nature of the Jewish problem: they denied not only their Jewish heritage but also the socialist foundations of their own thought. The Jews belong to one of the most oppressed people in the world, and instead of protesting against this oppression, Jewish socialists tended to overlook it in their criticism of the oppressive nature of contemporary bourgeois society. "Instead of first crying out as Jews and then raising their protest to the level of the universal . . . they did the contrary. They robbed the protest of its Jewish character, suppressed all reference to their Jewish origins, and thus became merely another variety of Jewish assimilationism."[12]

Thus the truly universal character of the protest of the Jewish socialists became twisted and distorted. According to Syrkin, cosmopolitanism does not mean just the positing of some generalized universal ideas but the construction of a universal vision of redemption steeped in reality, with all its particularistic elements, yet transcending this while always remaining aware of its concrete, historical background. By overlooking this particularism as a foundation, Jewish socialists arrived sometimes at an arid, lifeless, abstract universalism. Syrkin strongly emphasizes the link between socialism and national liberation movements and would like to see Jewish nationalism integrated into this universal context:

> The socialist movement staunchly supports all attempts of suppressed peoples to free themselves. Each national emancipation movement finds its moral support in socialist ethics and in socialist concepts of freedom. The [Socialist] International was the first to express solidarity with the Polish revolt against the Czar. The socialist masses of France and Italy hailed the rebellion of the people of Crete against Turkey. At the various national and international socialist congresses the right of every nation to self-determination has consistently been proclaimed as an ideal organically related to the ethic of socialism.[13]

This immanent link between socialism and national liberation movements has been firmly established, Syrkin argues. Only in the Jewish context has the absurd contention been made that in the name of socialist principles an oppressed nation was told to assume the identity, culture, and language of the oppressors:

> There are no socialist leaders, in any national group, who deny their own nationality and the need to assimilate to a dominant nationality. Only the bourgeoisie of oppressed nations deny their own nation and abandon it, unhesitatingly committing treason when it behooves them to do so for a profit. Thus, the Polish bourgeoisie betrayed Poland and Polish nationalism and was the first to join hands with the enemy. . . . Only in the case of the Jews, among whom everything is topsy-turvy, have the socialists inherited assimilation from the bourgeoisie and made it their spiritual heritage. In such a policy we can see only a lack of seriousness in their socialism and in their devotion to liberty. . . .[14]

Similar arguments would be heard many years later in the controversies between socialist Zionists and many communists and socialists of Jewish origin.[15] Syrkin also maintains that because socialist Zionism is an expression of an oppressed *people*, Jewish socialism is different from the socialist movements of other nations, for example, from German socialism, which may, albeit unwittingly, give expression to the interests of a great and domineering nation. The Jewish proletariat, on the other hand, if it will remain truthful to its historical roots, will express in its class struggle a twofold protest: that of its class oppression as well as that of its national oppression. Hence its revolutionary potential will be greatly enhanced. According to Syrkin, the Jewish proletariat will be able to restore the deracinated Jewish intelligentsia to its identity: "As a protest movement against Jewish suffering, socialism can become the common possession of all Jews, because Jewish suffering affects every class of Jewry—the proletarians as well as the intelligentsia, the middle class as well as the upper bourgeoisie."[16] The position of the Jewish proletariat is thus paradigmatic: it is, in a way, a truly universal class.

For Syrkin Judaism is based on fundamental nonconformism; similarly, Jewish socialism is to him not only the most crystallized expression of this Jewish nonconformist tradition but also a contemporary protest. The irony is evident: a Jewish socialist who does not relate to this Jewish revolutionary tradition denies not only his own national past but also its critical and nonconformist nature; and there can be no adequate revolutionary reason for dissociating oneself from such a tradition. In Jewish history, *protest and nonconformism are part of the tradition.* Therefore, "if Jewish socialism . . . wants to rise to the level of real moral protest, then it must acknowledge and proclaim in public that the Jewish protest is its basic motif."[17] In the Jewish context, any Jew who is not within the Jewish tradition with its nonconformism is not a revolutionary.

Moreover, Syrkin maintains that those Jewish socialists who think that the international class struggle can solve the problem of the Jewish intelligentsia without an explicit link to Jewish national renaissance are mistaken. On the contrary, the intensification of class conflicts will only radicalize anti-Semitism and tend to make the position of the revolutionary Jewish intelligentsia even more precarious. The position of the Jewish bourgeoisie will likewise become more unstable, not for class reasons but because it will be a convenient scapegoat for practically everyone. The socialist movement condemns anti-Semitism and rightly sees it as an enemy of progress and socialism; but under conditions of extreme political pressure, the socialist movement may, for tactical reasons, find it prudent to be less than forthright in its public struggle against anti-Semitism. Syrkin mentions the ambivalent attitude during the Dreyfus affair of the French Socialist party, which initially maintained that socialists need not get involved in a squabble about which of two reactionary officers is really guilty of treason. The fact that one of these officers, Dreyfus, was Jewish and became the focus for a violent anti-Semitic campaign was simply glossed over for a considerable time by the Socialist party. Syrkin also reminds his readers that on some occasions socialist leaders welcomed some outbursts of anti-Semitism and publicly defended their position by maintaining that while they, of course, condemn anti-Semitism as such, some aspects of such demonstrations may "objectively" develop within the working class a critical approach toward the capitalist system.

Be this as it may, Syrkin maintains that socialism as such, when it fails to look for a specific answer to the Jewish predicament, cannot be an adequate answer to the problem faced by the Jews in the modern age. Oddly enough, Syrkin calls all non-Zionist solutions to the Jewish problem utopian, while it is Zionism—seemingly the most utopian solution—which he welcomes as realistic and realizable. Zionism, according to him, "has its roots in the economic and social position of the Jews, in their moral protest, in the idealistic strivings to give a better content to their miserable life. It is borne by the active, creative forces of Jewish life."[18] In a way reminiscent of Hess, the Jewish messianic tradition becomes for Syrkin the foundation of a possible revolutionary transformation of society.

After arguing that Jewish socialists should embrace Zionism, Syrkin confronts the parallel argument: why Zionism has to be socialist. The question whether the future Jewish society will be capitalist or socialist is to Syrkin more than just a choice between two alternatives, since the historical status of these alternatives is not perceived by him as equal. Capitalism is a *fact* of human history; socialism is a *vision*. All existing societies are capitalist because they evolved that way within the historical process, not because they have been *consciously* formed as such.

Zionism is a conscious attempt to create a new society, and for human beings to establish out of their free will a capitalist society is to Syrkin unimaginable:

> It is inconceivable that people will agree to the creation of an autonomous state based on social inequality, for this would amount to entering into a *social contract of servitude*. No new social contract will ever come to be unless its foundation is freedom. Primarily, social inequality is the product of the impersonal forces of history. It is the aim of conscious social action to transmute the status quo along rational lines and to elevate it morally.[19]

The distinction here is central to the ethical nature of Syrkin's socialist thought. Capitalism is the dead weight of history, socialism is the fruit of conscious human praxis. Since Zionism is similarly a conscious human act of revolt, it shares this ethical element of will with socialism.

To this a pragmatic element is being added by Syrkin. The development of a Jewish society in Palestine on the basis of free competition and laissez-faire would be also highly impractical. The Jewish settlement of Palestine would be on a large scale and should call for an overall system of social planning. Such planning by itself will necessarily imply socialist models and will be incompatible with a capitalist market economy. The scale of the enterprise itself, which will have to utilize sophisticated agricultural machinery and set up large-scale industrial plants, will call for a structure completely different from the smallholders economy characterizing the first Jewish villages in Palestine or Baron Hirsch's Jewish villages in Argentina. Individual attempts for settling the Land of Israel that do not become historical, massive projects (like the immigration of 1882) can perhaps be based on private property, but even they eventually have to rely on some philanthropic support, like that of the Rothschilds. Such patronage, to Syrkin, is a mere substitute for overall national planning. A major effort at transforming the economy and demography of Palestine could succeed only if accompanied by large-scale planning. Land will be publicly and not privately owned, and the initial capital will have to be national and not private.

Moreover, a Jewish state based on private property will not be able to address itself to the needs of the most oppressed of Jewish classes in the Diaspora—the Jewish proletariat; and only this class would be able to supply the Jewish commonwealth with a firm sociological and demographic infrastructure. A Jewish state based on capitalism is thus, according to Syrkin, doomed to failure, whereas

> only by fusing with socialism can Zionism become the ideal of the whole Jewish people—of the proletariat, the middle class, the intelligentsia. All Jews will be involved in the success of Zionism, and none will be indifferent. The messianic hope, which was always the greatest dream of exiled Jewry, will be transformed into political action.[20]

The present political impotence of homeless Jews, together with their revolutionary-messianic potential, makes Zionism in its socialist variant a possible socialist model that could be realized in the new Jewish state even *before* socialism became victorious in other countries. For, in the context of Palestine, Syrkin argues, one does not need to abolish an already existing capitalist class society; all one has to do is start from scratch in a socialist direction. Out of the unusual conditions of the Jewish people, its renascent state may become the first socialist commonwealth on earth, a light unto the nations.

Dialectically, the Jewish tragedy would thus be transformed into a new dawn for all of human civilization:

> [The Jews] have therefore been presented with the opportunity to be the first to realize the socialist vision, because they are placed in an unusual situation that they are forced to find a homeland and establish a state. This is the tragic element of their historic fate, but it is also a unique historical mission. What is generally the vision of a few will become a great national movement among the Jews; what is utopian in other contexts is a necessity for the Jews.[21]

Syrkin's historical vision of the Jews as the eternal nonconformist minority is thus combined in his thought with a realistic assessment of the dilemmas faced by the Jews in a modern society torn by national and class conflicts. This vision and reality are then turned by Syrkin into an equally pragmatic analysis of the dynamics needed for a massive settling of the Land of Israel and the socialist structures imperative to realize such a grandiose scheme. In this, Syrkin prescribed much of what later became the mainstream in the Zionist movement—the pioneering, constructive social praxis of Labor Zionism.

CHAPTER 13

BOROCHOV: ZIONIST MARXISM

T HE PROCESS OF CONFRONTING SOCIALIST IDEAS WITH ZIONist thought, started by Syrkin, gained tremendous momentum with the development of the revolutionary socialist movement in Eastern Europe in the first decades of the twentieth century. Many of the activists and theoreticians of the revolutionary movement in the czarist empire were of Jewish origin. The message of universal human salvation, inherent in socialism, drew to its banner a large number of young Jewish intellectuals, who had left the traditional mode of life of the Jewish ghetto yet found society closed to them. Joining one of the various revolutionary underground movements became for many of these young men and women the only way for social and spiritual emancipation. Through the socialist revolution, so they felt, the whole structure of oppressive czarist society would come tumbling down. This would also signal the death knell to anti-Semitism and would solve the Jewish problem through an integration of the young Jewish intelligentsia within the general context of universal human redemption. This young Jewish intelligentsia had consciously cut itself off from traditional Jewish culture. After being rejected by the dominant Russian culture, Marx's slogan "The proletarians have no homeland" represented, in a way, their social existence and their messianic hopes perhaps even more than was true for the actual Russian proletariat who was, after all, deeply embedded in the national and historical culture of the Russian people.

Moreover, the largest and most developed socialist organization within the czarist empire at the turn of the century was the Jewish Workers Association (*Bund*). For many years its membership was larger than that of any other socialist organization in Russia, and the quality of its intellectual activities was truly impressive. The *Bund* acknowledged the uniqueness of the Jewish problem in the general economic and cultural context of Eastern Europe and did not deny that the emancipation of the Jewish masses in Russia would have to take place within social and cultural structures specifically related to Jewish social history. It is for this reason that the *Bund* advocated the development of Yiddish culture, which it saw as the language of daily Jewish life, carrying within it the social struggle of the Jewish masses—a clear Jewish echo to Russian populist traditions. In this frame of thought, Yiddish as the language of the toiling masses was juxtaposed to the Russian and Polish languages adopted by the assimilationist Jewish bourgeoisie and to Hebrew, which was conceived as the clerical language of the past and of the old religious establishment. The future was perceived by the theoreticians of the *Bund* as the integration of the Jewish proletariat, conscious of its own cultural heritage, within the general revolutionary proletarian movement; in future socialist society the cultural and linguistic heritage of the Jewish masses would be preserved just as the Russian, Ukrainian, and Polish languages would remain the focus of identity for the non-Jewish proletariat within the general structure of universal revolution.[1]

At the same time, the cultural nationalism of the *Bund*, which by itself was one of the expressions of the Jewish quest for national identity in the modern age, radically opposed any attempt to revive a Jewish political nation in Palestine: immigration to Palestine, the revival of the Hebrew language, the establishment of a Jewish society in the Land of Israel—all this was perceived by the *Bund* as narrow, reactionary nationalism, isolating the Jewish problem from the context of universal solutions and pushing the Jews back into their own past and into a new, Middle Eastern ghetto. According to the *Bund*, the Jews, just like the proletariat at large, have only one homeland: the Revolution.

It is in this context that one has to understand the intellectual direction of Ber Borochov's polemical writings. Born in Poltava, in the Ukraine, in the home of a *maskil* close to the Hovevei Zion movement, Borochov (1881–1917) grew up close to the Russian socialist revolutionary movement and its many branches with their plethora of Jewish activists. On this background of conflicting claims between a national vision and revolutionary socialism, he developed a systematic program which later became the unique synthesis associated with his thought: an integration of Jewish nationalism with orthodox Marxist doctrine. Thus a Zionist Marxism, or a Marxist Zionism, was developed and became the ideological foundation of Poalei Zion [Workers of Zion], which was, first in Russia and Poland and later in Palestine, the most influential Labor Zionist movement.[2]

Intellectually, such a synthesis between Marxism and Zionism was not an easy undertaking. Classical, orthodox Marxism viewed nationalism as merely a "super-structural" phenomenon. In Marxist doctrine, as developed by Friedrich Engels, Karl Kautsky, and Georgi Plekhanov, the dominant interests of the class war are the determining factors of historical development, and the national idea is nothing else than an "ideology" concocted by the bourgeoisie to give it a quasi-general legitimacy for its narrow, particularist class interests. According to this view, the proletariat has to uncover this truth lurking behind the national verbiage, to unmask its bourgeois nature, and to forge, through international proletarian solidarity, the basis for the redemptive universalism of world revolution.

There is no doubt that such a view did not make it easy for the socialist movement in areas like Eastern Europe, where national, linguistic, and cultural conflicts were central to political consciousness at the beginning of the twentieth century. At least one Marxist socialist movement—the socialist party emerging in the multiethnic Austro-Hungarian Empire—attempted to develop a more differentiated and less simplistic attitude to the national question. This school of thought, vaguely called Austro-Marxism, advocated granting legitimacy to national and cultural structures and to identifiable proletarian groups possessing distinct ethnic-linguistic traits; it also acknowledged that in the multiethnic context of the Hapsburg Empire, ethnic distinctions have elements of class differentiation built into them.[3] Thus, Austro-Marxism developed a theory of social revolution that allowed proletarian groups of Czech, Croatian, or Hungarian origin to develop political and social activities in their own languages, without trying to force upon them the majority language of the German ruling classes of the empire. It also envisaged the future in highly federalist and pluralistic terms.

Borochov's attempt to find a legitimacy anchored in Marxism for socialist Zionists owed much of its impetus to the sociological studies of such Austro-Marxist writers as Otto Bauer, Max Adler, and Karl Renner, whose basic argument was that in the context of multinational societies, class emancipation may have to go hand in hand with national emancipation, since so many of the socially oppressed were also oppressed because of their nationality. Nationality is thus embedded in the social structure of such societies and is not merely "superstructural."

Borochov follows a similar approach. In his first major study, *The National Question and the Class Struggle* (1905), Borochov tries to suggest that Marx's own writings on the national question are more nuanced than is usually perceived. As a doctrine, Borochov maintains, Marxism addresses the question of class warfare; but numerous side remarks by Marx and Engels encapsulate the basic ingredients of the national struggle as well. Quoting an article by Engels and some remarks by Marx in volume 3 of *Das Kapital*, Borochov points out that the founders of Marxism were themselves conscious of a certain pluralism about the impact of conditions of production on different historical contexts. To explain the concept of this pluralism, Borochov quotes Marx's dictum that "the very same economic bases . . . can develop in different ways: widely different variations can arise from actually different situations, natural causes, social relations, and external historical influences."[4]

Bringing out these pluralistic elements in the Marxist doctrine softens the mechanistic economic determinism that was becoming associated with Marxism under the influence of Kautsky and Plekhanov. It enabled Borochov to develop his view that, parallel to the vertical division of mankind into classes, there exists also a horizontal division; those "groups of mankind, divided according to the differences in the conditions of their relatively distinct production systems, are called societies, or socioeconomic organisms (tribes, families, peoples, nations)."[5] Class struggle occurs always, according to Borochov, *within* this horizontal social-national group; hence class warfare has in every historical context a specific given character, determined by the particular history of that national society.

Where a class struggle is integrated into a national struggle, Borochov sees it as developing even further specific characteristics.

When a whole ethnic group has been conquered and subjugated by another ethnic group, the conquering group tries to impose its own class structure. The proletariat of the subjugated society finds itself in double thralldom—subjugated as a class by the bourgeoisie of the conquering nation, and subjugated linguistically and nationally to the entire conquering nation. The Austro-Marxists realized that the subjugation of conquered nations—like the Czechs—has been exacerbated by the fact that their overall social structure has been fragmented by the disappearance of the Czech ruling classes and by their substitution by a German-speaking ruling class. Subjugation thus means leaving the conquered nation with a distorted social structure. Similarly Borochov maintains that among the oppressed peoples nationalism appears in a more peculiar form. These oppressed peoples constantly exist under abnormal conditions of production; abnormal for the reasons that we have mentioned before, namely, the lack or deficiency of territory and its protective forms—political independence, freedom of language, and freedom of cultural development. Such abnormal conditions bring the varying interests of all individuals of the nation into harmonious agreement. It is due to external pressure, which hinders and disorganizes the influence of the conditions of production, that the relations of production and the class-struggle itself are hindered in their development. For the proper course of the mode of production is thus hindered, class antagonisms become abnormally dulled, and national solidarity derives greater strength.[6]

Under such conditions, the national struggle becomes transformed into a social struggle of the exploited classes against the exploiting classes of the dominant national society:

> Apart from the fact that the separate interests of each particular class are adversely affected by this external pressure; apart from the fact that the bourgeoisie suffers from a lack of markets, and that the proletariat lacks the freedom to control completely its workplace—this pressure is also felt by all the individuals of the nation. All feel and all comprehend that the pressure is a national one; it has its origin in a foreign nation and is directed against their own nationality as such. The language, for instance, now assumes an importance far exceeding that of a simple expedient devised for the purpose of protecting the market. When freedom of language is interfered with, those who are thus oppressed become more closely attached to it. In short, the national question of an oppressed people becomes sharply divided from the connection it normally has with

its basis—with the material conditions of its productive life. Cultural needs then assume an independent importance and all members of the nation become concerned about the freedom of national self-determination.[7]

In such situations, Borochov continues, various trends and nuances appear within the national movement itself. The traditional groups of the subjected nationality (the petite bourgeoisie, the clerical circles, the educated classes) associate their nationalism with traditional, conservative, and reactionary ideas. But the true historical products of the national movement are the progressive elements within the subjected nation—the intelligentsia and the working class; these can prevent the national movement from becoming chauvinistic and ethnocentric and endow it with a universal significance and truly internationalist goals; for these groups

the process of liberation is essentially not nationalistic, but national. And among the progressive elements of an oppressed nation there develops genuine nationalism. It does not dream of preserving its traditions; it does not exaggerate their importance; it is not deluded by the sham of national unity; it has a clear comprehension of the class-structure of society; it does not stifle the genuine interests of anyone. . . .

Genuine nationalism is the nationalism which does not obscure class-consciousness. It is to be found only among the progressive elements of oppressed nations. . . . Within the organized revolutionary proletariat of an oppressed nation, genuine nationalism is expressed in the firm, lucidly formulated demands . . . of its minimum program: . . . the establishment of the nation under normal conditions of production.[8]

According to this view, only after being emancipated from foreign subjugation can the proletariat of an oppressed nation start waging a real class struggle within its own society. So long as national society is subjugated, the class struggle remains distorted, and therefore national liberation is necessary for carrying out a successful class war.

Having thus attempted to integrate national struggles for liberation into the class structure of society, Borochov can berate "orthodox Marxist dogmatists"[9] for failing to recognize how national differences contribute to variations within the structure of bourgeois, capitalist societies. He can thus further distinguish between forms of nationalism—between the nationalism of the great landowners, that of the great bourgeoisie, that of the petite bourgeoisie, and that of the proletariat—and separate them into "reactionary" and "progressive" forms of nationalism. Those who view nationalism as just a carryover from the past not only are mistaken but also overlook the concrete, material basis of nationalism in the mode of production:

> Nationalism has thus, from its very beginning, not the slightest connection with tradition. . . . Utterly shallow and ignorant are those who belittle nationalism in general as something obsolete, reactionary, a matter of tradition. Nationalism is a product of bourgeois society. . . . Nationalism must be given the same consideration as any other phenomenon of bourgeois society. . . .[10]

Giving nationalism its place in historical development is thus, to Borochov, not a deviation from Marxist doctrine but an application of the Marxist materialist interpretation of history to one of the most powerful phenomena of modern society.

In *The National Question and the Class Struggle* Borochov attempted a general theory of the relationship between nationalism and the class structure. One year later, in 1906, he published *Our Platform*, in which he tried to apply these general principles to the Jewish problem.

His point of departure is a restatement of the conclusions in his first essay. "National movements do not transcend class divisions; they merely represent the interests of one of several classes within the nation. . . . Hence the great varieties of nationalism and national ideologies."[11] In the Jewish context Borochov distinguishes three main social groups, each of them developing its own attitude toward nationalism: (1) the upper bourgeoisie; (2) the middle class, including the intelligentsia; and (3) the working class with the lower middle classes in process of proletarianization.

The Jewish upper bourgeoisie, Borochov writes, usually tends toward assimilation. Those groups nearest to assimilation are the well-established and comfortable strata of Jewish society, and there exists a marked relationship between social class and the tendency to assimilate. Because upward social mobility came easier to Jews in the West than in Eastern Europe, assimilation is more prevalent among Western Jewry, "and were it not for the 'poor *Ost Juden*,' the Jewish upper bourgeoisie would not be disturbed by the Jewish problem. The continuous stream of immigration of East European Jews and frequent pogroms remind the [Jewish] upper bourgeoisie of Western Europe only too often of the miserable lot of their brethren."[12] For itself, this upper bourgeoisie has managed to solve its existential problems through its economic success and its integration into capitalist society. Nevertheless, anti-Semitism poses a serious threat to the integration of the Jewish upper bourgeoisie into bourgeois society at large, because it reminds everybody of the Jewish identity and connections of even the most assimilated strata of Jewish society. Therefore, despite their wealth and economic status, members of the Jewish upper bourgeoisie do not feel secure. Ultimately, anti-Semitism threatens the upper bourgeoisie just as it threatens the poorer classes. This, to Borochov, proves that overlooking the national aspect in analyzing the social position of the Jewish upper bourgeoisie is unrealistic. Otherwise, how can one explain the precarious position of this class? Jewish capitalists are viewed by society at large not merely as capitalists but as Jews as well, and therefore a merely economic analysis of their position, as some dogmatic Marxists would advocate, does not supply an adequate understanding of their position.

Anti-Semitism transcends social classes despite its distinct social and economic origins. Faithful to his Marxist interpretation of history, Borochov maintains that the roots of anti-Semitism are economic. "Anti-Semitism flourishes because of the national competition between the Jewish and non-Jewish petit bourgeoisie and between Jewish and non-Jewish proletarianized and unemployed masses."[13] Yet it threatens the Jewish peddler as well as the Rothschilds and the whole Jewish plutocracy. This, according to Borochov, poses an agonizing dilemma to the members of the Jewish upper bourgeoisie:

> Two souls reside within the breast of the Jewish upper bourgeoisie—the soul of a proud European and the soul of an unwilling guardian of his Eastern coreligionists. Were there no anti-Semitism, the misery and poverty of the Jewish emigrants would be of little concern to the Jewish upper bourgeoisie.... In spite of themselves and despite their efforts to ignore the Jewish problem, the Jewish aristocrats must turn philanthropists. They must provide shelter for the Jewish emigrants and must make collections for pogrom-ridden Jews. Everywhere the Jewish upper bourgeoisie is engaged in the search for a Jewish solution to the Jewish problem and a means of being delivered of the Jewish masses. This is the sole form in which the Jewish problem presents itself to the Jewish upper bourgeoisie....[14]

In contrast to this external, merely philanthropic manner in which the Jewish problem presents itself to the Jewish upper bourgeoisie, anti-Semitism is much more of an immediate problem to the Jewish middle classes and to the Jewish intelligentsia. It is these classes who are in every society the bearers of the national movement, and in the Jewish context these classes find themselves in the cross fire of conflicting development. The more any society develops toward capitalism, the more democratic and open it becomes—and at the same time the stronger nationalism becomes as well. The Jewish middle classes are thus pushed, through liberalism and the democratization of society, more and more into key positions in society—and at the same time they find themselves growing more alienated from their counterparts in non-Jewish society. Because of social mobility many more Jews become doctors, lawyers, engineers, journalists, and entrepreneurs—and at the same time, their opposite numbers in non-Jewish society view them as alien interlopers. This alienation from the parallel strata in non-Jewish society tends to develop very strong feelings of Jewish cultural nationalism among these groups. They seek to express their distinct identity through a link to Jewish history, language, and consciousness:

> Lacking any means of support in their struggle for a market, they tend to speak of an independent [Jewish] existence and of a Jewish state where they would play a leading political role. . . . But as long as they succeed in retaining their middle-class position, as long as the boycott and the isolation brought about by anti-Semitism have not yet undermined their material well-being, the center of gravity of their political interests continues to be in the Diaspora. . . . True, the Jewish position is a cause of certain discomfort to the middle class, but the class is not sufficiently hard pressed to desire a radical change in its condition.[15]

The Jewish upper bourgeoisie thus relates to the Jewish question only in a philanthropic fashion, while the Jewish middle classes develop a cultural and intellectual, yet ineffective, *Salon-Zionismus* (Parlor-Zionism). From Borochov's theoretical point of view, these classes cannot become the bearers of a national liberation movement, since their economic mode of production is still deeply embedded, for all its precariousness and their own social isolation, in the economic infrastructure of Jewish existence in the Diaspora.

According to Borochov there exists only one class of Jewish society whose misery is so radical that it cannot continue to exist under prevailing conditions, and it is necessarily pushed to seek for itself another economic base. This is the Jewish working class, accompanied by the massive Jewish lower middle class, whose social existence is being pulverized by recent economic development and which is thus pushed into the ranks of the proletariat. For Borochov, these two classes form one social entity that cannot continue to exist in Eastern Europe. Emigration to America is the *passive* response of these classes to their plight because it accepts as a given the very existence of bourgeois society in the United States and seeks a solution within the existing socioeconomic structure. Emigration to Palestine will, according to Borochov, be their *active* response to the radical predicament facing them because it is necessarily combined with the creation of a new society, a whole new infrastructure, and the emergence of a novel and revolutionary society there. The Jewish proletariat and the proletarianized lower middle classes, who have no place and no future in East European society, thus become a radical social subject for a national transformation of the Jewish people.

Borochov gives a number of reasons why emigration to America will not solve the plight of the Jewish proletarian and near-proletarian masses. The processes of proletarianization will overtake these groups in America, and they will become part of the immigrant labor force. Because the Jewish immigrants are concentrated in a number of urban centers—New York, Philadelphia, Chicago—a new antagonism will emerge between this identifiably Jewish immigrant proletariat and other working-class immigrant groups. The masses of Jewish immigrants thus bring the Jewish question to countries and continents which have not known it before; therefore, the scope of anti-Semitism will be broadened to include areas and classes not previously affected by it.[16] The attempts of Jewish immigrants to integrate into a productive labor force will similarly fail, and the Jews will again be pushed into marginal occupations; and the inverted pyramid of the Jewish social structure—a narrow productive base, heavy at the top with a middle class and an intelligentsia—will repeat itself in the New World.

What the Jewish problem, as a national problem, calls for is, according to Borochov, a territorial solution:

> The impossibility of penetrating into higher levels of production creates the need for concentrated immigration into an undeveloped country. Instead of being limited to the final levels of production, as is the case in all other countries, the Jews could in a short time assume a leading position in the economy of the new land. Jewish migration must be transformed from immigration to colonization. This means a territorial solution to the Jewish problem.[17]

After looking into the various choices for such a territorial solution, Borochov reaches the conclusion that only in Palestine would it become feasible. Only there would it be possible to create a Jewish society from its very foundation; only there could a Jewish peasantry and a Jewish working class be created and sustained. Such a process would be carried both by the spontaneous process (*stychia*) of the Jewish masses being pushed out of Eastern Europe and by the *conscious* effort of the Jewish proletariat to transform radically the social structures of Jewish society. A people cannot be independent unless it controls its own economic infrastructure; therefore Jewish economic independence is possible only in a territorial context in which the Jews would form also the basis of the social pyramid. This could happen only in Palestine, and it can be achieved only through the conscious activity of the Jewish proletariat to create such an infrastructure in the Land of Israel. The Jewish bourgeoisie, by moving its business from Europe to the Middle East, would not be able to create such a transformation, and therefore Borochov maintains that "the emancipation of the Jewish people either will be brought by Jewish labour, or it will not be attained at all."[18]

According to Borochov, the Jewish proletariat needs such a social revolutionary transformation more than any other class because its misery is more acute, both in comparison with other proletariats as well as in comparison with other classes of Jewish society. For this reason the Jewish proletariat will become the standard-bearer of the Jewish social revolution which would necessarily be a national revolution as well. Only the victory of the proletariat will emancipate all Jewish society from its dependence on non-Jewish economic structures, and only those who control the economic infrastructure can attain national independence:

> The country into which Jews will immigrate will not be highly industrial nor predominantly agricultural, but rather semiagricultural. Jews alone will migrate there, separated from the general stream of immigration. The country will have no attraction for immigrants from other nations.
>
> This land will be the only one available to the Jews; and of all the countries available for immigrants of all lands, this country will provide the line of greatest resistance. It will be a country of low cultural and political development. Big capital will hardly find use for itself there. . . . The land of spontaneous concentrated immigration will be Palestine. . . .[19]

According to Borochov, it is the anomaly of Jewish existence in the Diaspora that does not enable Jewish socioeconomic development to follow the general pattern of universal development. In this polemic against those Jewish socialists who saw in world revolution pure and simple a solution to the Jewish problem, Borochov does not flee from the universal to the particular. On the contrary, he says, only through the establishment of a Jewish society in Palestine can the historical Jewish class struggle be integrated into the universal struggle of the world proletariat. An attempt to carry on such a struggle when the Jews—all of them, bourgeois and proletarian alike—are minority groups within a non-Jewish society is doomed to distortion and failure, precisely because it gives rise to antagonisms *within* the social classes themselves—between non-Jewish and Jewish proletarians as well as between non-Jewish and Jewish bourgeois.

Thus Borochov does not see himself as abandoning a universal vision by advocating a Jewish society in Palestine. Only through the establishment of a Jewish society, controlling its own economic infrastructure, can the Jews be integrated into the universal revolutionary process. In Borochov's language, "political territorial autonomy in Palestine is the ultimate aim of Zionism. For proletarian Zionism, this is also a step toward socialism."[20] True internationalism leads through nationalism, not by overlooking it.

CHAPTER 14

GORDON: LABOR AND REDEMPTION

AHARON DAVID GORDON (1856–1922) WAS ONE OF THE most untypical pioneers of Zionism in the pre-1914 period, yet he came to represent that generation more than any other person. He was the first significant Zionist thinker whose ideas emerged through the confrontation with reality in Palestine itself. While most pioneers of the Second Aliyah (the wave of immigration between 1904 and 1914) were youngsters, Gordon came to Palestine in 1904, when he was forty-seven years old. Unlike many of the younger pioneers, who were active prior to their immigration in various Labor Zionist groups in Eastern Europe, he came from a very different background. He had behind him a successful career in Russia as the manager of a large agricultural estate belonging to a family relative. However, because of financial problems and family complications, Gordon, at middle age, had to start a new career, and he decided to emigrate to Palestine and devote himself to physical, agricultural labor there. Several years later he succeeded in bringing his family there, and all the while he worked as an agricultural laborer, first at Petah Tikva and later in the new cooperative venture in the Galilee and the Jordan Valley, destined to become the first kibbutz.

Gordon never saw himself as a socialist in any doctrinaire way, yet his thought became the guiding ideology of Hapoel Hatzair

(The Young Worker), the Labor Zionist party that attracted those pioneers of the Second Aliyah who did not follow the Marxist socialism of Poalei Zion, the party of Borochov, Ben Zvi, and Ben Gurion. This connection with the beginning of the kibbutz movement and Gordon's insistence that manual labor is central to both personal and national salvation made him one of the more influential thinkers of the Labor Zionist movement. The principles of Gordon's thought are still visibly present in the whole intellectual atmosphere permeating the kibbutz movement and the ideology so crucial to its structure of self-realization through physical labor. Through the later mentors of the kibbutz movement, like Yitzhak Tabenkin and Meir Yaari, whose politics were much more radical, Gordon's basic principles were preserved and further developed in the course of the labor movement in Israel.

Despite the specifically Jewish context of Gordon's thought, the problems of transition from life in the Diaspora to life in the Land of Israel, there are some very unmistakably universal elements in his thought. Its resemblance to Tolstoy's ideas about physical labor and agricultural life has been repeatedly pointed out. His rejection of urban culture because of its alienation from immediate contact with nature can be understood within the context of the late nineteenth-century neoromantic mood in Europe. Gordon's emigration to Palestine meant for him not only leaving the Diaspora for Zion but also rejecting decadent European society. This protest against the degeneration of bourgeois European culture is shared by Gordon with many of his European contemporaries. But unlike others, his protest did not dissolve into a mere literary mood or a desperate attempt to re-create a primeval world of innocence in Tahiti. Rather it became the foundation for a practical program of radical social reform, with the critic himself as the first practitioner of the New Creed. This element of affirmation through self-realization also distinguishes Gordon's approach from the wide gap between theory and praxis that characterized so much of the cultural protest of the fin de siècle.[1]

In an essay written in 1911 called "Some Observations," Gordon poses the two alternatives with which, to him, the Jewish community in Palestine is faced. One he calls "the practical way of the world wise . . . the continuation of Exile (*Galut*) life, with all its shortsighted practical wisdom," and the other leads to "the real life of national rebirth."[2] Exile to Gordon is not just a geographical place, it is also a psychological and existential context, and a exilelike existence is possible in Palestine just as anywhere else. Exile means the lack of self-reliance, exile means dependence on another, an estrangement from creative life. Exile and alienation go together:

> There is only one way that can lead to our renaissance—the way of manual labour, of mobilizing all our national energies. . . . We have as yet no national assets because our people have not yet paid the price for them. A people can acquire a land only by its own effort, by realizing the potentialities of its body and soul, by unfolding and revealing its inner self. This is a two-sided transaction, but the people comes first—the people comes before the land. But a parasitical people is not a living people. Our people can be brought to life only if each one of us re-creates himself through labour and a life close to nature. This is how we can, in time, have good farmers, good labourers, good Jews and good human beings. On the other hand, if in Palestine we continue the life of the Galut, with its petty trading and all that goes with it, the continuing generations will pursue the same road even more vigorously.[3]

Gordon's views about Jewish life in the Diaspora are integrated here into his more fundamental anthropological and psychological thought about human existence. To Gordon, a human being is only fully human through immediate contact with nature's inherent energy. This can only be done through physical labor, where the human and the natural are integrated into a new whole. The existence of the Jewish people in the Diaspora has been a distorted mode of existence because the people not only lost its homeland but also lost its land and the labor involved in it and had been pushed into the marginal existence of trade and commerce. A Jewish national renaissance will not occur, according to Gordon, just by a geographical migration to Palestine. It has to involve a "Return to the Self" through manual labor, and this is only possible for the Jews on a massive scale in the Land of Israel. Emigration to Palestine without radically revolutionizing Jewish social structures is nothing else than a transference of Exile to the Land of Israel. This explains Gordon's utter abhorrence, very much like that of his contemporary, the writer Joseph Chaim Brenner, at discovering a gradual transformation of erstwhile pioneers to Palestine into landowners and merchants dependent upon the labor of others.

Gordon thus joined Labor Zionism not because he was committed to the idea of class war or to the vision of a universal socialist redemption. For him Labor Zionism meant an attempt to create an economic infrastructure for a Jewish community in Palestine founded on the Jews' own labor. This for him was the *conditio sine qua non* of Jewish renaissance. Zionism for Gordon was not merely or even primarily a political revolution but a socioeconomic and psychological revolution as well, without which the political revolution would remain hollow and meaningless.

Gordon is aware of the far-reaching consequences of such a radical analysis demanding, as it does, a total transformation of Jewish life. The way of "true rebirth" is much more difficult than the so-called practical wisdom of the life of Exile. The way of national rebirth

> embraces every detail of our individual lives. Every one of us is required to refashion himself so that the Galut Jew *within him* becomes a truly emancipated Jew; so that the unnatural, defective, splintered person within him may be changed into a natural wholesome human being who is true to himself; so that his Galut life, which has been fashioned by *alien* and *extraneous* influences, hampering his natural growth and self-realization, may give way to one that allows him to develop freely, to his fullest stature in all dimensions [italics added].[4]

Exile is in the human soul: from there it has to be banished.

Like other Zionist thinkers, Gordon also suggests that paradoxically, traditional Jewish life in the Diaspora was much fuller and richer than post-Emancipation life. The pre-Emancipation Orthodox Jew did indeed look for a life that included physical comfort, but this was a legitimate aim for him "provided it also enabled him to carry out the precepts and commandments of his religion. . . . Any other life had no meaning for him. The ordinary Jew of today who emigrates to America or Australia, or even to Palestine, sees the real meaning of life in economic advancement."[5] But this sole pursuit of material good—even if carried out in the Land of Israel—sacrifices the real, meaningful life. A true renaissance requires "a radical change, a complete revolution."[6]

Gordon devoted much study to this connection between what he calls "real, natural life" and physical labor. In some of his writings he even uses the phrase "Religion of Labor." This aspect of his thought is developed at some length in another essay written in 1911, called *Labor*. Through labor, Gordon maintains, a people is linked and connected with its land and its homeland; once a people is torn away from agricultural work, it becomes deracinated and is on the way to ultimately losing control of its homeland. This is what happened to the Jewish people, and the consequence is a distorted, emasculated people with a value system totally out of focus. Gordon's views of what Exile did to the Jews are far from flattering. He maintains that over time the Jews became well accustomed to their distorted and alienated nature; even Zionist thinkers are not always aware how far-reaching changes must be for Jews to live a self-supportive national life in their own country:

> A people that was completely divorced from nature, that during two thousand years was imprisoned within walls, that became inured to all forms of life except to a life of labour, cannot become once again a living, natural, working people without bending all its willpower toward that end. We lack the fundamental element: we lack labour [not labor done because of necessity, but labor to which man is organically and naturally linked], labour by which a people becomes rooted in its soil and its culture.[7]

Gordon admits that "to be sure, not every individual among other peoples exists by labour." But in the case of other peoples, this is always a minority; every people, according to Gordon, has a vast majority who live by their labor. This is not so among the Jews:

> We despise labour. Even among our workers there are those who work because of necessity and with the continual hope of some day escaping from it and leading "the good life." We must not deceive ourselves. We must realize how abnormal we are in this respect, how alien labour has become to our spirit, and not alone to the individual life, but also to the life of the nation.[8]

Being cut off from labor thus appears to Gordon as a deep, historical flaw in the Jewish people. It is not only that Exile created this alienation from labor. Alienation from labor, whatever its historical origin, also contributed to the continuation of Exile; it enabled Jews to come to terms with Exile, to accommodate to it, and to survive in it. A people more deeply connected with labor would have done much more to go back to its land. Labor has become alien to the Jews, and consequently Gordon is pessimistic about what might happen in this context even in Palestine:

> Now let us assume that somewhere we already have settled a goodly number of Jews. Will this attitude of ours change there of itself? Will a transformation of our soul take place without a radical cure? Will not our Jewish people at all times prefer trading, speculation, especially business in which others will labour while they will manage the enterprise?[9]

A cultural revolution is thus needed, according to Gordon. But looking at the debate about Jewish culture as conducted in Zionist congresses and assemblies, Gordon finds it utterly unsatisfactory. The Russian Populist distrust of "intellectualism" echoes very clearly in Gordon's statement that those engaging in the Zionist debate about culture are "concerned mainly with ideas," while truly speaking, "a living culture embraces the whole of life," and populist ideas of social revolution are quite apparent in his forceful plea for a total transformation of Jewish life. In this context Gordon is specifically addressing the Jewish problems, but he reflects the *Zeitgeist* of European and Slavophile romanticism:

> Whatever man creates for the sake of life is culture: the tilling of the soil, the building of homes, of all kinds of buildings, the paving of roads, and so on. Each piece of work, each deed, each act is an element of culture. Herein is the foundation of culture, the stuff of which it is made. Arrangement, method, shape, the way in which a thing is done—these are forms of culture. What a man does, what he feels, thinks, lives, while he is at work, and while he is not working, the conditions arising from these relations—these mould themselves into the spirit of culture. From these, higher culture draws its nourishment—science, art, beliefs and opinions, poetry, ethics, religion. Higher culture or culture in its restricted sense, the culture which we mean when we speak of culture, is the *butter* of culture in general, of culture in its broader sense. But is it possible to make butter without milk or will man make butter from the milk of others, and will the butter then be his very own?[10]

Therefore, what Zionism has to bring about in Palestine is not a mere academic culture. There is no doubt that a High Culture, to use Gordon's expression, has to be established in the new homeland of the Jewish people, and it will have to include "beliefs, opinions on life, the art of life, the poetry of life, the ethics of life, the religion of life." But all this cannot be achieved on a superstructural level without the emergence of an integral popular and social life, without all labor in the Jewish community being carried out by the Jews themselves:

> [We have] to work with our very own hands at all things which make up life [in Palestine], to labour with our own hands at all kinds of works, at all kinds of crafts and trades from the most skilled, the cleanliest and the easiest to the coarsest, the most despised, the most difficult. We must feel all that the worker feels, think what he thinks, live the life he lives, in ways that are our ways. Then we can consider that we have our own culture, for then we shall have life.[11]

This element integrating man as *homo faber* into the spirit of the nation is called by Gordon *am adam*—literally, "man-nation," a human nation. The ability to create a new Jewish "man-nation" is the challenge facing Zionism, Gordon maintains. Nationalism is not merely a problem of a linguistic, historical, or religious affinity. In an article on "Our Tasks Ahead" (1920), Gordon again mentions the cosmic element—the link between man and nature—which has been lacking until now in Jewish existence in the Diaspora. It is this cosmic element which Zionism aims to restore:

> Jewish life in the Diaspora lacks this cosmic element of national identity; it is sustained by the historic element only. . . . We, who have been uprooted, must first learn to know the soil and prepare it for our transplantation. We must study the climate in which we are to grow and produce. We, who have been torn away from nature, who have lost the savour of natural living—if we desire life, we must establish a new relationship with nature, we must open a new account with it.[12]

For this reason Gordon does not favor linking the Labor movement in Palestine with the struggle of the international proletariat, whose problems and concerns are very different. The dilemma of Jewish creativity is different from the problems of the industrial working class; and the Jewish effort, precisely because it is so tremendous and has to fight against such formidable historical and psychological odds, should not be sidetracked. All energies should be focused on the radical Jewish transformation. However, Gordon warns against making the Jewish community in Palestine into a mere outpost of Diaspora Jewry and maintains the centrality of the Land of Israel in his scheme of things:

> What we seek to establish in Palestine is a new, recreated Jewish people, not a mere colony of Diaspora Jewry, not a continuation of Diaspora Jewish life in a new form. It is our aim to make Jewish Palestine the mother country of world Jewry, with Jewish communities in the Diaspora as its colonies—and not the reverse.[13]

The institutional consequences of Gordon's radicalism are far-reaching—though not perhaps immediately apparent—and they are in a way much more political than his anthropological and quasi-apolitical language may at first suggest. Gordon's call for transferring the focus of the Zionist movement and the Jewish people from the Diaspora to Palestine was motivated by his anthropological understanding of the enormity of the radicalism of the

Zionist revolution; this became a political reality in the 1930s under the hegemony of the Labor movement in Palestine, when leadership in the Zionist movement shifted from the middle-class Diaspora Zionists to the Labor movement in Palestine itself. The centrality of the Land of Israel and of the Labor movement as the social subject carrying out the Zionist revolutionary transformation of the Jewish people are the political consequences of Gordon's anthropological radicalism.

Historically speaking, Gordon emerges as a pessimistic thinker, expressing the unease about civilization traceable in European thinking from Rousseau to Dostoievsky and Freud. It is in this general context that Gordon views with fear the strength of the spiritual and psychological forces that have torn the Jewish people away from productive labor and consequently from its homeland. Exile resides in the soul, according to Gordon; and Zionism, for him, is always a desperate revolt against two thousand years of Jewish history and Jewish accommodation to Exile and alienation. To him, if this radical revolt will not succeed in exorcizing this internal Exile and alienation from the reality of Jewish life, the end result of a merely political Zionism may turn out to be a terrible disappointment.

The relevance of Gordon's thought thus obviously transcends its impact in the 1910s and 1920s on the pioneering generations of the Second and Third Aliyah. For him, Zionism is not a mere bundle of political slogans or a series of diplomatic fiats. It is an actual praxis, to be carried out by all those who want to participate in this momentous revolt of the Jewish people against its own history. Dialectically, Zionism is, thus, also close to the basic tenets of Jewish religion as a practical way of life, not merely as a set of doctrines or ceremonial rites. This gives Gordon the theoretical justification to view his "Religion of Labor" as having quasi-religious connotations within the Jewish tradition, despite all its radical rebellion against this tradition itself.

CHAPTER 15

JABOTINSKY: INTEGRALIST NATIONALISM AND THE ILLUSION OF POWER

VLADIMIR JABOTINSKY (1880–1940) WAS NOT ONLY ONE OF the most controversial figures in the development of the Zionist movement, he was also, without doubt, one of the most colorful personalities to emerge from the intellectual and social ferment brought forward by Zionism. He was a gifted journalist, an orator with mass appeal, a writer whose novels show considerable talent, and a sensitive aesthete who at the same time called on his people (in the language of Samson, the hero of his most famous novel) to gather iron. As a progeny of the Russian turn-of-the-century intelligentsia, Jabotinsky was a polished European gentleman and towered high above all the other Zionist leaders between both world wars in his culture, sensibilities, and intellectual horizons. In hundreds of essays, articles, and notices, written in several languages, he proved his almost uncanny ability to be at home in many different societies, to attach himself to various schools of thought, and integrate into his thought many of the most modern strands and fashions of European cultural life. None of the leaders of Zionism could rival him in the rich variety of his activities as poet and translator, essayist and novelist.

According to his own testimony, Jabotinsky started his career under the influence of socialist doctrines. However, he became more attuned to the cultural and social convulsions of his age than any of his contemporaries in the Zionist leadership and thus developed a theory of integralist nationalism deeply influenced by parallel developments on the general European scene.

If there was something lacking in the kaleidoscopic richness of his intellectual baggage, it was the specific Jewish cultural ingredient. Even Jabotinsky's most devoted disciple has to admit that the person who expressed perhaps more than any other a theory of Jewish nationalism based on national pride is rather lacking in his own Jewish heritage. His Hebrew is rich and mellifluous (his translation of Edgar Allan Poe's *The Raven* is one of the masterpieces of modern Hebrew literature), but anyone who goes carefully through the twenty volumes of his collected works will learn more about Russian, Italian, German, and even Ukrainian culture than about Jewish culture.

This shallowness of the Jewish component in his intellectual heritage is similar to Herzl's spiritual makeup—despite the difference, of course, that Herzl had no working knowledge of Hebrew. Yet in Jabotinsky's case it raises a few questions. Herzl never attempted to speak from a position of national pride or ethnic uniqueness and always stood for the most cosmopolitan and universalistic elements in Zionist thought. Jabotinsky's doctrines, on the other hand, became identified with a worldview considered largely ethnocentric, and yet while most of Jabotinsky's disciples are usually coated with a thick layer of *Yiddishkeit,* Jabotinsky evinces a certain distance and alienation from values and symbols directly connected with the Jewish tradition, be it religious or secular. It may not be wholly accidental that his didactic historical novel *Samson* deals with the most pagan of biblical heroes, and Jabotinsky's Samson evokes memories of Greek or Nordic mythical figures. This Samson also expresses deep admiration for the Philistines' vitalistic power cult and their pagan worship of nature. Similar themes can be found in modern Hebrew literature in the writings of Shaul Tschernichowsky and Micha Yosef Berditschevsky, but in Jabotinsky's case this was not a mere literary pose but a base for a political, practical program.

Jabotinsky's testament, written in 1935, is another example of this deep alienation from some very basic Jewish cultural traits. On one level, this is a highly political testament. "My bones," Jabotinsky writes, "if I be buried outside of the Land of Israel, should be transferred to the Land of Israel only at the express order of the Jewish government of that country when it will be established." But Jabotinsky appears utterly equanimous to the question whether he would be buried according to Jewish ritual. "I wish to be buried or cremated (*it is the same to me*) at the place in which death will find me [italics added]."[1] Cremation has always been considered, even by secular Jews, as a most un-Jewish way of disposal of the dead, and it certainly is a unique phenomenon to find a Jewish national leader expressing such nonchalance about whether he will be buried according to Jewish ritual or not. It may have been this utter alienation from Jewish cultural values that caused Jabotinsky, in his quest for self-identity, to come out with an overstated and highly overcharged version of integralist nationalism by way of compensation.

These questions, however, belong more to the biographical aspects of Jabotinsky's life—and there is no doubt that he could be a fascinating subject for such a study. The biographies written about Jabotinsky until now have, in most instances, been too much involved in propagating a political thesis and have thus missed, in most cases, much of the fascination of his personality as a true fin de siècle character. The discussion here is limited to his ideas, but because these have been a subject of so much controversy, some aspects of his thought will be examined more closely than would have otherwise been called for.

Jabotinsky was born in Odessa, the son of a wealthy merchant who was infused with the Enlightenment character of this unusual Russian city. In his *Autobiography*, Jabotinsky recalls that while *kashrut* was rigorously observed at home, "I had at that time no internal connection with Judaism except through the study of Hebrew." As for the private school to which he was sent, he does not recall "anything Jewish there, be it Jewish history or prayers," though he studied Hebrew from an early age.[2] The cosmopolitan atmosphere of Odessa was deeply imprinted on Jabotinsky's intellectual development, and in the 1930s he devoted a novel in Russian (*They Were Five*) to the evocation of this ambience. In his autobiography Jabotinsky writes about Odessa that

out of the void has this city been established a hundred years before my birth, and in a dozen languages did its inhabitants speak, yet none of them did they fully master. . . . I have never seen such an easygoing city—there is no city like Odessa when it comes to the mellowness of joy or the light scent of intoxication floating about the air. It is utterly free from any shadow of psychological complexity or moral tragedy.[3]

Despite the early death of his father and the economic hardships imposed on his family as a consequence of this loss, Jabotinsky's home maintained its cosmopolitan atmosphere and through his father's library and his relatives, Jabotinsky became acquainted with European, especially German, culture. As a teenager he translated poetry from Hebrew and English into Russian, and supported by his relatives he went to study law in Switzerland and Italy.

According to his own account, his first encounter with Zionism occurred during his studies in Berne, when he attended a lecture by Nachman Syrkin on socialist Zionism. On that occasion, Jabotinsky writes, he made his first Zionist speech; the episode is recounted in his *Autobiography* in the following slightly surprising manner:

> I spoke Russian, in the following vein: I do not know if I am a socialist, since I have not yet acquainted myself with this doctrine; but I have no doubt that I am Zionist, because the Jewish people is a very nasty people, and its neighbours hate it, and they are right; its end in the Diaspora will be a general Bartholomew Night, and the only rescue is general immigration to Palestine.[4]

Too much importance should perhaps not be attached to this retrospective report, neither to its prefiguration of Jabotinsky's later radical insistence on the tragedy awaiting the Jewish people in the Diaspora nor to the telling commentary that those who hate the Jews "are right." But it certainly suggests a pronounced train of thought, to be accentuated much later.

The major impact on Jabotinsky's intellectual development was to come later—in Italy, where he moved after Berne and where he stayed for three years. Italy, not Russia, became the experience that molded his spirit, as he says in his *Autobiography*:

> If I have a spiritual homeland, it is Italy, much more than Russia. . . . From the day of my arrival there I became fully integrated into Italian youth, and its life I lived until I left Italy. All my views on problems of nationalism, the state and society were developed during those years under Italian influence; it was there that I learned to love the art of the architect, the sculptor and the painter, as well as the Latin song. . . . At the university my teachers were Antonio Labriola and Enrico

Perri, and the belief in the justice of the socialist system, which they implanted in my heart, I kept as self-evident until it became utterly destroyed by the red experience in Russia. The legend of Garibaldi, the writings of Mazzini, the poetry of Leopardi and Guisti have enriched and deepened my superficial Zionism: from an instinctive feeling they made it into a doctrine.[5]

Italian nationalism—with its pathos and rhetoric, the heroism of Garibaldi's volunteers—more than a direct link with the immediate problems of Jewish existence determined the nature of Jabotinsky's views on nationalism. At the same time, Jabotinsky's sensitivity made him aware of the new trends already appearing on the Italian intellectual horizons. The demise of liberalism, the appearance of modernist aesthetic schools, like Futurism, attuned him to the first rumblings of the developments that would culminate in fascism:

If I would be asked to suggest a word underlying the common denominator of all the trends of political thinking then vying for public attention in Italy, I would have chosen that old-fashioned term—liberalism. That term was already then the common laughing stock of all, and to-day it is utterly discredited and viewed with disgust by the Italian youth as well as by young people all over the world. What is liberalism? It is a broad concept, vague because of its all-encompassing nature; it is a dream about order and justice without violence, a universal dream woven of sympathy, tolerance, a belief in the basic goodness and righteousness of man. At that time one did not feel in the air even an intimation of that cult of discipline, which later expressed itself in fascism; if I recall in my memory any signs for a change in attitudes, then its prophet was not Mussolini but Marinetti. Its tendency was toward that literary and philosophical school which called itself, years later, Futurism—a school whose historical role has been, perhaps, to become a prelude to Mussolini. . . .

Among my student friends . . . I heard people saying, "A day will come and we'll send to hell all those tourists who insist on seeing Italy as a mere museum. It is our life, it is the smoking chimney which are the true and real Italy . . ." It is as if an early echo to Marinetti's view could be heard here: the noise of an airplane is more beautiful than the vibrations of a Neapolitan song; the future is more beautiful than the past; Italy is the land of industry and cars and electricity, it is not just the promenade for international do-nothings who look for aesthetic recreation. The New Italian is organized and orderly, meticulous in his accounts—a builder and a conqueror, obstinate and cruel.

This is the first origin of fascism.[6]

How much Jabotinsky shared this critique of the weaknesses of liberalism can be seen from a very early essay, "Man Is a Wolf to Man" (Homo homini lupus), written in 1910, in which he declares liberalism dead and irrelevant for the modern age. Here Jabotinsky maintains that there is no foundation for the classical liberal humanistic view according to which "anyone who has himself suffered for a long time under the yoke of a stronger one will not oppress those weaker than he."[7] Jabotinsky mentions the Polish population in Galicia, then under Austrian rule, which oppresses the Ukrainian minority while at the same time it is itself being oppressed by the German-speaking Austrians:

> Sometimes we base too many rosy hopes on the fallacy that a certain people has itself suffered much and will therefore feel the agony of another people and understand it and its conscience will not allow it to inflict on the weaker people what had been earlier inflicted on it. But in reality it appears that these are mere pretty phrases. . . . Only the Bible says "thou shalt not oppress a stranger; for ye know the heart of a stranger, seeing ye were strangers in the land of Egypt." *Contemporary morality has no place for such childish humanism* [italics added].[8]

Early intimations of Italian *sacro egoismo* can be found in this article, which does not deal at all with the Jewish question. This is theoretically significant, for when Jabotinsky deals later with the acute Jewish problem in the 1930s, his utter concentration on Jewish interests is to be understood not as a response to the specific (and unique) Jewish agony of that period but as a general expression of how the world is built.

In words recalling the cult of power so prevalent in many intellectual circles in pre-1914 days, Jabotinsky closes his essay "Man Is a Wolf to Man,"

> It was a wise philosopher who said "man is a wolf to man"; worse than the wolf is man to man, and this will not change for many days to come. We will not change this through political reforms, nor through culture and even bitter experience will not change it. Stupid is the person who believes in his neighbour, good and loving as the neighbour may be; stupid is the person who relies on justice. Justice exists only for those whose fists and stubbornness make it possible for them to realize it. When I am criticised for my insistence on apartness, on not believing in anyone and on other matters which are difficult for delicate persons to accept, I sometimes want to answer: I am guilty. Do not believe anyone, be always on guard,

carry your stick always with you—this is the only way of surviving in this wolfish battle of all against all.[9]

The later development of Jabotinsky's political and national thinking has to be understood against the background of his intensive literary and public activity in the years following his stay in Italy. He returned to Russia and served for several years before World War I as a roving correspondent for a number of influential Russian newspapers, where he published most of his articles up to the outbreak of World War I. These were sometimes signed with his own name, sometimes appeared under his pen name of Altalena.[10]

This period also saw the beginnings of his Zionist activity. He became involved in the first attempts at self-defense in the wake of the Kishinev pogroms (1903), attended Zionist congresses and the Helsingfors Conference; after the revolution of the Young Turks he spent some time in Istanbul as an editor of a number of Zionist journals; in 1912 he presented his dissertation entitled "On Autonomous Government of a National Minority" for a Diploma in Law at the University of Yaroslavl. When the war broke out, he was sent by his newspaper to tour Europe and the Middle East and thus reached Egypt and participated in establishing the First Zion Mule Corps; later, in London, he was active in forming a Jewish Regiment in the British Army. After the revolution in Russia stopped his journalistic work, he joined the Jewish Regiment and arrived in Palestine after its occupation by the British. Here he was one of the first to demand a permanent Jewish armed force under British supervision and was imprisoned by the British authorities for a short time during the 1920 Arab disturbances. His insistence on the political-military aspect in preference to the policy of settling pioneers on the land brought him into early collision with the official Zionist leadership in the 1920s. The origins of this split can be seen in his opposition to the attempt to maintain a Jewish presence, albeit small, in the Upper Galilee, which was then in the French zone of occupation. Jabotinsky was against Trumpeldor's desperate insistence that Tel Hai should not be evacuated—and the fact that years later he named the youth order he established, Betar, after Trumpeldor, is perhaps one of the many ironies connected with the development of his policies.[11]

During the years in which the structure of the Jewish community in Palestine, the Yishuv, was formed through an increasing rise in the power of the labor movement, the rift between Jabotinsky, who resided mostly in Paris, and the official Zionist leadership became deeper and more bitter, and in 1925 Jabotinsky founded the Revisionist Zionist Organization within the Zionist movement. Ten years later he and his followers left the official Zionist movement and founded the New Zionist Organization. Against official Zionism, which combined settlement activities in Palestine with cautious diplomacy, Jabotinsky offered a novel and radical Zionism, which, while it appeared strident and implacable to his rivals, gathered an enormous following among Jewish masses in Central and Eastern Europe at a time when the position of the Jews there was becoming more and more precarious with the rise of nazism and other anti-Semitic movements.

According to his own testimony Jabotinsky regards his Italian experience as decisive in the development of his political ideas; and indeed, from the beginning of his journalistic career, Jabotinsky's articles abound with discussions of problems of nationalism. It is not only Jewish nationalism which appears central to his interests but also the problems of nationalities in Europe in general, and this continues even at the time of his most intensive Zionist activities. In this context, Jabotinsky views nationalism as a supreme value, and following Garibaldi, he says that "there is no value in the world higher than the nation and the fatherland, there is no deity in the universe to which one should sacrifice these two most valuable jewels."[12]

This theory about the supremacy of the nation is accompanied in Jabotinsky's writings by a clear and decisive view of the role of races in world history. His views are expressed unequivocally in several articles during various periods of his life. The first detailed discussion appears in a long article, "On Race," published in 1913, in which he says,

> It does not matter whether "pure" races exist or not; what matters is that ethnic communities are distinguished from each other by their racial appearance, and it is in this sense that the term "race" acquires a most definite and scientific meaning.
>
> We are entitled then to say that generally speaking almost every nation has a specific racial component, which is common to each individual within it. In this sense (and not, of course, in a political or juridical sense), nation and race overlap each other. What follows from this?
>
> Physical nature and intellectual activity are interconnected, they show a psycho-physical parallelism. . . . It is impossible to

describe the racial psyche, yet nonetheless there is no doubt that a racial community (in this sense) is endowed with a special racial psychology, which appears in one form or another, in every member of the community despite all their individual differences.[13]

Against the materialist determinism derived from Marx, which Jabotinsky rejects, he proposes in this article a determinism defined by race:

If the types of the economy and its specific ingredient, its social organization, et cetera, are necessarily imprinted by the racial psychology of the community—this is true *a fortiori* with regard to religion, philosophy, literature and even legislation, in short—with regard to all of spiritual culture, whose immediate nexus with the national psyche is even more clear and evident.[14]

This identity between the national and the racial is presented by Jabotinsky as a model for the "absolute nation." He is well aware that this ideal type can never be attained in reality in its pure form, but it can serve as a criterion for judging existing and emerging nations:

Let us draw for ourself the ideal type of an "absolute nation." It would have to possess a racial appearance of marked unique character, an appearance different from the racial nature of that nation's neighbours. It would have to occupy from times immemorial a continuous and clearly defined piece of land; it would be highly desirable if in that area there would be no alien minorities, who would weaken national unity. It would have to maintain an original national language, which is not derived from another nation. . . .[15]

The racial component remains for Jabotinsky the essential element of the nation after all the other, secondary elements have been distilled away:

You are forced to say: territory, religion, a common language—all these are not the substance of a nation, but only its attributes; true, these attributes are immensely valuable, and they are even more valuable for the stability of national existence. *But a nation's substance, the alpha and omega of the uniqueness of its character—this is embodied in its specific physical quality, in the component of its racial composition. . . .* [italics added].

For the scholar, who is interested not only in the facts and necessities of daily political life or in mere phenomena of psychological life, but looks also for primary, objective causes—for him, when all externalities derived from history, climate, surrounding nature will be removed, then the nation will be reduced to its racial kernel.[16]

Such ideas about race were perhaps not that significant politically when published in 1913, but Jabotinsky continued to maintain them even later, when the appearance of racial theories became politically far more significant. In a pamphlet published in Yiddish in Warsaw in 1933, called *A Lecture on Jewish History*, Jabotinsky makes much of the same arguments:

> Every race has a different spiritual mechanism. This has nothing to do with the fact whether there exist "pure" races or not; of course, all races are "mixed," and this includes us, the Jews. But the mixture is different from case to case. . . .
>
> The nature of the spiritual mechanism depends on race; the degree of intelligence, a stronger or weaker tendency to look for novel experiences, the readiness to acquiesce in the existing situation or the courage to make new discoveries, the stubbornness or, conversely, the kind of character which gives up after the first unsuccessful attempt: all these modes are themselves a product of race. . . .
>
> Every race possessing a definite uniqueness seeks to become a nation, i.e., to create for itself an economic, political and intellectual environment in which every detail will derive from its specific thought and consequently will also relate to its specific taste. Such an environment a specific race can establish only in its own country, where it is the master. For this reason, every race seeks to become a state . . . because only in its own state will it feel comfortable.[17]

Such a detailed discussion of problems of race is accompanied in Jabotinsky's writings by a parallel debate about the superiority and inferiority of races. This appears in a spirited and subtle dialogue held by an imaginary Russian and an imaginary Jew about the question of racial superiority. The dialogue, called *An Exchange of Compliments*, was published in 1913 as a response to an anti-Semitic tract called *An Inferior Race*. The dialogue opens with the Russian stating that there exist superior and inferior races, and according to his criteria, the Jews constitute an inferior race. The Jew's initial position is that for him all races are equal despite the enormous differences separating them from each other. But in the course of the dialogue the Jew subtly shifts his position, and he sets out criteria according to which, in a hypothetical comparison between the races, the Jews and not the Russians (or the Aryans generally) emerge as a superior race. Here is the crux of the Jew's argument:

> According to your view, the criterion for a superior race is creativity and versatility. . . . I, on the other hand, would like to suggest another

criterion for a superior race: self-awareness. Such a superior creature will be a scholar among barbarians or an aristocrat in a rabble. At every moment will he be aware of his own value, an awareness which cannot be uprooted and is not even responsive to his own will. Externally, this self-awareness will express itself in modes which we call by different names—usually we call it pride. This is the same trait due to which King Lear does not cease to be a king even when dressed in rags: his consciousness tells him that he is king, and he cannot detach this from his own self. This feeling which a person has that he is an aristocrat is the primary and main sign of his true aristocracy. True, sometimes a *parvenu* comes along and claims to be an aristocrat; on the other hand, even the Bushmen believe that the rest of mankind is inferior to them. But a common person who has risen in the world, suffice it for him to meet a true grandee— and the internal order of his consciousness will appear immediately: he will feel ill at ease, he will not be able to strike the right note— and will *feel* his inferiority. The same applies to the Bushman, when he will meet a white person: ultimately, and despite everything, he will be impressed by the white man's supremacy. Both believe in their own superiority, but in the white man's heart it will not be impaired, while in the Bushman's feeling it will be contested and destroyed and will finally disappear. Ultimately, the white man will rule the Bushman not only by force, but his domination will also be that of spiritual superiority.[18]

This example firmly expresses Jabotinsky's conviction that the issue of racial superiority is not just a matter of mutual subjective feelings and notions but is destined to be internalized by those races who are inferior. Furthermore, what characterizes racial superiority is the rejection of alien elements—a superior race (the Jew in Jabotinsky's dialogue maintains) takes care not to be contaminated by external alien influences:

First of all, a superior race has to possess self-awareness; it possesses a kind of pride which can withstand everything: not, of course, through sheer bragging, but through valiant steadfastness, through a feeling of respect for its own spiritual values. For such a race, the very idea that it will accept the authority of an alien element, is organically disgusting and detestable.[19]

The Jew goes on that according to these criteria, it is Russian culture which has always adapted itself to foreign elements and is basically derivative, whereas the Jews have always maintained their originality and their rejection of external and alien elements. The Jew reiterates toward the end of the dialogue that his basic position still is that all races are equal, yet he adds, "But if we are going to make comparisons, everything depends on the criteria to be used, and then, you should know, I will insist on my own criterion: he who is steadfast in spirit—he is superior. . . . He who will never give up his internal independence, even when under foreign yoke—he is superior. . . . We are a race that will never be harnessed."

Jabotinsky's concept of the nation is also imbued with vitalistic and activist elements, and this calls for the subjugation of all spheres of social life to the primacy of the national experience. Literature, art, music—all have to be immersed in the totality of national life. In an article published in 1919 Jabotinsky praises the appearance of a Hebrew translation of Henryk Sinkiewicz's *By Fire and Sword* and views it as a model for a national literature. According to Jabotinsky, there are two kinds of literature—contemplative and activist—and he feels that the main defect of modern Hebrew literature has been its undue focusing on the contemplative:

> We, as an emerging nation, need without doubt an activity-inducing literature. We need a generation of founders and builders, a generation ready for all kinds of adventures and experiences, a generation that can find its way in the most dense forest. We need young people who can ride horses and climb trees and swim in the water and use their fists and shoot a gun; we need people with a healthy imagination and a strong will, striving to express themselves in the struggle for life. A Dostoievsky or a Knut Hamsun will not educate such a generation. In the future epoch about to begin, we have no place and no use for a complex creature, contemplating his own soul and minutely measuring all its feelings, their length and depth and intensity. Our *true* internal world has not yet been created, and there is nothing to contemplate. It is the external world that awaits us, and there we will act and there will we build.
>
> Our original literature (and by this I mean our fiction) is not up to this national task. Generally speaking, there is no action in it, no movement, no great events, no dynamism. . . .[20]

Jabotinsky's commitment to the values of nationalism *qua* nationalism leads him to one of the more surprising positions taken by him—an endorsement of Ukrainian nationalism and its national literature—and to a positive evaluation of the greatest Ukrainian national poet, Taras Shevchenko. Of all the new and emerging nationalist movements of Eastern Europe, Ukrainian nationalism was characterized more than any other by an extreme xenophobia and a virulent anti-Semitism. While among Jewish intellectuals there are expressions of support for Polish or Italian nationalism, with their humanistic background, it is quite unusual and surprising to find a Jewish thinker coming to the defense of Ukrainian nationalism, usually identified in Jewish consciousness with pogroms and a particularly vicious kind of anti-Semitism.

Jabotinsky's essay "Shevchenko's Jubilee" (1911) is a general defense of Ukrainian nationalism and Ukrainian culture against those "Great Russian" protagonists who viewed Ukrainian as a mere debased form of a provincial peasant patois. Jabotinsky, on the other hand, discovers in Ukrainian nationalism vitality, originality, and authenticity. These traits are to Jabotinsky central to the development of a national movement, which is characterized by him through its rejection of alien and foreign elements. Jabotinsky does not overlook the fact that because of this, Ukrainian nationalism in general—and Shevchenko's poetry in particular—is imbued with an extreme lack of tolerance vis-à-vis other cultures. But this xenophobia is for Jabotinsky just another aspect of the authenticity and nonderivative nature of Ukrainian nationalism, hence it should be praised and welcome:

> Shevchenko was a national poet, and herein lies his strength . . . He is a national poet also in the subjective sense, i.e., he is a nationalist poet, and this includes all the defects involved in nationalistic attitudes, including explosions of wild fury against the Poles, the Jews and other neighbors. . . . But what is more important is . . . that he has given to his people, as well as to the whole world, a clear and solid proof that the Ukrainian soul has been endowed with talent for independent cultural creativity, reaching unto the highest and most sublime spheres.[21]

This is not the only instance in which Jabotinsky expressed sympathy and empathy for Ukrainian nationalism. In the essay "Man Is a Wolf To Man," published at about the same time, Jabotinsky endorsed the Ukrainian position in Galicia against Polish nationalism.

This feeling of support for Ukrainian nationalism because of its authenticity, despite its terrible anti-Semitic overtones, may also have had some practical political consequences. At the twelfth Zionist Congress convened in 1921 in Carlsbad, Jabotinsky proposed to a rather stunned audience a scheme for cooperation with the anti-Communist Ukrainian independent regime of Semyon Petlyura. Jews have come to identify Petlyura's regime and his legions with brutal pogroms and massacres, and prior to the emergence of Hitler the very name of Petlyura conjured in the Jewish mind the archetypical anti-Semite. Jabotinsky's proposal, which was consequently rejected, has been defended on grounds of expediency and Jabotinsky's own strong anti-Communist feelings. But there might have been more to it than just such instrumental considerations. Jabotinsky's feelings of deep affinity with Ukrainian nationalism and even his empathy for its greatest anti-Semitic poet indicated that the roots of his proposed agreement with Petlyura were deeply imbedded in his historical and aesthetical admiration for what he considered to be the vitalistic authenticity of Ukrainian nationalism and culture.

Another element in Jabotinsky's nationalist theory is his insistence on the nation's internal unity—the monistic principle (*Had-Ness*). This principle has two aspects—the nation's hegemony toward both the individual and partial associations like classes.

This hegemony of the whole toward the individual expresses itself in Jabotinsky's insistence on discipline. Discipline is what holds a nation together, Jabotinsky argues, and discipline is what characterized the organizational structure around which he built Betar, the youth order of the Revisionist movement. In an article, "The Idea of Betar" (1934), Jabotinsky writes,

> *Betar* is structured around the principle of discipline. Its aim is to turn *Betar* into such a world organism that would be able, at a command from the center, to carry out at the same moment, through the scores of its limbs, the same action in every city and every state. The opponents of *Betar* maintain that this does not accord with the dignity of free men and it entails becoming a machine. I suggest not to be ashamed and respond with pride: Yes, a machine.
>
> Because it is the highest achievement of a multitude of free human beings to be able to act together with the absolute precision of a machine. . . .[22]

As in other expressions of the cult of discipline characteristic of integralist nationalism in the 1920s and 1930s, the role of the leader is another aspect of the same development. In the same article, Jabotinsky also maintains that

> discipline means that a multitude submit to the authority of one who directs them, and this one submits in his turn to the authority of another one higher up, and so on. . . . We all have one will, we all build one structure, and therefore we have all responded to the call of the one architect whose building abilities have been accepted by us . . .
>
> The Commander, the Conductor, the Architect—he may be one person or a collectivity. . . .[23]

Jabotinsky is well aware of the connotations and associations implied in such a theory in the thirties, and in an article, "On Militarism" (1933), he tries to address the criticism voiced against Betar's insistence on military discipline, hierarchy, parades, and paramilitary uniforms. In that article he admits that militarism is "a nasty word" but suggests that "mature people should not be taken aback by the sound of a word but can be expected to analyse every term and distinguish between the positive and negative elements in it." He then goes on to extol the aesthetic beauty implied in the action of a disciplined human mass as expressed in parades and mass rallies:

> You can imbue, for at least one minute, the worst assimilationist with Jewish national enthusiasm by a simple device: take a few hundred Jewish youngsters, dress them in uniform, and let them parade before his eyes—in a well-ordered march, where every step of these two hundred lads will sound like thunder, like a machine. There is nothing in the world as impressive as the ability of a mass of human beings to feel and act at certain moments as one entity, imbued with one will, in one rhythm. This is the difference between a multitude, a mob, and a nation.[24]

Jabotinsky's aesthetic preference for the collective over the individual expresses itself also in his musical taste. In another article, also written in 1933, he says:

> It is a pity that we, the Jews, do not value massed choirs. Among the Baltic people, especially the Estonians, the roots of their national movement go back to choir singing. It is an enormously effective means for the development of unity and discipline.[25]

Such deep emotional admiration for mass rallies in which a multitude of human beings act as one organism at the command of their leader is also expressed by Jabotinsky most forcefully in his historical novel *Samson* (1927). On becoming acquainted with the pagan social and political system of the Philistines, Samson expresses deep admiration for the disciplined order of their polity ("a precise, well-planned, intricate hierarchy"). He then recalls an episode of a religious pagan festival at which he was present—and anyone reading this in the 1920s or 1930s could not but recognize the phenomenon. It is perhaps one of the most powerful passages in the novel, and it should be quoted in full, despite its length:

> One day, he was present at a festival at the temple of Gaza. Outside in the square a multitude of young men and girls were gathered

for the festive dances. There were several thousand of them, one to each of the flagstones in the square. All were dressed alike in white garments: the young men in short, belted tunics, the girls in dresses with tucked hems that reached to the ground. The girls' dresses fitted close over the hips, and had the usual long sleeves, but in front they were cut away leaving the breasts exposed. The dancers had been arranged in two groups according to height, the young men on the right and the girls on the left.

A beardless priest led the dances. He stood on the topmost step of the temple, holding an ivory baton in his hand. When the music began the vast concourse stood immobile, the dancers on the flagstones and the spectators who looked on from the wooden stands, the roofs of surrounding houses and the unpaved sides of the square. The roar of surf could be heard from the distant quay of Mayim, the harbor of Gaza. Not a fold moved on the dancers' dresses, and scarce a sign of breathing could be seen on the bared breasts of the girls. The beardless priest turned pale and seemed to submerge his eyes in those of the dancers, which were fixed responsively on his. He grew paler and paler; all the repressed fervour of the crowd seemed to concentrate within his breast till it threatened to choke him. Samson felt the blood stream to his heart; he himself would have chocked if the suspense had lasted a few moments longer. Suddenly, with a rapid, almost inconspicuous movement, the priest raised his baton, and all the white figures in the square sank down on their left knee and threw their right arm toward heaven—a single movement, a single, abrupt, murmurous harmony. The tens of thousands of onlookers gave utterance to a moaning sigh. Samson staggered; there was blood on his lips, so fiercely had he bitten them.

The whole dance consisted of similar movements, dictated by the baton of the priest. Sometimes they were sudden, sometimes slow and sweeping. It did not last long, but Samson left the place profoundly thoughtful. He could not have given words to his thought, but he had a feeling that here, in this spectacle of thousands obeying a single will, he had caught a glimpse of the great secrets of the builders of nations.[26]

Jabotinsky raises this ceremonialism, always accompanying inte-gralist nationalism in Europe, to the level of a supreme principle, saying that "the highest achievement . . . is to be able to act with the absolute precision of a machine." In a eulogy for the first member of Betar hanged by the British, Shlomo Ben Yosef, Jabotinsky in 1938 goes one step further, making ceremony into the supreme human achievement:

Man's pre-eminence above a beast is—ceremony. The difference between a civilized person and a brute is—ceremony. Everything in the world is ceremony. How do we conduct a trial in a court of justice, if not by ceremony? The presiding judge opens the session and calls upon the prosecutor, then upon the counsel for the defense. And how are the witnesses summoned? Prior to giving testimony, the witness is asked for his name, despite the fact that his name is known; it is known that he is an honourable man—but still, an oath is administered to him; it is likewise known that the second witness is a liar—yet an oath is equally administered to him, and if the most minute ceremonial detail has been overlooked, the verdict is null and void and open to challenge.

And liberty, what is it if not an expression of a certain ceremony? Elections—even if they will be held according to all the details and regulations of the most democratic election ordinance—if one superfluous ballot will be discovered in the urn, the elections will be declared null and void even if the candidate would have in any case been elected with a sweeping majority. Without ceremony, there is no liberty.[27]

The other aspect of Jabotinsky's monism relates to his views about class organization. In his youth Jabotinsky had, according to his own testimony, been deeply influenced by some of the central figures in Italian socialism. Despite the fact that he has never been an avowed socialist, this sensitivity to social issues appears in his writings throughout his life. But it is accompanied by an underlying conviction that any class organization, and especially an organization of the working class, is detrimental to the integrity and unity of the nation and endangers its very existence.

This opposition to proletarian class organization and to the socialist movement has been enhanced by the fact that Jabotinsky's chief opponents in the Zionist movement have been the Labor Zionist parties. These parties vied with the Revisionists for the votes of the same uprooted and proletarianized Jewish masses in Eastern Europe, and in Palestine it was the Labor parties that established at that time their hegemony in the Jewish community through their central position in creating the cooperative and collective agricultural and industrial infrastructure of the country. Consequently, Jabotinsky's polemic tone became acerbic and bitter in the 1930s. A collection of essays *Problems of Labour,* published in 1933, included articles with titles like "Yes, Let Us Smash Them!" and "The Red Swastika."

But these polemical excesses were accompanied by similarly charged language from the labor movement. What is significant in this debate is that Jabotinsky's views on these subjects were not merely rhetorical flourishes but were deeply integrated into his general political philosophy.

In an article called "Class," Jabotinsky expounds his view that giving the working class any sort of special status is basically "reactionary," as it injures the primacy of national unity. In this context Jabotinsky does not distinguish between communists and socialists or between Stalinists and social democrats. The nationalist movement should conduct a remorseless struggle against any sort of working-class ideology and organization:

> I do not believe that there exists any difference between communism and other forms of socialism based on class views. . . . The only difference between these two camps is a difference of temperament—the ones rush ahead, the others are slightly slower: such a difference is not worth the value of the inkdrop necessary to describe it in writing.[28]

The operational consequences following from this denial of any distinction between social democrats and bolsheviks determined to a large degree Betar's violent tactics against the Labor hegemony emerging in the 1930s in the Jewish Yishuv in Palestine. It did, however, require an answer to the question of class relations, and it is in this connection that Jabotinsky develops his views on social organization, which call for the establishment of a corporate society, largely modeled on the Italian experience of Mussolini's Italy, Salazar's Portugal, and Dollfuss's Austria.

In response to the socialist concept of class warfare, Jabotinsky developed his ideas of mandatory arbitration. Arbitration to Jabotinsky is not just a device through which class antagonisms are being decided and mitigated. It should be a substitute for all trade union activity, with the National Arbiter supplanting strikes and any separate working-class activity by the integrationist policies of national arbitration. In an article published in Warsaw in 1928, "On a New Zionist Economic Policy—Second Article," Jabotinsky says:

> The problem has to be solved not through an agreement between two well-defined groups active in the economic sphere, but on the basis of an overall national interest, solely determined by the idea of Zionist statehood. There is no doubt—in arbitration all groups have to be represented, but the Arbiter, who determines and decides, cannot represent any group. He stands for the national interest.[29]

From this idea of substituting National Arbitration for trade union activity, Jabotinsky goes on to suggest the reorganization of social and economic life in Palestine along lines derived from the ideas of the Corporate State. He does not suggest that the Representative Assembly of the Jewish community in Palestine (the highest organ of Palestinian Jewry at that time) be abolished but proposes that alongside this parliamentary body another, Upper Chamber, be established, a so-called Trades' Parliament. Every person should elect his representatives to this body according to the corporation or guild to which he belongs, and Jabotinsky clearly spells out how the ideas of National Arbitration and such corporative representation are two aspects of the same vision of a new social order, transcending the class differences of present society and its democratic-parliamentary representation:

> If one wishes to endow the System of Arbitration true and significant prestige, it has to be realized in all aspects of the internal structure of the *Yishuv*, to make it into the basis and cornerstone of the Jewish organization in the Land of Israel.
>
> This leads some of us to think about the idea of a Trades' Parliament. . . . First of all, one has to create in the *Yishuv* the idea of professional corporations, corporations in which will be associated all those who take part in one of the branches of Jewish economic life in industry, commerce, agriculture, banking and finance, trade, transportation, professional occupations, clerking, etc. Those branches in which there is a clear distinction between the three elements—employers, clerks and wage-earning workers—will be granted adequate representation.
>
> After such an overall organisation will materialize, each corporation will elect its representative to a new National Committee—this will be the Trades' Parliament. Its role will be, first of all, to control all economic life—to oversee all problems of agriculture, commerce, industry, credit, loans, represent the *Yishuv* vis-à-vis the [British Mandatory] Government in matters of taxation, commercial treaties or customs tariffs; secondly, this Trades' Parliament will establish the Arbitration System from the top downwards, and this system will regulate all the relations between the various economic groups.[30]

This is a very clear political and economic program. Jabotinsky's alternative to the hegemony of the socialist movement then emerging in Palestine is not a laissez-faire, liberal economic order. His alternative is a hierarchical, state-controlled corporate order, modeled on the etatist ideologies prevalent in the 1930s.

The picture that thus emerges is clear and definite. Jabotinsky's views on nationalism were very largely determined through his Italian experience and mirror the prevalent ideas of post–World War I European thought. Thus his nationalism is imbued with ideas about race, leadership, hierarchy, and a vision of etatist corporatism. From this point of view, Jabotinsky, who lived in Europe in the 1920s and 1930s, was much more responsive to the new ideas of integralist nationalism than the left-wing pioneers who settled in Palestine a decade or so earlier. Jabotinsky was much more European and cosmopolitan that these pioneers who mainly came from the atmosphere of the Pale of Settlement in Eastern Europe. Their early emigration to Palestine also cut them off from the main currents of European thought between the two wars; hence they were much more provincial and much less open to new ideas than Jabotinsky, who witnessed these developments firsthand in Europe.

Jabotinsky's sensitivity to the new ideas of integralist nationalism and the cult of power relate also to his artistic perceptions. The immediate aesthetic experience, so central to the neoromanticism of integralist nationalism, is best expressed by Jabotinsky in what might be seen as an unusual context—an essay on "Introduction to Economic Doctrines" (1938).

In this essay, Jabotinsky attempts to present an alternative to the materialist conception of history. Like many other thinkers of integralist nationalism who have been influenced in their early life by socialist doctrines, Jabotinsky also devoted much of his polemical writings to an attempt to combat socialist ideas. Jabotinsky maintains that materialism is basically wrong in attributing historical development to merely one motive—need. There is, according to Jabotinsky, always another motive, variously called by him the element of *play* or of *enjoyment* or of *luxury*. The difference between them is clear-cut. "The element of need is passive, that of playfulness is aggressive, always attacking, trying to extend its experiences, more precisely: to extend its domination."[31] Moreover, Jabotinsky maintains,

> Every play, be it in our scientific or normal sense, is a *will to power*, a striving for kingship [*malchut*]. Try to analyse the satisfaction of human desires: it always expresses itself in domination. This is the . . . instinct or impulse for kingship.[32]

Dealing with the great men of history, Jabotinsky clearly follows Carlyle's theory about the role of great men and the will to power as the motive force in history. In a parallel way, another of Jabotinsky's ideas, that of *Pan-basilea* (Every Man Is a King) also fits into this scheme; its roots are not egalitarian, as sometimes maintained, but aggressive. Every man is a king, according to Jabotinsky, because all men partake of this impulse or instinct to power and domination.

This centrality of the national experience in Jabotinsky's thought raises the question of his views about Arab nationalism. And again, the issue here is not that of Jabotinsky's tactical considerations but the theoretical foundations of his position and policies.

On the one hand, it could be assumed that a person of Jabotinsky's background, who sees nationalism, national uniqueness, the national will to separate oneself from alien elements, and national pride as the central focus of political and historical development, would also be at least somehow responsive to the stirrings of Arab nationalism. A person who was able to feel empathy even toward Ukrainian nationalism with its anti-Semitic overtones; who was also much involved with arguing for the national rights of Serbs, Croats, and Albanians; and who could become enthusiastic about Estonian massed choirs and their nationalist significance might be expected to integrate the national feelings of the Arabs of Palestine into his general scheme of things.

Yet this is not the case. There is no appreciation of the force, authenticity, let alone legitimacy of Arab nationalism in Jabotinsky's writings. It is true that the confrontation with Arab nationalism has always been a contentious point with many Zionist thinkers, but to a person who viewed nationalism *in general* as such a central force in world history as did Jabotinsky, this omission is even more surprising. Moreover, in what Jabotinsky wrote and said about the Arabs generally there is a certain tone of condescension, if not outright contempt.

It is true that Jabotinsky maintains, with all his pathos, that the Arabs living in the future Jewish state would enjoy equal civil rights as *individuals*. But when it comes to Jabotinsky's general attitude to the Arabs as a cultural and political force, he is far less generous.

The reason for this is found in Jabotinsky's basic view about the superiority of European versus non-European culture. To him, Zionism is an expression of European culture, and this superiority is evinced in his view of the relative merits of Zionism versus the Arab world. His writings consequently abound with instances in which he insists—counter to other nuances in Zionism—that in returning to its ancestral land in Palestine, the Jewish people is *not* returning to the fold of the Orient: on the contrary, to Jabotinsky the Jews are, and should always remain, an Occidental, European nation, and he condemns any sort of idealization of the Orient, which sometimes became very popular in Zionism and modern Hebrew literature.

In 1927 Jabotinsky argues this point very strongly in an article called "The Arabesque Fashion," in which he reiterates his views that the Jews are a European people, deeply embedded in European culture, and that in the Occident, and not in the Levantine Orient, lies the cultural future of the Jews. He even goes so far as to maintain that the Sephardim possess a European, and not a Middle Eastern, culture:

> We, the Jews . . . have no connection with that "Orient," perhaps even less than other European people.
>
> It cannot be argued that we belong to the Orient because we came originally from Asia. All Central Europe is full of races who also came from Asia—and at a much later period than we. All the Ashkenazi Jews, and certainly half of the Sephardi ones, have been resident in Europe for two thousand years. This is a sufficient long time for spiritual integration.
>
> Moreover, not only have we been resident in Europe for many generations, not only have we learnt a lot from Europe, we are also one of the peoples who have created European culture—and we are one of the most important creators of that culture. . . .
>
> The spiritual atmosphere of Europe is ours, we have the same rights in it just like the Germans and the English and the Italians and the French. . . . And in Palestine this creativity will continue. As Nordau has put it so well, we come to the Land of Israel in order to push the moral frontiers of Europe up to the Euphrates. . . .[33]

In the same year, 1927, Jabotinsky wrote another article, "The Pedlars of Culture," in which he insists that medieval Arab culture was not Arab at all, not even Muslim. Most of the glorious names in this firmament, he argues, were not Arabian but Syrian, Jewish, Persian, Afghan, et cetera. The point is not, of course, whether Jabotinsky's distinctions are historically tenable. After all, these distinctions themselves are part of the shifting of cultural identities involved in the emergence of modern Arab nationalism. The point is that the same person who cited every shred of historical evidence to demonstrate that the Ukrainians possessed a specific national identity, reversed himself completely with regard to the Arabs.

This belittling of the historical role of Arab culture is extended by Jabotinsky to include the whole world of Islam. In an article published in 1925, "On Islam," Jabotinsky points to a number of historical instances in which a handful of European soldiers were able to overpower much more numerous Arab and Muslim forces. The Italian victory over the Senoussis in 1911 in Tripoli, the victory of the French Expeditionary Force over Faisal in Damascus in 1920—these and other examples are to Jabotinsky a proof of the essential superiority of the West:

> I am not writing this in order to humiliate the Arabs or make fun of them. I harbour no doubts about their martial qualities. . . . Yet in modern times, war is a scientific and financial enterprise. It is beyond the powers of backward nations.[34]

Jabotinsky did not view this backwardness as a temporary phenomenon. Consequently, the Western powers, and Great Britain in particular, have nothing to fear from Muslim reprisals if they support Zionism. The Muslim world, Jabotinsky claims, is not and will never become a political force:

> There are perhaps 100 million people or more who believe in Islam. But Islam as a unified factor in international relations does not exist. . . . Today just as a hundred years ago, one can clash with every and any Moslem nation without getting entangled in a confrontation with Pan-Islamism.[35]

This view is at the root of Jabotinsky's attitude to Arab nationalism. Its consequences for his political arguments against Arab claims in Palestine are self-evident. In his evidence in 1937 before the Royal Commission on Palestine (the Peel Commission), Jabotinsky calls for the establishment of a Jewish state covering the whole area of the original Palestine Mandate, including Transjordan. He admits that this would turn the Arabs in such a Jewish state into a minority, but he denies that it would involve any infringement of their rights or aspirations:

> We maintain unanimously that the economic position of the Palestinian Arabs, under the Jewish colonization and owing to Jewish colonization, has become the object of envy in all the surrounding Arab countries, so that Arabs from those countries show a clear tendency to immigrate into Palestine. I have also shown to you already that, in our submission, there is no question of ousting the Arabs. On the contrary, the idea is that Palestine on both sides of the Jordan should hold the Arabs, their progeny, *and* many millions of Jews. What I do not deny is that in that process the Arabs of Palestine will necessarily become a minority in the country of Palestine. What I do deny is that *that* is a hardship. It is not a hardship on any race, any nation, possessing so many National States now and so many

more National States in the future. One fraction, one branch of that race, and not a big one, will have to live in someone else's State. Well, that is the case with all the mightiest nations of the world. I could hardly mention one of the big nations, having their States, mighty and powerful, who had not one branch living in someone else's State. That is only normal and there is no "hardship" attached to that.[36]

Turning the Arabs of Palestine into a minority is not to Jabotinsky the lesser of two evils or a hardship. Individual rights they will, of course, possess in the future Jewish state that will encompass both Palestine and Transjordan, but *national* rights will not be granted to them. Ironically, here Jabotinsky echoes what some European liberals were ready to grant the Jews as individuals, but not as a nation: "To the Palestinian Arabs as individuals—everything; to the Palestinian Arabs as a community—nothing."

Jabotinsky's major contribution to the politics of Zionism and the root cause of his disagreement with the official Zionist leadership under Weizmann and later Ben Gurion was this implacable insistence on the immediate establishment of a Jewish state and of a Jewish armed force.

No person expressed this demand in a more unequivocal way than Jabotinsky. Weizmann and the Labor movement saw the demand for a Jewish state as a general final goal which should be publicly expressed or suppressed according to the exigencies of the tactical demands of the political struggle of Zionism. Meanwhile, they insisted, the Zionist movement should not waste its time on declaratory politics but create in Palestine the socioeconomic infrastructure which would make such a demand into a viable possibility at the right moment. For Jabotinsky, on the other hand, the idea of a Jewish state was of such basic importance that he could not accept its being trivialized through complex tactical maneuvers. Nor is there any doubt that Jabotinsky, who lived in Europe, felt much more than the leaders of Labor Zionism in Palestine (or Weizmann in England) the immediacy of the Jewish plight in Europe in the 1930s.

Yet it is here that Jabotinsky became entangled in a web of internal contradictions between his politics and his political philosophy. He demanded a Jewish state in the name of strength and power, but ultimately he found himself begging for it. For Jabotinsky a state was an expression of a nation's might and prowess, but here he was, speaking out of the abysmal vulnerability of the

Jewish people, *asking* for a Jewish state so that Jews could be saved from the Nazis. This was not Jabotinsky's tragedy: it was the tragedy of the whole Jewish people. But precisely because Jabotinsky had always identified nationalism with the ability to express power, his appeal now from a position of such pathetic weakness was even more tragic.

This appears most eloquently—and tragically—in Jabotinsky's already quoted evidence before the Peel Commission. Here his call for a Jewish state is buttressed by two arguments—the impending Jewish tragedy *and* the community of interests between the aims of Zionism and the British Empire.

There could be no greater theoretical and practical contradiction than the attempt to adopt simultaneously these two arguments. When Jabotinsky demanded a Jewish Legion and the establishment of a massive Jewish military force in the Middle East, this political demand mirrored his basic principles that only military might establishes itself in the world. ("We all realize, that of all the conditions necessary for national renaissance, the ability to know how to shoot is unfortunately the most important one," he wrote in 1933.[37]) On the other hand, such Jewish power did not exist, and the only way for Jabotinsky to bring it about was to try to establish it under the protection, patronage, and permission of Great Britain. Here and there Jabotinsky managed to get permission to establish training camps for Betar in Mussolini's Italy or in Pilsudski's Poland—but how far removed were these minuscule attempts from the power and the glory of Garibaldi's legionnaires!

Moreover, the official Zionist policy of gradually changing the demographic and geographic composition of the Jewish population in Palestine could be undertaken without direct support of the British government and sometimes had to be reached through direct confrontation with British regulations about immigration and the purchase of land. Even the establishment of a semimilitary, semiagricultural militia like the Palmach could be brought about through cat-and-mouse maneuvers vis-à-vis the British administration. But Jabotinsky's explicit insistence on a massive and legal Jewish force, which was undoubtedly the most radical demand from the nationalist point of view and expressed most specifically Jabotinsky's identification of nationalism with military power, could be achieved, paradoxically, only with the support and help of the British government.

This concept determined Jabotinsky's whole attitude toward Britain even though he was involved in daily skirmishes with the British during the short period of his residence in Palestine in the early 1920s. The demands of the Revisionists from the British were undoubtedly most radical; but Jabotinsky's basic premise was a massive and comprehensive collaboration and cooperation with the British Empire, in Palestine and the whole Middle East. Zionism, Jabotinsky maintains, was an offshoot of Europe in the Middle East. Therefore a Jewish Legion could be a better defense for British imperial interests in the area than any other force. According to Jabotinsky, there exists an absolute identity between British and Zionist interests in the Middle East, and the British are (unfortunately) mistaken in assuming that their support for Zionism might diminish their power in the Arab world. In an article, "What Do the Revisionist Zionists Want" (1928), Jabotinsky most strongly maintains the strategic importance of Zionism for the West:

> It is untrue that England is doing us a favour without getting anything in return. Through our help England gained quite a lot and is about to gain even more in the future. Among all the countries of colonization of the European powers, there is only one country developing at a quick pace . . . and this is Palestine. There are big powers in Western and Eastern Europe who openly envy the cooperation between England and the Zionists. Public opinion in England, as well as the government in England, understand this only too well, despite the attempts of diplomats to deny it. Moreover, in the Mediterranean, that corridor of England to the Orient, on whose eastern and southern shores anti-European dangers coalesce— there the Jews build the only sustaining basis which belongs morally to Europe and will always belong to it.[38]

Jabotinsky does not envisage a mere pragmatic and temporary coalescence of interests between Britain and Zionism. For him it is a fundamental, spiritual bond, premised on the European nature of Zionism as he sees it. He is aware, however, that wide sectors of public opinion in Britain, let alone the British government, view the matter in another way. But, Jabotinsky maintains, the British are mistaken about where their true interests lie, and a "political offensive" of information will ultimately convince public opinion in Britain who is their true ally: "We fully believe that every just opinion, if it will be only defended wisely, energetically and courageously, will find a responsible ear among the British people."[39]

Such an attempt at a political offensive is undertaken by Jabotinsky in his impressive evidence before the Peel Commission:

> We utterly deny that [establishing a Jewish state on both sides of the Jordan] means bringing Great Britain into conflict with world Islam; we utterly deny that it means a real physical conflict with the neighbouring states. . . . Given a firm resolve, made clearly known to both Jews and Arabs, all this would be performed with the normal smoothness of any other equally big colonization enterprise.[40]

A first step in the transfer of power from Britain to the Jewish population is seen by Jabotinsky in the establishment of a Jewish Legion endowed with responsibility for internal security in Palestine. The justification for entrusting internal security in Palestine to the Jewish population is seen by Jabotinsky as analogous to the practice of British colonial rule in Kenya, where the white population has been officially and legally armed against the dangers threatening them from the blacks:

> We said [to the government]: "Remember that we have children and wives; legalize our self-defense, as you are doing in Kenya." In Kenya until recently every European was obliged to train for the Settlers Defense Force, Why should the Jews in Palestine be forced to prepare for self-defense underhand, as though committing a legal offense. . . . The Jews have never been allowed to prepare for the holy duty of self-defense, as every Englishman would have done.[41]

Viewing the position of the Jewish community in Palestine as analogous to that of the European settlers in Kenya is in line with Jabotinsky's equation of Zionism with European expansion. How much British public opinion did, or could, share such a view is, of course, a different question. What such a view did to the Arab perception of Zionism is no less complex a problem. In any case, Jabotinsky's argument hardly had any chance of being accepted by British official opinion—and herein lies his ultimate tragedy.

For there have been few more authentic outcries than Jabotinsky's *J'accuse* when he confronted the Peel Commission with the unanswered question, "What are you going to advise us? Where is the way out?"[42] The moral force of this question, asked by a persecuted and terrorized Jewish people in the 1930s, cannot be challenged. But according to Jabotinsky's philosophy, it is not morality but power that decides among the nations, and hence his moral claim, buttressed by unspeakable suffering but having no legions to support it, is doomed to failure in accordance with Jabotinsky's own premise. If you require a state or a military force in the name of power, you do not have to ask or beg for it; if you have the power, you take what you feel is yours. But if you are weak and persecuted, as the Jewish people were in the 1930s, how can you demand anything in the name of power if you do not try, first of all, to create even a minuscule infrastructure in Palestine itself? Who will voluntarily share power with the weak?

Jabotinsky's way out of his own dilemma of impotence was the failed attempt to base his demands from the British government not on sympathy but on a community of interests between the Zionist movement and the British Empire, overlooking almost completely the importance of the Arab factor in British calculations. Ben Gurion and the Labor movement had also felt, despite their socialist ideology, that there was a context for cooperation with Britain. But they always held that this was a limited partnership, not an immanent identity of aims, for the British and the Zionist interests were not and could not be basically identical.

Jabotinsky, on the other hand, believed until his very last day that there existed an essential common ground between imperial Britain and the Zionist movement. For this reason he opposed more radical views within his own movement (as, for example, among the Betar leadership in Poland) that called for a rebellion against the British.

When Jabotinsky died in 1940 he was already a tragic figure even within his own Revisionist movement because of this deep dichotomy between his awareness of the terrible weakness of the Jewish people and his insistence on developing Jewish power—when this power could be developed, according to him, only through cooperation and collaboration with the British. When in 1944 the Irgun Zwai Leumi, under Menachem Begin, declared its rebellion against Britain, the declaration was couched in Jabotinskian language and terminology. But there may perhaps be no better proof of the utter failure of Jabotinsky's theoretical and strategic doctrine, which always called for reliance on Britain and collaboration with British imperial interests, than the fact that when his own disciples set out to achieve the independence of Israel, they did it through a rebellion against British rule, not through cooperation with it.

CHAPTER 16

RABBI KOOK: THE DIALECTICS OF REDEMPTION

ZIONISM EMERGED AS THE RESPONSE TO THE ENLIGHTENMENT and Emancipation by nineteenth- and twentieth-century Jews whose world had become increasingly secularized. But the responses of traditional rabbinical thinkers like Alkalai and Kalischer notwithstanding, Zionist ideology and the Zionist movement were generally viewed with suspicion, if not outright hostility, by the Jewish religious establishment; Zionism was modernizing, nonreligious, and secular. For all the deep differences between East European Orthodoxy and the more liberal Reform movement in the West, both shared a fundamental opposition to Zionism, albeit for different reasons. Most Zionist activists thus found themselves, both in Eastern as well as in Western Europe (and in America), having to confront a hostile religious leadership that viewed Zionism as another ill-fated false messianism.

Yet despite this very fundamental religious objection to Zionism, there was, from the very beginning, a parallel development, attempting to combine religious Orthodoxy with a supportive attitude to some of the more practical expressions of the rebuilding of the Land of Israel. Within the Hovevei Zion movement there was a religious group, which was later incorporated into the Zionist movement and connected with rabbinical leaders like Shmuel

Mohiliver and Yitzhak Yaakov Reines. In Palestine, Yehiel Michal Pines tried to fight the religious establishment of the Old Yishuv and lay the foundations for a Zionist alternative within Orthodoxy itself.[1]

It was some time until religious Judaism was able to develop an ideological structure for dealing with the novel phenomenon of a basically secular Jewish national movement. Religious Judaism always knew how to deal with assimilation and conversion to Christianity, but a secular Jewish nationalism—people who said they were Jews and would emigrate to Palestine but proclaimed themselves nonreligious—was radically new and unsettling. It is true that Rabbi Mohiliver did write, in his memorable epistle to the first Zionist Congress, that

> the resettlement of our country—that is, the purchase of land and the building of houses, the planting of orchards and the cultivation of the soil—is one of the fundamental commandments of our Torah; some of our ancient sages even say that it is equivalent to the whole Law, for it is the foundation of the existence of our people.[2]

Yet most religious Jews—and practically all rabbis—thought and acted differently. Pines recognized the depth of this challenge of secular Zionism to the religious tradition by creating a new and modern focus for Jewish identity. He tried to prove that Jewish nationalism itself has religious connotations and cannot be based on a secular conception of nationalism.

But these were isolated voices, and their intellectual impact on the religious Jewish community was extremely limited. Only in the writings of Rabbi Abraham Isaac Kook (1865–1935), who became the first Ashkenazi Chief Rabbi of Palestine under the British Mandate, is there a systematic attempt to integrate the normative centrality of the Land of Israel within the religious tradition into a radical and revolutionary reinterpretation of the political and practical activity of Zionism and the resettling of Palestine. During Rabbi Reines's leadership, the religious Zionists still found it possible to vote for a temporary "night asylum" in Uganda. Rabbi Kook is the one who finally presents a comprehensive Zionist religious-national philosophy, and thus the gap between religious Judaism and modern Jewish nationalism could be closed.

The richness and variety of Rabbi Kook's thought makes it much more difficult to give an adequate account of his ideas in a short context than is the case of other Zionist thinkers.[3] It is relatively

life in the Diaspora would not have developed as it did and the symbiosis between religiosity and Exile would not have emerged. What Rabbi Kook is attempting here is a radical attack on the whole Jewish religious tradition of accommodating oneself to life in Exile, of accepting it and learning to live with it. At the same time, it is clear that such a radical religious attack on Jewish religious quietism could emerge only after Zionism, with its secular and this-worldly approach, opened new avenues for Jewish identity.

The People of Israel, the Torah, and the Land of Israel are One, maintains Rabbi Kook, and this synthesis cannot and should not be undone in the historical practice just as it cannot be undone in theory. As the Reform movement showed during the nineteenth century, cutting Judaism loose from the Land of Israel amounts to cutting it loose from its very roots. Anyone who relinquishes the belief in the Return to Zion ultimately relinquishes his belief in the identity of the Jews as a nation. It is not the celestial Jerusalem of prophetic visions (*Yerushalayim shel ma'ala*) which concerns Rabbi Kook but the actual, real, terrestrial Jerusalem (*Yerushalayim shel matta*). The first lives merely in human imagination, the last is inextricably woven into the reality of human lives. Therefore, Rabbi Kook maintains,

> a valid strengthening of Judaism in the Diaspora can come only from a deepened attachment to Eretz Israel. The hope for the return to the Holy Land is the continuing source of the distinctive nature of Judaism. The hope for the Redemption is the force that sustains Judaism in the Diaspora; the Judaism of Eretz Israel is the very Redemption. . . . [On the other hand, in the Diaspora] the very sins which are the cause of our exile also pollute the pristine wellspring of our being, so that the water is impure at the source. . . .[6]

Ascribing such a profound meaning to the attachment to the real Land of Israel enables Rabbi Kook to move toward a revolutionary view, from the religious point of view, of the secular Zionist efforts to settle and revive the country. The religious Jewish community, in Palestine and abroad, slowly became aware that Zionism was confronting it with a difficult dilemma. Initially, some rabbis would ceremoniously excommunicate the Zionist pioneers by pointing to the radically anticlerical and antireligious character of most of the newcomers, especially those of the Second Aliyah, who had been greatly influenced by the Russian revolutionary tradition. Yet the dilemma persisted. Those pioneers were, after all, engaged in a project which could not be brushed aside by the religious establishment. They were rebuilding the Land of Israel, sacrificing their careers in the Diaspora, sometimes even their lives, for a goal that could not leave religious Jews totally unmoved. These pioneers might be atheistic socialists, men and women living a promiscuous life, not caring about kosher food or the Jewish holidays, but they were adding to the number of Jews in the Land of Israel, establishing new villages and towns in the country, kindling the spark of the Love of Zion among many Jews who otherwise might have turned to assimilation or joined the non-Jewish socialist movement abroad.

The consequences of all this might even lead to the establishment of a self-governing Jewish society in Palestine. How should a religious Jewish person relate to such a novel phenomenon? Can one really condemn Jews who sacrifice so much for the sake of living in Palestine just because they are not observant? And why is it that the old dream of rebuilding Jerusalem is being carried out by atheists? Is there, perhaps, a hidden meaning in all this, or is this just one more of those inscrutable divine puzzles?

Rabbi Kook's response to this challenge follows the dialectical subtleties already used by Kalischer and Alkalai, who had contemplated the idea that the ultimate religious redemption might be preceded by practical developments related to the more profane realities of emigration to the Land of Israel and other preparatory steps, all in the secular realm. Kook develops this idea by suggesting a comprehensive theory within which it could be fitted.

The pioneers coming to Palestine, Rabbi Kook maintains, are indeed highly hostile to the Jewish religious tradition and are motivated, according to their own understanding, by secular ideological considerations which are basically alien to the religious structures of Judaism. The legitimacy given by them to their actions is similarly not related to religious sources but draws its inspiration from non-Jewish European revolutionary ideas as nationalism or socialism. Yet, Rabbi Kook argues, this subjective understanding of their own motives is only one side of the picture. In the divine cosmic order, where every detail has its own place and *telos*, the true meaning of a person's action may be unknown to himself. He may fancy himself as motivated by A, yet the ultimate meaning of his action may be B. The same applies to the Zionist pioneers. They may subjectively *think* they are motivated by secular, political ideas, but truly they are acting within a cosmic scheme of a divine will, in which their seemingly secular and even atheistic motivation is nothing else than an external cover for the true meaning of their action as related to God's redemptive structure. These people may contribute toward the ultimate messianic coming even while they deny it; hence they have to be seen as tools and vessels in the hands of Divine Providence. Unbeknownst to themselves, they serve the labor of the Divine. It is the objective meaning of their project that is important, not their subjective motivation or their external deeds. In language tauntingly reminiscent of Hegel's theory of the Cunning of Reason, according to which not subjective motivation but objective, historical products count philosophically, Rabbi Kook says,

> Many of the adherents of the present national revival [*ruah ha-uma*; literally, the national spirit, *Volksgeist*] maintain that they are secularists. If a Jewish secular nationalism were really imaginable, then we would, indeed, be in danger of falling so low as to be beyond redemption.
> *But what Jewish secular nationalists want they do not themselves know:* the spirit of Israel is so closely linked to the spirit of God that a Jewish nationalist, no matter how secularist his intention may be, is, despite himself, imbued with the divine spirit even against his own will. An individual can sever the tie that binds him to the source of life, but the House of Israel as a whole cannot. All of its most cherished possessions—its land, language, history, and customs— are vessels of the spirit of the Lord (italics added).[7]

In this way, the resettlement of the Land of Israel, even by blasphemous atheists, is a step on the road to salvation. The revival of the Hebrew language—an anathema to the Orthodox traditionalist, who saw in the process a profanation of the Holy Tongue, which should be used only for matters divine—is likewise a landmark toward redemption.

These dialectics lead Rabbi Kook to maintain that religious Judaism should view Zionism not through its external form but through its immanent content. Religious Judaism should grasp the underlying meaning of Zionism and discern, beyond its external, secular forms, the divine spark evident in the heart of an atheistic Zionist pioneer who sacrifices himself for the Land of Israel even as he vilifies the religious tradition. Rabbi Kook goes further to suggest that the inherent meaning of Zionism will ultimately surface to the level of explicit consciousness; the godless Zionists are destined, in the fullness of time, to acknowledge the truly religious meaning of their endeavor:

> How should men of faith [that is, religious Judaism] respond to an age of ideological ferment which affirms all these values in the name of nationalism and denies their source, the rootedness of the national spirit in God? To oppose Jewish nationalism, even in speech, and to denigrate its values is not permissible, for the spirit of God and the spirit of Israel [that is, Jewish nationalism] are identical. What they must do is to work all the harder at the task of *uncovering the light and holiness implicit in our national spirit, the divine elements which are its core. The secularists will thus be constrained to realize that they are immersed and rooted in the life of God and bathed in the radiant sanctity that comes from above* [italics added].[8]

The secular Zionist pioneers are, therefore, not godless blasphemists but servants in the House of the Lord, unaware, as yet, of their true mission. Religious Judaism has thus a double educational task: not to oppose secular Zionism but to divine, beyond the veil of externality, its true kernel. Similarly, one has to educate religious Jews to recognize the Hidden Light immanent in Zionism. The pioneers should not be anathemized but drawn nearer to traditional Judaism. Ultimately, those who are seeking a partial, purely secular salvation will come to realize that they are only a part of the integral wisdom of the Creator:

> Our quarrel with them must be directed only to the specific task of demonstrating their error and proving to them that all their efforts to fragmentize the higher unity of Israel is doomed to failure. . . . Once this truth is established, our opponents will ultimately have to realize that they were wasting their efforts. The values they attempted to banish [that is, religiosity] were nonetheless present, if only in an attenuated and distorted form, in their theories, and the result of their labours could only be spiritual hunger, narrowed horizons, and the loss of any true sense of direction. One path will be open to our adversaries: to acknowledge the truth proved by experience and to cleave to the *entire* living and holy content of the fully manifest Light of Israel. Their souls will then no longer be tortured by nebulous and ghostlike ideas from which they could neither free themselves nor find in them clear illumination of the spirit.[9]

Just as secular Zionism is, unbeknownst to itself, an integral part of Jewish religiosity, and just as Eretz Israel is of central cosmic significance in this Jewish existence, so Rabbi Kook views the Redemption of Israel as part of a universal process. In the world as it now exists, not only is the existence of the Jewish people distorted and corrupted because the Jews live in Exile, but the whole world is disordered because the People of Israel is not in its allotted place in the teleological structure of the universe. Just as influential trends in the Kabbalah and Hasidism saw Exile as a cosmic alienation, as the distortion of the principles of creation, and consequently viewed Redemption as a cosmic restoration (*tikun*), so Rabbi Kook views the salvation of the Jewish people not merely of particular importance but as a universal restoration (*tikun olam*). God did indeed choose Israel as his people, but the whole world is his Creation, and every human being, Jew and non-Jew alike, was created in his image. Let not the tribulations of the Jews make them so much involved with themselves as to forget this universal message. Hence the rebirth of Israel, and the Ingathering of the Exile, will not mean a particularist, ethnocentric redemption only. The whole universe will be redeemed, and this is the truly divine, universal, meaning of Jewish redemption:

> All the civilizations of the world will be renewed by the renaissance of our spirit. All quarrels will be resolved, and our revival will cause all life to be luminous with the joy of fresh birth. All religions will don new and precious raiment, casting away whatever is soiled, abominable, and unclean; they will unite in imbibing of the dew of the Holy Lights, that were made ready for all mankind at the beginning of time in the well of Israel. The active power of Abraham's blessing to all the peoples of the world will become manifest, and it will serve as the basis of our renewed creativity in Eretz Israel.[10]

This universal vision is accompanied by another aspect, which has occasionally been overlooked by some of Rabbi Kook's disciples. Rabbi Kook does not see in the establishment of a Jewish state an end unto itself, and sometimes he is even skeptical whether it is desirable at all. The rebuilding of the Land of Israel is absolutely desirable, but the reality of power is much more problematic. Central to Rabbi Kook's religious thought is the real Land of Israel, and from this there follows his support for even secular and atheistic pioneers who are engaged in the rebuilding of the country. But he is aware that the moment Judaism reenters the practical, historical arena, it might become entangled in the game of power politics and be tainted by it. A nation that is powerless and landless need not get involved in these issues and can thus remain relatively free from the corruption of power. Rabbi Kook is aware that if a Jewish state were to be established in a yet unredeemed world, such a state, in order to survive in a world of *homo homini lupus*, would itself have to behave like a wolf among wolves. Such a state could not become a state of righteousness and of justice and hence could not be a vessel of divine redemption. Therefore, a true and final redemption for the people of Israel would become possible only if the whole world would be redeemed and the Jewish state would not have to be involved in the power struggles of an unredeemed world.

Such a view also involves a second look at the initial exile of the Jewish people from its ancestral land. While all previous religious thinkers—as well as modern secular Zionists—saw Exile as a catastrophe imposed on the Jews by external forces, Rabbi Kook sees in the destruction of the Jewish polity some hidden reason connected with the meaning of Judaism as a religion of peace and righteousness:

> External forces compelled us to leave the political arena of the world, *but our withdrawal was also motivated by an internal will, as if to say that we were awaiting the advent of a happier time, when government could be conducted without ruthlessness and barbarism.* That is the day for which we hope. Of course, in order to bring it about, we must awaken all our potentialities and use all the means that the age may make available to us: everything evolves by the will of the Creator of all world. But the delay is a necessary one, *for our soul was disgusted by the dreadful sins that go with political rule in evil times* [italics added].[11]

The loss of political independence and sovereignty in the past is, therefore, of deep religious significance. It was not, as traditional rabbinical literature would have it, just a retribution for the sins committed by the Jews; it also prevented Judaism from being contaminated by the dialectical necessity of applying brute force even for the loftiest ideas in an imperfect world. Christianity and Islam became entangled in this contradiction and were not, ultimately, very selective in the means employed to force their faith on an unwilling world and maintain it. The paradox for Rabbi Kook involves the fact that it was precisely during the biblical period of the First Commonwealth, when Judaism as a religion had not yet attained its full blossom, that Jewish sovereignty was prominent, while at the time of the Mishnah and the Talmud, when Judaism emerged into full development, Jewish independence went into abeyance because of the dialectics of "external forces . . . also motivated by internal will." Therefore Judaism—stateless, power-less, and weak—never needed an Inquisition, nor did it inscribe its faith on the sword, because the loss of sovereignty freed Judaism, dialectically, from the enslavement to power. It was precisely the most enslaved and subjugated people in history who could maintain its distance from the corruption of power. The politics of the world as it is—an unredeemed world—is based on power and corruption. Therefore, Rabbi Kook forcefully maintains,

> It is not fitting for Jacob [that is, the people of Israel] to engage in political life at a time when statehood requires bloody ruthlessness and demands a talent for evil.[12]

Rabbi Kook's redemptive vision requires, therefore, also a global transformation of the world of politics. Hence accompanied by his advocacy of the rebuilding of a Jewish Palestine, there always remains a skepticism about the desirability of the Jews gaining political power so long as the world is not redeemed. Redemption will not be achieved through holy wars, Rabbi Kook maintains, but through the complete salvation of all mankind. Writing in the 1930s and fully aware of the menacing clouds of war and destruction, Rabbi Kook realizes that the crisis of the twentieth century is posing a threat not only to the Jewish people but to the world at large. Therefore the solution to this crisis cannot be just a particularist redemption of the Jews; it will have to involve a universal redemption. "World civilization is crumbling, the human spirit is weakened, and darkness is enveloping all the nations."[13] Therefore, the time is ripe for universal redemption, and the redemption of Israel is thus entwined in world history and in the radical necessity for such a universal solution. The dream envisaged by Rabbi Kook was not one of national-religious domination but a vision of universal salvation, in which the Land of Israel, the people of Israel, and the brothers and sisters of Israel—all the nations of the world—will be redeemed. With Israel back in its land and its allotted place, Providence itself will return to where it should be, and all the universe will be its abode.

CHAPTER 17

BEN GURION: THE VISION
AND THE POWER

AVID BEN GURION (1886–1973) WAS A MAN OF CONTRADIC-
tions: a socialist, who in the 1920s wished to adopt Soviet
models for the organization of Jewish labor in Palestine,
yet, after the establishment of Israel, found himself identified with
its army and hailed as a military leader; a social and economic
thinker, who as the first Secretary of the Histadruth Labor Federation laid the foundations for its economic power, yet as Prime Minister always enjoyed saying that he did not understand economics;
a contentious man, always quarreling with his friends as much as
with his opponents, who came to symbolize the unity of the people of Israel; and an avowed agnostic, who nonetheless frequently
quoted the Bible and forged the political coalition between Labor
and religious Zionism, which became the basis for the Israeli political system until 1977. He was a self-taught student of philosophy,
immersed in Plato and Buddha, whose sartorial tastes in a crucial
period of his life as Minister of Defense focused on uniformlike
khaki; he was a political leader always surrounded by hosts of
admirers, who left no successor worthy of his name. He realized
the Zionist dream of Jewish sovereignty but quarreled after 1948
with the Zionist leadership and called for the dissolution of the
Zionist movement after the State of Israel had been established.

208 | THE MAKING OF MODERN ZIONISM

Ben Gurion was the most charismatic leader of Israel's largest Labor party, who was, however, thrown out of his own party a few years before his death by controversial quasi-legal proceedings.

Ben Gurion was a much-glorified military leader whose strident rhetoric sometimes verged on the arrogant; he was, however, filled with existential fears about the destiny of the State of Israel. Yet behind the tough facade of aggressiveness in his public rhetoric, which coined such controversial phrases as "What matters is not what the Gentiles say, but what the Jews do," or "UNO-Shmuno," can easily be discerned a complex personality, extremely sensitive to the weaknesses of the Jewish people even in its own state, much aware of its surrounding dangers against whom it will never be able to fight without the support of outside powers. It was this complexity that was responsible for his unique blend of aggressive rhetoric and extremely cautious politics.

Only a detailed biography can do justice to such a person and to his historical contribution.[1] Yet all the vicissitudes of Ben Gurion's political career contain elements of continuity in the basic tenets directing his policies. Although he was never a systematic thinker, distinct traits stand out in his writings and actions. To a very large extent, the State of Israel, with its achievements and failures, is a mirror as well as a monument to Ben Gurion's own achievements and failures, and no history of Israel can be written without focusing on the dominant role played by him, for better or for worse, in its development.

For anyone looking for the theoretical foundations of Ben Gurion's Zionist thought, they can be encapsulated in two principles: first, Zionism is a revolt against Jewish tradition; second, to carry out this revolution, it will not suffice to announce it, but one has to seek the social subject able to carry it out. This historical subject Ben Gurion finds in the Labor movement and its practical activity in creating the social infrastructure for a Jewish society in Palestine. To this, Ben Gurion always added the necessity of finding an adequate political power within whose context Zionism could become a reality. This calls for a cool identification of the power structures active in the international arena. Such forces are dependent on the changing diplomatic and strategic fortunes of the Great Powers, and the Zionist movement (as well as the State of Israel) would always need to have an adequate reading of that scene. Otherwise, Zionism and Israel might find themselves isolated and pitted against stronger, richer, and more ruthless antagonists.

The idea that Zionism is a revolt against the continuity of Jewish history has been voiced by many who preceded Ben Gurion. But he expresses this recognition in a most pronounced way. In a series of articles included in the volume *From Class to Nation* (1933), this is reiterated time and again:

> The very realization of Zionism is nothing else than carrying out this deep historical transformation occurring in the life of the Hebrew people. This transformation does not limit itself to its geographical aspect, to the movement of Jewish masses from the countries of the Diaspora to the renascent homeland—but in a socioeconomic transformation as well: it means taking masses of uprooted, impoverished, sterile Jewish masses, living parasitically off the body of an alien economic body and dependent on others—and introducing them to productive and creative life, implanting them on the land, integrating them into primary production in agriculture, in industry and handicraft—and making them economically independent and self-sufficient.[2]

Or in another instance:

> Zionism in its essence is a revolutionary movement. One could hardly find a revolution that goes deeper than what Zionism wants to do to the life of the Hebrew people. This is not merely a revolution of the political and economic structure—but a revolution of the very foundations of the personal lives of the members of the people. The very essence of Zionist thinking about the life of the Jewish people and on Hebrew history is basically revolutionary—it is a revolt against a tradition of many centuries, helplessly longing for redemption. Instead of these sterile and bloodless longings, we substitute a will for realization, an attempt at reconstruction and creativity on the soil of the homeland. Instead of a people dependent on others, instead of a minority living at the mercy of a majority, we call for a self-sufficient people, master of its own fate. Instead of a corrupt existence of middlemen, hung-up in mid-air, we call for an independent existence of a working people, at home on the soil and in a creative economy.[3]

The essence of this revolution is, then, not merely geographical immigration to the Land of Israel—but it requires an overall restructuring of the Jewish socioeconomic fabric. A Zionist movement that would be satisfied with the creation in Palestine of a Jewish society that replicates the traditional Jewish occupations in Plonsk, Brisk, or Warsaw will be doomed to failure. Jewish political independence in Palestine will never be established unless preceded by Jewish economic independence there—that is, by the creation of a self-sufficient Jewish community in Palestine, not dependent on the labor of others and controlling its own economic structure. The reverse is also true. A Jewish society created in Palestine, not economically independent but dependent on donations from abroad and internally dependent on non-Jewish labor, will be doomed to lose its political independence as well. Ben Gurion's materialist conception of history, derived as it was from the somewhat simplistic Marxist materialism of Poalei Zion, always returned to this cruel underlying truth: there is no political power without economic power. In the Zionist context this meant that without a Jewish economy, there can be no Jewish state.

From this followed the struggle for ensuring that the Jewish economic enterprises in Palestine would be based on Jewish, not Arab, labor. This was an insistence not always understood, and rarely welcomed, by the European socialist sister-parties of the Zionist labor movement. But before the eyes of the pioneers of the Second Aliyah, there was always the fate of the first settlers of the First Aliyah. The first settlements attempted to create a class of Jewish peasants, but they slowly introduced Arab labor and before too long Jewish latifundia, exploiting Arab labor, emerged. Without the insistence on Jewish labor, Ben Gurion argued, such attempts might result in the creation of a class of Jewish *effendis* and *colons* in the Middle East. But a Jewish nation would not emerge from such an experiment.

Ben Gurion was deeply aware that the transition to physical labor in Palestine could be even more difficult than the very act of immigration itself. It is from this that he develops his views about the centrality of the working class in the Zionist renaissance and the necessity to spread the newcomers all over the country and not limit Jewish immigration to a few urban centers.

According to Ben Gurion, this transition to all aspects of primary production would call for a move from urban to agricultural occupations. In the Diaspora, the Jews became an urban people, severed from agricultural life and immediate production, and the Zionist revolution has to reorder this aspect of Jewish life as well. Decentralizing the Jewish population of Israel and spreading it all over the country, particularly to the Negev, became one of Ben Gurion's obsessions as prime minister. Yet the roots for this view can be found in a much earlier realization of the nexus between economic base, social structure, and strategic power. In 1935, in an article called "Our Action and Our Direction," Ben

Gurion argues against those in the Zionist movement, mainly the Revisionists, who belittle the importance of establishing new agricultural settlements. Evoking a slightly surprising historical example, Ben Gurion argues for the importance of creating a social and economic infrastructure for the Jewish community in Palestine:

> World history recalls one frightening example which should be a lesson to us. Anyone who has learned Roman history remembers the drastic chapter called the Punic Wars. In our language we should say the Canaanite Wars. Once there was a great Canaanite military leader, from a stock close to the ancient Hebrews. He had a Hebrew name and a Hebrew title: Hannibal, the Judge from Qeret Hadath [Carthage]. He was one of the greatest military leaders of all times, perhaps the greatest of them all, and he fought against the young Roman state. He showed marvelous feats. He headed an army of mercenaries, made up of various tribes and races, and he led them from North Africa to Italy, through the Alps, and created havoc in the Roman camp. Against him was pitted a large Roman army, larger than his own, and he defeated them time and again.
>
> Yet ultimately all his heroism and all his military and political genius did not sustain him—and he was not only a strategic genius, but also a statesman of genius. Eventually he was defeated, despite the fact that his adversaries were rather mediocre generals with no talent. Roman mediocrity defeated Canaanite genius. For Carthage was a *city-state*, whereas Rome was a *village-state*, and in the desperate conflict between a city-people and a village-people, the village-people proved victorious, and all the commercial wealth of Carthage and the ingenuity of its military leaders were to no avail. Hannibal's heroism was broken by the obstinate warfare of the Roman peasants. These peasants were not taken aback by the successive defeats inflicted on them—because they were integrated into their soil and tied to their land. And they overcame Carthage and wiped it off the face of the earth without leaving a trace.[4]

For all the centrality Ben Gurion accords to the working class, his analysis is far from that of an orthodox Marxist. For him, no class war is at the center of his thought, especially as he realizes that the anomaly of the Jewish people was its lack of a viable working class. For Ben Gurion, Zionist socialism does not mean the hegemony of the working class but the creation of a Jewish working class through emigration and settlement of the Land of Israel. Since the creation of such a working class is to Ben Gurion the social expression of the Zionist revolution—a revolution that will recreate for the Jewish people its productive economic base and enable it to rely on its own labor—he views the "class function" and the "national function" of the Jewish proletariat in Palestine as merely two different aspects of the same historical phenomenon.

This also leads Ben Gurion to maintain that in the long run the outcome of the Zionist endeavor will depend on the productive infrastructure in Palestine, not on the Zionist associations in the Diaspora. The changing and revolutionary reality in Palestine is the focus of Zionism, not Zionist organizational activity abroad. Even before World War I, Ben Gurion wrote in the journal *Ha'ahdut*, published in Jerusalem by Poalei Zion, that the destiny of Zionism will ultimately be decided neither by the World Zionist Organization nor by the worldwide political and diplomatic efforts of Zionism. The outcome will be decided "here, in the Land of the Turk" ["*Kan, be-Tugarma*"]—in the Ottoman Empire, in Palestine.

On the face of it, this is utopian and pretentious: that the future of Zionism will be determined in the Land of Israel, whose Jewish population numbered at that time less than one hundred thousand people and whose new pioneering population amounted to a few thousand, that such a minuscule Yishuv will determine the fate of the nation—and not what the Jewish people in the Diaspora will do, with all its wealthy, well-educated, and diplomatically and politically influential Jews—this was really hubris and *chutzpah*. On the other hand, such an unorthodox approach truly understood the nature and source of real Zionist strength.

For the focus of this strength was the social praxis changing the nature of Palestine and with it the nature of the Jewish people, and this praxis was happening "here, in the Land of the Turk." This was Ben Gurion's great practical achievement—first as secretary of the Histadruth and later in the Zionist Executive. He was the first to grasp the meaning of the shift from Zionist *activity* in the Diaspora to Zionist *reality* in the Land of Israel. The Holocaust finally stamped the realization of this shift on general public opinion, but many decades earlier, it was Ben Gurion who first gave this shift its practical and normative centrality.

The consequence of this all is fairly simple. Political power has to reside where real social praxis is being carried out. Just as the center moves from Diaspora Zionism to Zionist reality in Palestine, so hegemony in the Zionist movement should pass from the middle-class, quasi-philanthropic Zionist leadership in the West to the leadership of the Zionist Labor movement in Palestine. Ben Gurion's election to head the Jewish Agency and the Zionist Executive in Jerusalem in the 1930s signifies this double shift: from the Diaspora to Palestine, from bourgeois Zionism to the Labor movement.

For Ben Gurion, bourgeois Zionism, which continues in Palestine the same modes of Jewish existence as those that prevailed in the Diaspora, cannot become the basis for the Zionist revolution. The Labor movement is made up of people who, on emigrating to Palestine, have *changed* the structure of their existence, consciously becoming workers and farmers and thus rejecting their middle-class origins in Europe. Each Zionist pioneer who left his bourgeois background in Europe in order to engage in primary production in Palestine has carried out a far-reaching personal transformation. Such a transformation, when viewed collectively, becomes the infrastructure for the social transformation of the whole Jewish people. A middle-class merchant or intellectual who on emigrating to Palestine continues to do what he had been doing abroad just extends the traditional modes of Jewish existence from the Diaspora. By replicating Diaspora structures, the Zionist revolution will not be carried out. The Jewish nascent working class in Palestine, consciously created by middle-class immigrants convinced of the necessity of making themselves into proletarians, is to Ben Gurion the truly "national class" in the sense used by Marx when he wrote that the universal, national class *is* the class whose interests "must genuinely be the aims and interests of society itself, of which it becomes in reality the social head and heart."[5]

For this reason Ben Gurion does not see Zionism and socialism as two separate elements merely welded together historically in the phenomenon of Labor Zionism. They are two sides of the same coin, permanently joined to each other in the crucible of the Zionist revolutionary experience. In his speech at the opening of the convention of the Mapai (the Labor Party) in 1950, Ben Gurion reiterated the same formula used by him decades earlier:

> Socialist Zionism is not an artificial aggregation or a mechanical combination of two separate visions and wills, Zionism on one hand and socialism on the other. . . . Neither Zionism nor socialism come to us from the outside; they originate in the will and the urges of the person who lives by his own labour. . . . The terms Zionism and socialism are but two different expressions and manifestations of the same praxis: the creative praxis of the working Jewish person and his vision, aiming at moulding national and general human life according to his own image; for only an image of a creative society of workers, free and enjoying equal rights, can guarantee

independence, liberty and equality to all members of the Jewish
people and all the nations of the world.[6]

In *From Class to Nation* Ben Gurion insists that only socialist Zionism is pure Zionism, all other forms, to him, having been adulter-
ated by other elements:

> Socialist Zionism does not mean Zionism alloyed with anything
> else which does not organically belong to Zionism; on the contrary,
> socialist Zionism is distinct from other forms of Zionism precisely
> by being not mixed with foreign alloys. . . . Socialist Zionism means
> a full Zionism, distilling into itself all the historical contents of
> the redemption of the Jewish people without any condition or
> afterthought, without any compromise or concession. This is a sort
> of Zionism which will not be content with redeeming only a part of
> the people, but aims at the complete redemption of all the people
> of Israel: this is a sort of Zionism which envisages the Land of Israel
> as a homeland not only for a few privileged and wealthy but wants it
> to be a homeland for every Jew who returns there—a homeland that
> equally provides for all her children, revives them, makes them into
> citizens and redeems all of them without discrimination.[7]

In another essay included in *From Class to Nation* Ben Gurion
spells out the constructive, society-building role of the Labor
movement in the Jewish community in Palestine:

> The Hebrew worker came here not as a refugee, clutching at any
> reed offered to him. He came as a representative of the whole
> people, and as an avant-guarde pioneer in the grand enterprise of
> the Hebrew revolution did he capture his position in the labour
> market, in the economy, and in settlement activities. In all his
> deeds and activities, be they small or large, in his work in village
> and town, in the creation of his own agricultural and industrial
> economic structures, in conquering language and culture, in
> defense, in fighting for his interests at work, in satisfying his class
> interests and his national interests, in the creation of his institutions
> and the building of his *Histadruth*—in all this the Jewish worker was
> conscious of the historical task destined to be carried out by the
> working class, preparing the revolution which would make labour
> and work into the dominant elements in the life of the country and
> the people. The Hebrew worker combined in his life work national
> redemption and class war, and in his class organization created the
> content of the historical aims and needs of the Jewish people.[8]

Ben Gurion tried to encapsulate these ideas in the slogan
"From Class to Nation." The extreme left wing of socialist Zionism,
grouped in the Poalei Zion-Left movement, saw socialist Zionism

as a vehicle for the realization of the proletarian revolution in the Jewish context. Ben Gurion, on the other hand, realized that in the Jewish context the first task is the very *creation* of a Jewish working class, and according to him such a Jewish working class could be created only through the Zionist effort itself in the process of settling Palestine. Left-wing socialist Zionism advocated class warfare within the nascent Jewish population in Palestine; Ben Gurion and his movement realized how sterile and mechanistic such an adaptation of the concepts of class warfare would be to the conditions of the minuscule Jewish population in Palestine. How can a working class that does not yet exist emancipate itself from the fetters of a capitalist bourgeoisie which itself hardly exists? For this reason Ben Gurion did not advocate class warfare in the 1920s and 1930s but called for "constructive socialism"—a socialism that would create in the Land of Israel a nation through building its economic infrastructure along public and cooperative lines. In such an economy, publicly directed and controlled, the Jewish working class and its political representatives would naturally become the hegemonic factor. Not through class warfare but through creating its own economy, would the emergent Jewish working class become the dominant influence in the new homeland of the Jewish people.

In 1931, a year after the establishment of the Mapai Labor Party, Ben Gurion writes in the party weekly, *Hapoel Hatzair*:

> Our movement has always maintained the socialist idea that the party of the working class, unlike the parties of other classes, is not merely a class party, caring only for class interests, but is also a national party, responsible for the future of the entire nation and viewing itself not just as a particular party, but as the nucleus of the future nation. In this [Zionist] Congress, this idea became political reality. The Labor movement, which fifteen years ago hardly existed as a visible entity, has today become a corner-stone of Zionism, qualitatively and quantitatively: we have become the largest faction, directing and deciding the fortunes [of the whole Zionist movement]. What has happened a few months ago at the Representative Assembly [of the Jewish community in Palestine] has now been repeated at the [Zionist] Congress. In the Land of Israel we are turning from a party to a mainstay of the community.[9]

Once the Labor movement became hegemonic in the Zionist movement because of its central position in the infrastructure of the Yishuv, Ben Gurion turns to broadening the base of its power through a coalition with other elements within the Zionist movement which are not necessarily identified with the liberal, bourgeois General Zionists. In the same article Ben Gurion calls for Labor to become a focus for "the toiling circles of the Eastern communities, especially the Yemenites, the craftsmen, clerks and free professions, small farmers and shopkeepers who do not exploit the labor of others." This is a true profile of the wide social base of Mapai in Palestine and Israel at the height of its power.

Ben Gurion's position has a paradoxical element in it. On the one hand, his insistence on "constructive" socialism rather than on a Marxist model of class warfare distinguished him from the more doctrinaire attitudes of the left wing of socialist Zionism; on the other hand, his strategy has some very distinct Leninist elements in it. Lenin's main innovation in his polemic against the Social Democratic Mensheviks was his insistence that in the conditions of Russia, the power of a revolutionary socialist elite will precede the full-fledged development of a capitalist system in Russia and the mature development of a working class there. Under Russian conditions that meant a violent revolution based ultimately on repression and terror. In a way, Ben Gurion's position was similar. He maintained that the strategy of the Zionist Labor movement could not be gradual and could not wait until a capitalist economy developed in Palestine to try to overturn it through class warfare.

Precisely because Jewish Palestine, just like Russia, did not yet possess a fully developed capitalist system and hence had no widespread working class in the country, the Labor movement could become hegemonic through a dialectical leap. In Russia it may mean an elitist dictatorship, in Palestine its course would be different—identifying the Labor movement with the general national aims and thus turning it into a hegemonic power in the emergent economy and society. Making the Histadruth central to the creation of a cooperative economy in the country would turn it into a much stronger force than the feeble private sector, always split among numerous individual proprietors. Since the Jewish community in Palestine before 1948 lacked coercive state power and was necessarily based on the voluntary association inherent in the Zionist movement, Ben Gurion's elitist notions did not lead to anything as oppressive as a Leninist dictatorship. In the context of the Yishuv and the Zionist movement, this created the basis for Labor to achieve a parliamentary majority in the Zionist congresses and helped the Labor movement channel Jewish contributions from abroad, coming mainly from middle-class Jews, into cooperative and collective socialist enterprises in Palestine and later in Israel. Socialist Zionists never had to expropriate by force the property of the bourgeoisie, for there hardly existed a significant Jewish bourgeoisie in Palestine at that time. But Labor's control of the Zionist movement helped to transfer money from Jewish bourgeois sources in the Diaspora to socialist enterprises in the Land of Israel which were central to the national aims of the Zionist movement. Thus a unique coalition was forged between the leaders of socialist Zionism in the Land of Israel, headed by Ben Gurion, and significant sectors of the Jewish community abroad, notably in the United States. As a result the real strength of the Labor movement in Israel has always been much greater than its mere numerical showing in parliamentary elections. It became the real Establishment of Israeli society and still retains much of its power even after losing in the 1977 parliamentary elections.

This may also explain the interest Ben Gurion himself showed in the Soviet experience. As secretary of the Histadruth, Ben Gurion traveled to the Soviet Union in the 1920s, ostensibly to visit an agricultural exhibition, and his visit raised many eyebrows in the Zionist movement. Ben Gurion's visit was not motivated by any admiration for the Soviet system, which he detested and combated politically throughout his life; nor was he so naive, as the Webbs have been, to be taken in by the more obvious Soviet successes while overlooking the abhorrent nature of the system as a whole. Yet for Ben Gurion, Soviet Russia was a challenge. As in Zionism, a social revolution was consciously undertaken, which drastically changed the whole social structure of the nation. True, in the Soviet context it was based on coercive state power, while in the Zionist case it was based on voluntary affiliation and immigration. Nonetheless, some of the problems were the same. How does an avant-garde elite succeed in changing long- and well-entrenched social, economic, and cultural structures? How does such a change take place? What are the material and spiritual forces sustaining it? The new Soviet culture fascinated Ben Gurion not because of its contents nor because he wanted to emulate its values. It was its morphology and its mechanisms that he wanted to study. Here the whole fabric of national life was being changed, perhaps for the first time in history. And this is what Zionism had set as its revolutionary task.

When Ben Gurion said, "Socialism is not only an end, but also the means through which Zionism will be realized," he announced the unity of means and ends that characterized the realistic approach undertaken by him as a political strategist. Ben Gurion realized that the methods through which states are established are also the methods through which they will be governed. If the Land of Israel is built by private enterprise employing Arab labor, a Jewish colonial society will be established in the Middle East. If, on the other hand, the Zionist homeland is established through collective and nationally controlled funds and with Jewish labor, then the nature of the state that will thus emerge would also be collectively and socially oriented. The social class that will be seminal in establishing a Jewish society in Palestine will also be, eventually, its hegemonic force. Ben Gurion was thus able to combine his insistence on the ideological structures of socialist Zionism with a harshly realistic political infighting within the Zionist movement. Hence his alliance with the petite bourgeoisie of artisans and small shopkeepers was to forestall a right-wing majority; his coalition with religious Zionism (and the price he was ready to pay for this) was to forestall the creation of a joint Revisionist-national religious coalition of the sort that came to power in 1977. His ruthless partisan fight was against the extreme left in socialist Zionism (called first the Poalei Zion-Left, and in the 1950s the unified Mapam), against its doctrinaire views about the centrality of class war, which he found utterly irrelevant in a society still creating its classes, especially its working class, from the truncated social structure of Jewish life in the Diaspora.

For with all his polemic against doctrinaire Marxism, Ben Gurion always realized the prime importance of economic infrastructures; without them, there is no political power. This was the basis of his violent opposition to Revisionist Zionism as expressed by Jabotinsky. He maintained that stressing maximalist political and military aims without a firm foundation in the country and without real allies leads to empty rhetoric and to strategic and political weakness. Spectacular feats may be achieved in this way, but a sustained national effort cannot be achieved through such a combination. On the internal scene this was proved in 1948 on two levels. It was the Haganah, with its social infrastructure in hundreds of Jewish settlements all over the country and sustained by the collective enterprises of the Histadruth, which was able to repel the Arab military onslaught. The Irgun and the Stern groups, for all their fervor and idealism, were not able to do it. Conversely, the relative ease with which Ben Gurion and the Haganah overcame the internal military threat of the Irgun and the Stern groups also bore out his analysis about the social roots of political power.

Ben Gurion's insistence on the self-supporting nature of a Jewish community in the Land of Israel somehow became dissipated over the years under the impact of the terrible realities of nazism and the Holocaust. Before the rise of the Nazis, Ben Gurion and the Labor movement preferred selective immigration to Palestine, focused on pioneers who would be educated to a new life based on labor awaiting them in the new land. After 1933 and certainly after 1945, there was no way to maintain such a *halutzic*, avant-garde, and elitist concept. When hundreds of thousands of survivors tried to reach the country after 1945, there was no way to select or educate them prior to their immigration. Similarly, when the establishment of Israel in 1948 and its wars with the Arab countries made the existence of Jewish communities in the Arab world precarious, if not altogether impossible, there was no way to stem the tide of a massive Ingathering of the Exiles. The consequence was a drastic change in the social structure of Israeli society. Newcomers had to be educated to the realities of the Zionist revolution *after* immigration, and it was only natural that such a massive educational effort was far from successful, given the constraints under which Israel then had to operate.

A similar shift occurred in the structure of the financial aid flowing from world Jewry and other external forces to Israel. Before World War II, Ben Gurion's movement was adamant that all Jewish contributions to the Zionist effort should be channeled to constructing the social and productive infrastructure of the new society, not for direct consumption. Mass immigration after 1948 made it necessary to find enormous funds for the daily and immediate upkeep of masses of new immigrants, and slowly the distinction between investment and immediate consumption became blurred. The enormous defense burdens of Israel, proportionally larger than those of any other nation at present, meant creating another link of dependence on external forces, very much against the initial socialist Zionist idea of self-reliance. It is no wonder that after 1948 Ben Gurion could not easily sustain many of his original positions, and a certain sense of gloom and desperation crept into his vision. The Zionist dream did become reality, but Ben Gurion, for all his glorifying the reemergence of Israel and its military strength, was more aware than many others how different was the realization of that dream from the original vision.

Ben Gurion's views about the international context in which Zionism must act were similarly characterized by a sober, and sometimes cruel, realism. The tough rhetoric used during his prime ministership notwithstanding, Ben Gurion understood very well that in any international equation—be it regional or global—the Jewish people will always be the weaker part. This harsh truth never left him even after the establishment of the Jewish state and its spectacular military feats. In the David-Goliath equation, Ben Gurion always knew Israel was the perpetual David, and never (perhaps with the exception of a few days after the Sinai campaign of 1956) did this sobriety leave him. He realized that for all its military accomplishments, Israel's defensive capability was not autonomous but financially and politically dependent on outside sources, that Israel would always need allies and should never maneuver itself into a war situation without such support. Yet he also knew that such outside support would always be contingent and conditional, and that in the long run, for Israel there would be no constant allies.

During the British Mandate, Ben Gurion rejected the doctrinaire views of the Zionist extreme left which condemned any cooperation between the Zionist movement and imperial Britain. As a socialist Ben Gurion realized the ideological difficulties inherent in such cooperation; yet he remained convinced that no other outside element could give Zionism similar support. On the other hand, he equally rejected the uncritical enthusiasm for Britain and the British Empire expressed by the Revisionists, who envisaged a basic alliance between Zionism and the British Empire. Ben Gurion maintained that this was wishful thinking; British interests in the Middle East were much too complex to allow Britain's uncritical support of the Zionist movement. For Ben Gurion, cooperation with Britain was always pragmatic, not ideological. At the outbreak of World War II he was able to express his complex attitude most succinctly, when he said, "Let us fight against Hitler as if we had no differences with the British, and let us continue our political struggle against Britain as if there were no war against Hitler." Less sophisticated and less subtle minds were not able to follow such a strategy.

In an article written in 1936, "Our Balance Sheet with the English," he expressed this critical assessment of the link with Britain:

England allowed 350,000 Jews into the country. She built a harbour at Haifa, and Haifa became a city with a Jewish majority. She built roads connecting the Jewish settlements, and she supported, albeit not sufficiently, Jewish industry. The English are not a nation of angels, and I know only too well the terrible things done by them in Ireland and other places; but the English have also done many positive things in the countries under their rule. They are a great nation, with a rich culture, and not a people of exploiters and robbers. And to us, the English were far from being just bad. They recognised our historical right to this country—they were the first to do so—proclaimed our language an official language, permitted a large-scale immigration—and if we are to judge, let us judge justly and fairly.[10]

It was in a similar vein that Ben Gurion addressed the no-less-complex problem of Israel's relation to the United States after 1948. Here again, his sobriety and realism stand out. He rejects, on the one hand, Mapam's ideological pro-Soviet anti-Americanism, yet does not fall into the opposite pitfall of believing that Israel could ever achieve a full identity of interests with the United States. Contrary to those who, during Ben Gurion's own lifetime and later on, tried to explain how the interests of Israel and the United States were fully identical and therefore the United States should know it had no better ally in the Middle East than Israel, Ben Gurion always realized that such simplistic views would not help Israel in forging what could be a pragmatic, yet limited, community of interests with America. He pointed out that occasionally Israel would have to use American public opinion judiciously to move the U.S. administration to a more friendly attitude toward Israel. In an article called "Our Foreign Policy" Ben Gurion formulated views in 1951 that remain relevant to this very day:

> American assistance to Israel is the outcome of the sympathy of the American people toward us, and only if we shall know how to maintain relations of friendship and trust between ourselves and the American people will we be able to rely, more or less, on the support of the American government.
>
> But I have to warn against illusions: despite the fact that we achieved great results in this sphere in the last years, both politically and materially, let us not fool ourselves in thinking that America ever identified or will ever identify in the future with the State of Israel. No state ever identifies with another, because there is no identity of interests between a world power, powerful and affluent as is the United States, and a small and poor nation in the faraway corner of the Middle East. And just as America does not identify itself with

us, we do not identify with America. America has never committed itself, nor will it ever do so, to stand behind us in all of what we shall do or want. The United States has its own considerations, and they are sometimes different from ours, and sometimes they are even fully contradictory to ours. And we have our considerations. They do not have to be contrary to those of America but neither do they have to be identical with them.

Yet despite the fact that there is no identity, and there can be no identity, there exists an ever-growing partnership—a partnership linked to human freedom and to a democratic system of government, based on liberty, government freely elected by the people, freedom of thought, freedom of speech, freedom of debate.[11]

"Exile has planted into us distrust of all governments. We were a people perpetually in opposition to all government, because we were not in control of our own fate." In those words, voiced in 1953, Ben Gurion expressed one of the most central thoughts of his later period: his deep doubts about the internal difficulties facing the Jewish people in its attempt to lead the life of a nation-state, to obey the law and bear the burden of running a state. In the public debate of the late 1950s and 1960s, these doubts came to the fore in Ben Gurion's insistence on *Mamlachtiyut*—the primacy of the state.

There is no doubt that this concept has obvious etatist connotations, and for this reason Ben Gurion's usage of it was very critically attacked by many within his own party. For the Labor movement, always basing itself on voluntarism and being publicly identified with voluntary associations as the Histadruth and the kibbutz, such a term was far from welcome. The fact that Ben Gurion also tended to focus on *Mamlachtiyut* in extolling the virtues of the army certainly gave credence to these fears, especially as many of Ben Gurion's followers, lacking his historical insights and nuances, translated *Mamlachtiyut* into a somewhat uncritical cult of the military and defense establishment. Such views were occasionally also sanctioned by Ben Gurion in the heat of the political polemics at the end of his period as prime minister.

It appears, however, that something much deeper was involved for Ben Gurion himself. At the root of his views on educating the Jewish people to the idea of the primacy of the state was his pessimistic reading of Jewish history. Like Aharon David Gordon, Ben Gurion thought that the Jewish tradition of living on the borderline, of knowing how to get along under any regime and under any system, may in the end be the undoing of the Jewish commonwealth. Because Jews were living in exile, they lacked the immediate discipline of obeying laws, and the Zionist revolution to Ben Gurion meant not only immigration to Israel and transition to a life based on labor but also learning how to live within the law, not at its margin. These were very harsh words, yet Ben Gurion had no idealized view of the Jewish people. After all, it is a people in dire need of redemption precisely because Exile has corrupted its life and its values. In a long speech made in 1954, Ben Gurion put this in a most revealing fashion, and it may be worthwhile to quote this at some length because it deals with issues that became a subject for general concern in Israel only many years later. Yet Ben Gurion appears to have grasped them much earlier:

The people in Israel has not yet been sufficiently imbued with political, statelike [*mamlachti*] consciousness and responsibility, as befits a self-governing nation. In most countries of Exile, Jews have suffered from the hands of a hostile government, and they had to devise stratagems to outsmart the laws of the land and its discriminatory regulations. Such habits, developed over the generations, do not disappear in a few years, and a new immigrant, descending from the plane or boat, does not become overnight a patriot and a law-abiding citizen. A well-ordered state is not an outcome of well-ordered morals, but an outcome of well-ordered and educated citizenship. It is of course true that bad government makes it difficult to educate good citizens, yet government is not everything. And a people used to Exile [*am galuti*], oppressed, lacking independence for thousands of years, does not change overnight, by fiat or by a declaration of independence, into a sovereign, state-bearing people [*am mamlachti*], lovingly and willingly carrying the duties and burdens of independence. Because independence does not only grant rights, but it also imposes heavy responsibilities.

Most of our public knows how to demand from the state more than a hundred percent of what it owes the state. It demands from the state good and excellent services, but does not like paying taxes, without which no services are possible. At best everyone would easily agree that his neighbour pay taxes, but not he himself. And the many factions, which will never be asked to assume the responsibility of government, try to catch the support of voters by demanding opulent services and low taxes. And in this respect there is no difference between right-wing and left-wing factions.

In our country, even personal manners are deficient. Many of our inhabitants, including Israeli youth, have not learned how to respect their fellow-citizens and treat them with politeness, tolerance and sympathy. Elementary decency is lacking among us, that decency which makes public life pleasant and creates a climate of comradeship and mutual affection.

Once upon a time Zionist orators used to pray for the day when they will see Jewish criminals going to Jewish prisons. Such an ideal has been abundantly realized. We have in Israel black marketeers, smugglers, burglars, thieves, murderers, rapists and all kinds of other criminals. In that respect, we became like "all the nations"— and not necessarily like the more refined among them. And in what has been said here, not all the internal malfunctions of Israel and its people have been enumerated.

But we shall overcome![12]

From the defiant concluding exclamatory sentence, it can be seen that Ben Gurion believed that things could and would be changed. Just as he believed that a nation living by its own labor, and not exploiting the labor of another people, can be created in the Land of Israel, so he believed that Israeli society could be educated to become law-abiding and evolve a quality of life overcoming the terrible legacies of Exile.

Yet Ben Gurion never believed that this could be achieved by politics alone or merely through the instrumentalities of the state. For him, the Zionist revolution was not only a transition from dependence to independence, nor was the very existence of the state ever seen by him as an end to itself. Ben Gurion prided himself on being a student of Aristotle, which philosophically may have been slightly presumptuous. It was Aristotle who always maintained that while the state aims at preserving life, its ultimate goal, its *telos*, is the good life, the morally good life. This could also be said of Ben Gurion's view of the state. For all the somewhat uncritical glorification of the state that could be discerned in his writings and speeches in the 1950s and 1960s, the state to him never degenerated into a *Selbstzweck* (end unto itself); it always remained an instrument, basically a moral and educational instrument, through which a nation, not possessing a body politic for millennia, could rediscover the meaning of the *res publica*, of the commonwealth.

For Ben Gurion, a historically highly abnormal people like the Jewish people could maintain a state only if it would not be another run-of-the-mill "normal" state: a Jewish state will be able to exist, according to him, only if it will be a model state, a Good Society, based on the social and spiritual values of one's own labor (*avoda atzmit*), economic self-sufficiency, internal order, and abiding by the law. Precisely because Exile has so much distorted the fabric of Jewish life, the people of Israel cannot just try to have a state like all the nations; it does not possess a social structure like all the nations. There is nothing of the hubris of a Chosen People in such a view. On the contrary, it is a tragic appreciation of the baseness and corruption imposed on the Jewish people by its historical development. This calls for an extra effort, according to Ben Gurion, for a supreme social and intellectual endeavor, which may enable the Jewish people to emancipate itself from the terrible distortions imposed on it by Exile. Not only has the Jewish people to be taken out of Exile, Exile has also to be taken out of the Jewish people—to paraphrase in this context a Hasidic precept. For this reason, the Zionist revolution always remained for Ben Gurion not a merely political revolution. It had to be accompanied by a social and spiritual revolution as well.

EPILOGUE

ZIONISM AS A PERMANENT REVOLUTION

B Y ANY CONVENTIONAL STANDARDS, ZIONISM HAS BEEN A SUC-
cess story. But if one would like to identify more precisely
the specific successes of Zionism, one might be hard
pressed to find them within the traditional targets of Zionism. The
majority of the Jewish people, after all, did not return to Zion; and
the reasons for this cannot be attributed in most cases to external
forces but have to do with a reluctance on the part of most Jews to
immigrate to Israel. The State of Israel has been established, yet its
international status is still far from being as universally accepted
and regulated as that of France or, for that matter, Egypt. The army
of the Jewish sovereign nation is indeed defending the lives of its
citizens and inhabitants and has even managed to attain victories
that will be remembered by generations to come, not only in the
annals of Jewish history but also, in some cases, in the classics of
modern warfare. But for all the show of arms of the Israeli Defense
Forces, the lives of Israelis are still far from secure and tranquil;
and for all its glory, the Israeli army is most heavily dependent for
its armaments on external aid. In short, the dream of normalizing
the status of the Jewish people through the attainment of political
sovereignty is as elusive today as it was on the day Israel was established. Even the peace treaty with Egypt—an almost undreamed-of

achievement a few years ago—has, most paradoxically, complicated the position and status of Israel among the nations.

Yet one has constantly to recall that the central Zionist thinkers never believed that the very establishment of a Jewish state would conjure out of existence all the problems traditionally faced by Jews. Some of the more popular expressions accompanying Zionist political propaganda did indeed project such images, yet most Zionist thinkers knew better. Looking at the ideas of such divergent thinkers as Herzl and Ahad Ha'am, Gordon and Ben Gurion, Moses Hess and Rabbi Kook provides ample evidence that none of them held the naive and simpleminded belief that once a Jewish majority emerged in Palestine or a Jewish state was established there, all the ingredients that have made up the anomaly of Jewish existence would disappear overnight. What differentiated the Zionist thinkers from non-Zionist Jewish thinkers was only their insistence that *without* a territorial base in Palestine and without the establishment of a Jewish commonwealth there the beginning of those processes which could eventually transform the historical anomalies of Jewish life would never have a chance. Zionism essentially always believed—perhaps with the exception of Jabotinsky and his disciples—that the establishment of the state would be only a necessary condition for Jewish renaissance, never a sufficient one.

What then has been Zionism's essential achievement, if any?

It created a new *normative* and *public* focus for Jewish existence. In the pre-Emancipation period, religion and the *kehilla* served as this normative focus. Being Jewish in pre-Emancipation times was not only a matter of religious observance but also entailed being a member of a community, belonging to a public entity. Being Jewish meant not only personal commitment to a set of beliefs or norms but also belonging to a Jewish public. One could not maintain one's Jewishness in isolation from other Jewish people.

It was Graetz who succinctly brought out this political dimension of historical Judaism, which never became ossified in one form but underwent numerous transformations until it became finally institutionalized after the destruction of the Temple. What before the destruction of the Temple was implied by the political institutions of the Jewish polity in the Land of Israel, and the political ramifications of the linkages with the Temple itself, later became transformed into the normative meaning attached to the *kehilla* structure and to the individual's place with it. If the

Catholic Church maintained that there was no *salvation* outside the Church, the precept of Judaism could be formulated to read that outside the *kehilla* there were no *Jews*. As Graetz maintained time and again, for Judaism the question never focused on the salvation of the individual soul but on the collective meaning of individual existence.

The Enlightenment and Emancipation utterly changed the status and function of the *kehilla*, as poignantly expressed by Nordau in his address to the first Zionist Congress. Instead of a miniature *polis*, within whose confines public and political life flourished and which was the only source of significance to individual life, the *kehilla* and the synagogue now became a partial factor, one institution among many others in an open society, catering to limited and carefully circumscribed religious needs. From a total structure the *kehilla* turned into a particular function, and from a focus of identity, which determined the place and standing of a Jewish person in the social and even cosmic universe, it became an institution providing merely ritual services. This was the profound meaning of modernization for the structure of Jewish life.

Jewish identity thus lost its normative and public standing—its *peroussia*, or *parhessia* as it become known in Aramaic and Hebrew. The individual Jew, who became to a large degree emancipated from traditional religious structures in relation to personal beliefs and precepts, found himself without this public aspect of his existence as a Jew and for the first time had to face an external, albeit liberal, world as an individual.

The State of Israel put the public, normative dimension back into Jewish life. Without this having ever been defined or decided upon, it is a fact that to be Jewish today means, in one way or another, feeling some link with Israel. The contents of this relationship may be different from one individual Jewish person to another and varies greatly from one Jewish community to another. For some, it may mean seeing Israel as the true manifestation of the messianic yearnings of the Jewish people; for others it is the Israeli kibbutz and the vision of social justice so central to many aspects of Zionism that is a specific Jewish expression of a social, universal vision of redemption. There may be persons whose link to Israel is daily and continuous, as in the case of those involved in fund raising and political lobbying on behalf of Israel; and there may be others whose link to Israel manifests itself only in moments of grief and anxiety—or exultation and vicarious pride in the achievements of the Jewish state. These differences may be profound and quite meaningful, but they do not matter. For it is the State of Israel that unites more Jewish people all over the world than any other factor in Jewish life.

This is not an ideological claim or the expression of a pious wish that this is how it should be but a statement of fact. It is a fact that religion does not unite the Jews today as it did in the pre-Emancipation past. It is a fact that the majority of the Jewish people, both in the Diaspora and in Israel, defines itself in terms that are basically secular—ethnic, national, cultural—and the lifestyle of most Jews in the world today is utterly secularized. Jewish religion itself is split into at least three major trends (Orthodox, Conservative, and Reform), and the relationship between these trends sometimes divides Jews more than it unites them (the attitude of some Orthodox rabbis to the Reform movement is an example of how religion can divide rather than unite). Today there does not exist one idea or one institution around which all Jewish people can or do unite—with the exception of Israel. In the not too distant past, liberal Jewish reformers saw Judaism as identical with liberalism, and Jewish socialist revolutionaries saw International Socialism as the harbinger of Jewish redemption. Such simplemindedness is much less prevalent today and certainly is no longer the conventional wisdom of wide circles.

Today when Israel is faced with danger or beset with problems, its concern becomes the focus of Jewish activity, anxiety, nervousness, and even paranoia, in terms of both Jewish institutional activity and the personal concerns of individual Jews. One has only to recall the reaction of Jews in the Diaspora both to the anxieties and exhilarations of the Six-Day War and to the shock of the Yom Kippur War to realize how profound these feelings are. It is Israel and its destiny which can, more than any other thing Jewish, bring together religious and secular Jews—Orthodox, Conservative, and Reform, Hasidic and agnostic, right-winger and left-winger, Jews in the United States and in the Soviet Union. Materially this may mean that in many cases the normative focus of Jewish fund raising in North America is centered around Israel, even if a sizeable amount of the money thus raised is left in the local community. Through the concern for Israel's security and well-being, middle-class American Jewish communities may find it possible to finance the building of sometimes lavish community centers for themselves: another expression—albeit vulgar and usually resented when publicly mentioned by Israelis and American Jews alike—to the normative centrality of Israel in Jewish existence.

However, the concern for Israel is not the *only* concern activating Jewish communities around the world. The plight of Soviet Jewry, for example, has also motivated in the last years enormous amounts of energy among Diaspora Jews. But there seems to be a fundamental difference. The concern for Soviet Jewry is, at its base, an interest in the personal and individual fate, welfare, and safety of more than two million Soviet Jews; the concern for Israel does not exhaust itself upon the individual fate of three million Jews living in Israel. The concern for Israel has wider implications: for the communal, collective, and public fate of the State of Israel. It is not only what would happen to the inhabitants of Israel but what would happen to Israel as a body politic. Soviet Jewry can be moved somewhere else, and hence emigration from Russia is considered a way to salvation; a parallel activity involving Israeli Jews would be tantamount to another holocaust, because the very existence of Israel as a state is of normative significance and meaning to Diaspora Jewry.

This, then, is what distinguishes Israel from other Jewish communities. Other Jewish communities are merely aggregates of individuals, and as such they have no normative standing as a public entity. Israel, on the other hand, is conceived not only as an aggregate of its population, but its very existence has immanent value and normative standing.

Israel is thus the new *public* dimension of Jewish existence, the new Jewish *parhessia.* As such it replaces the old religious-communal bonds that circumscribed Jewish existence in the past. Today, due to modernization and secularization, Israel is the normative expression of this collective existence of the Jewish people, of *KM Yisrael.*[1] This may also explain why so many Jews continue to support Israel. It is their symbol of collective identity—even if they disagree with the policies of its government. Support for Israel is not necessarily support for a policy or even an ideology; rather it is an expression of Jewish self-identity.

This emergence of Israel, the historical outcome of the Zionist movement, as the public dimension of the Jewish people is indeed a far-reaching revolution in Jewish life. The Zionist movement started as a minority phenomenon among Jews, and until the 1940s it could not, by any stretch of the imagination, be viewed as the mainstream of Jewish life. Orthodox and Reform rabbis, bourgeois

assimilationists, and socialist revolutionaries, Bundists and Jewish communists alike—all of them viewed Zionism as a marginal
phenomenon, an aberration soon to disappear; and indeed, in its
beginnings Zionism was nothing more, both in terms of its normative standing among the Jews as well as in terms of sheer numbers.

Today the situation is totally different. The question is not
whether or not Jews around the world who support Israel are
Zionists: this, to a large extent, is a semantic quibble. Clearly they
are not Zionists in the traditional sense of the word—they do not
emigrate to Israel nor do they intend to do so. But they view Israel,
and their identification with it, as being more central to their own
identity and self-definition as Jews than any other factor involving
their lives. Israel not only is the focus of identity for those Jews who
live there but also defines, more than any other factor, the Jewish
identity of those Jews who do not live there but view it as central
to their own self-definition as Jews. To turn Israel for American
Jews into what Ireland or Italy has been for Irish-Americans or
Italian-Americans is a tremendous revolution. In fact it goes
beyond that: American Jews have become, on the whole, much
more involved in support of Israel than Irish-Americans or
Italian-Americans are in support of their countries of origin. In the
1930s most Jewish public and philanthropic institutions around
the world had very little identification with the Zionist effort in
Palestine; today there exist only a few very marginal groups who
identify as Jewish but divorce Israel from their concerns (Naturei
Karta and their American ultra-Orthodox counterparts would be
among these highly marginal groups).

The emergence of Israel as such a normative center for Jews
all over the world, nonetheless, is not an immutable given, whose
position is ensured by its very existence. Far from it. The historical
conditions that gave rise to Israel made it into what it has become
for world Jewry: the failure of Emancipation, the breakdown of the
dream of universal socialism as a solution to the Jewish problem,
the Holocaust, the mass immigration to Israel (The Ingathering
of the Exiles in the evocative language of Zionism), the stubborn
Israeli resistance to its surrounding enemies and its successful feats
of arms. All these dramatic and traumatic events have by their own
weight transformed the Israeli experience into something directly
shared by Jewish people all over the world. When it appeared
that the Jews might be exterminated from the face of the earth,
when both liberalism and socialism appeared powerless to solve

the problems of Jewish existence and identity, the emergence of a Jewish state, under such conditions, became an almost wonderous image of Jewish survival, of *netzah Yisrael.*

Yet once this novelty wears off—and some of it is already wearing off—such an almost automatic identification of world Jewry with Israel may be gradually eroded. When Jewish life was being threatened by extermination, when the Jewish state was in danger of being destroyed, the preservation of the very *existence* of Israel naturally became the highest priority. In the long run, however, it will be the *content* of Jewish life in Israel that will determine whether Israel will continue to be viewed by world Jewry as its normative center or become just one more aspect, among many others, of Jewish life, commanding no special standing and no special allegiance. If the content and quality of life of Israel will not make Jews all over the world proud to continue this identification, then this unusual bond will be severed. And, dialectically, it can continue to exist only if Diaspora Jewry is able to discover in Israel such qualities as it lacks in itself.

This is certainly one of the more perplexing dilemmas governing the relationship between world Jewry and Israel: Israel can continue to be the normative focus of identity for Jews abroad only if it is different from Jewish life in the Diaspora. If Israel becomes only a mirror image of Diaspora life, if it becomes, for example, just another Western consumer society, then it will lose its unique identification for world Jewry. If an American or French Jew discovers in Israel only those qualities which he already possesses (and cherishes) in his own society, then he will not be able to raise Israel to that normative pedestal with which he would identify. An Israel that is a Mediterranean Brooklyn or Los Angeles or Golders Green cannot serve as a focus of identification and self-definition for Jewish people from Brooklyn or Los Angeles or Golders Green.

This is, of course, not only ironic but also, to a large extend, quite hypocritical. Nevertheless, this is a characteristic of all identification that has normative dimensions. People do not endow normative standing to a mere mirror image of their own situation: anyone looking for normative identification does so to transcend his own existence and raise his sights to a horizon—different and more sublime—than his own mundane and quotidian life. So it is in religion, so it is in ideology.

For this reason much of what Ahad Ha'am, Gordon, Rabbi Kook, and Ben Gurion thought regarding the nature and quality of Jewish life in Israel is so relevant today and will remain so. This is also the unfinished dimension of the Zionist revolution, and some aspects of it might have even witnessed a regression in the last years.

If one of the criteria for the enduring centrality of the Zionist revolution for Jewish identification is the degree by which Israel is *different* from the Diaspora, then a far-reaching erosion of some of the revolutionary components of Zionism has taken place. Twenty years ago, the difference between the Jewish community in Israel and Diaspora Jewry—socially, intellectually, economically—was far greater than it is today. Not that Diaspora Jewry became similar to Israeli society, but Israel came to resemble the Diaspora.

Jewish life in the Diaspora has been characterized by an over-representation of Jews in the middle classes—be it the traditional commercial middle class or the modern educated, professional and intellectual middle class. The essence of the Zionist revolution has been to take those Jews immigrating to Israel from their traditional middle-class positions and turn them toward primary production, agricultural or industrial, and thus create in the new homeland an overall social structure, spanning the whole spectrum of socioeconomic occupations.

When Israel was established in 1948, it was much nearer to that ideal than today, as practically all the work done in the economy was carried out by Jews. Today, mainly due to the influx of Arab labor from the West Bank and Gaza, sizeable sectors of the Israeli economy have seen the disappearance of Jewish workers from manual jobs and their substitution by Arab laborers. In whole areas of agriculture, the building industry, and certain menial service occupations, most of the manual work is done by Arabs. This is occurring at a time when the relatively advanced standard of living of Israeli society is being maintained through sizeable overseas grants, and the Jewish population of Israel is becoming more and more concentrated in white-collar occupations. Such a society is much more reminiscent of the Diaspora than of Israeli society only twenty years ago. The degree of dependence of Israeli society today both on non-Jewish labor inside Israel and on overseas aid is greater than at any other time in its history, and not all of the external dependence can be attributed to the crushing burden of defense expenditure. The founders of the revolutionary Zionist society in Israel realized from the very beginning that independence, sovereignty, and self-determination involve not only a flag, ambassadors, and the pomp and circumstance of state occasions. Independence means first of all the existence—or creation—of a social and economic infrastructure to sustain a more or less self-supporting society. The question for the founders of Zionism never was only how many Jews would live in the Jewish state and what its boundaries were going to be. It also was what would be the quality of life lived by these people and what kind of society would they be establishing. In this respect Israeli society has recently developed some serious flaws.

The social and professional stratification of Israeli society today is much more reminiscent of the American Jewish community than of Israeli society in 1948. It is a society with a heavy concentration in white-collar service occupations and in commerce. There has been an unprecedented explosion of Israeli higher education—as against the somewhat naive yet significant traditional pioneering Zionist suspicion of the intellectual *Luftmensch*—and a flight from productive production to clerical occupations. The emergence of the stock exchange, that traditional fulcrum of so much of Jewish economic activity in nineteenth-century Europe, is a central facet of Israeli society and its preoccupations. All this suggests an erosion of Israeli society's social revolutionary uniqueness. Socially speaking, Israel is much nearer to Diaspora societies. As Gordon has said, Exile can emerge in the land of Israel as well as in the lands of the Diaspora itself.

A similar process can happen to Israel's military capability. There is no doubt that after two thousand years of lack of sovereignty, the very idea of the emergence of a Jewish military force engulfed Jews all over the world with feelings of pride and enthusiasm—the military feat of the Six-Day War proved this dramatically. To this very day, many Diaspora Jews get an enormous emotional lift through the very existence of the Israel Defense Forces—precisely because it is something they do *not* possess in their own countries. But even this novelty will eventually wear off. An army is something which every country possesses, and once it is accepted that Jews can fight just like everyone else, the question will be: how is a Jewish army different from other armies—and better? Then it becomes apparent that an Israeli army involved in nation building, in helping the desert blossom, in educational pioneering work will continue to arouse enthusiasm and identification among Diaspora Jews. But an army that will, over time, be more and more perceived in the public mind as involved in patrolling occupied Arab cities, imposing curfews on areas under military administration, chasing Palestinian school children out of the streets back into their classrooms—in short, an army that looks and acts like any other army, will cease to be a focus of identification for Diaspora Jews, even if many, or most of them, continue to justify the policies making such acts necessary. Even if Jews around the world remain conscious of the difference between such an army and, say, the French army, it would not serve any longer as an object of pride.

It is for this reason that the Zionist revolution has not ended nor been consummated by the very emergence of a Jewish state or the achievement of one or other military victory. Even the achievement of a final peace agreement with all Arab countries would not be tantamount to its completion. For the Zionist revolution is very basically a permanent revolution against those powerful forces in Jewish history, existing at least partially within the Jewish people, which have turned the Jews from a self-reliant people into a community living at the margin of and sometimes living off alien communities. Zionism is a revolution against the drift of Jewish life, which pushes so many Jewish people, precisely because of the determination and stamina acquired to overcome their tribulations—to look for relatively neat and easy occupations rather than to confront the challenge of building a national society, whose meaning is an overall responsibility and not just caring for oneself and one's own. Even the phenomenon of those Israelis who now leave Israel for other countries—the *yordim*—is, in its way, part of a long Jewish tradition of leaving the ancestral land of Israel for better climes and easier occupations. After all, the Jewish Diaspora was created not only by the forceful expulsion of Jews from their country by Nebuchadnezzar, Titus, and Hadrian; the flourishing Jewish communities in Alexandria and Babylon owed at least part of their origin to processes similar to those that led to the concentration of so many Israelis in certain areas of New York or Los Angeles. Now as then, life in Israel may be hard, the burden of maintaining a commonwealth is not easy; living in Exile frees one from many of these onerous burdens.

Zionism is a revolution against these trends in the Jewish people, which enabled the Jews to accommodate as individuals even to the harshest realities of Exile in situations of almost total powerlessness, yet perpetuated Exile as a way of life for the Jewish people as a whole. Zionism is an attempt to bring back into Jewish life the supremacy of the public, communitarian, and social aspects at the expense of personal ease, bourgeois comfort, and good life of the individual.

For this reason building a Jewish commonwealth in Israel always entailed—and will always entail—strong elements of hardship. For this reason Zionism had to be—and still is—also a far-reaching *social* revolution. Zionism is, after all, also a revolution against Jewish history, not only against the gentile world. Laissez-faire economics—so well attuned, as Milton Friedman pointed out, to Jewish existence in the West—cannot be squared with the ethos of social responsibility necessary for nation building in Israel, and the attempt to erect such an economy in Israel will always have catastrophic results for the social cohesion of its society. Laissez-faire in an Israeli context means bringing Exile back to Israel.

Therefore Zionism has ultimately no chance unless it constantly revolutionizes Jewish life in Israel and stops it from coagulating into the traditional historical molds of Jewish social and economic behavior. Israel can, therefore, remain for the long range the normative center for world Jewry only if it will remain a society different from Jewish Society in the Diaspora: the struggle for maintaining this difference will have to continue as the central facet of the permanent Zionist revolution.

This is the challenge facing Israel today.

EPILOGUE TO THE 2017 EDITION
AN INTERRUPTED REVOLUTION?

I N THE EPILOGUE TO THE FIRST EDITION OF THIS BOOK, I MADE the argument that since its inception Israel has become the normative focus of most Diaspora Jews. Jews living in free, democratic countries do not, with few exceptions, move to the Jewish state, but most of them view Israel as meaningful, in one way or another, to their identity as Jews. That Jews now have a country which they call their home and are also capable of defending it, if necessary, by the force of arms, signifies a tremendous revolutionary change from traditional Jewish identity which was basically rooted in religious affiliation.

Yet I also pointed out that this normative focus on Israel may be eroded if Jewish sovereignty and power came to be used only to defend the right of the Jewish people to national self-determination. If, I argued, the Israeli army "will, over time, be more and more perceived in the public mind as involved in patrolling occupied Arab cities, imposing curfews on areas under military administration, chasing Palestinian school children out of the streets . . . in short, an army that looks and acts like any other army, it will cease to be a focus of identification for Diaspora Jews, even if many, or most of them, continue to justify the policies making such acts necessary."

The cruel paradox is that since these words were written, the 1993 Oslo Accords between Israel, headed by Prime Minister Yitzhak Rabin of the Labor Party, and the Palestinian Liberation Organization, headed by Yasser Arafat, gave hope for the emergence of an historic reconciliation between the two national movements. As a first step, the Accords promised to serve as a bridge toward a two-state solution. Yet more than twenty years later, negotiations between the two sides have failed to bring about the desired final status agreement. Tensions and mutual fears have deepened and a peaceful resolution of the conflict now seems even further away than before. It is easy to lay the blame on specific politicians, but more fundamental developments have been at work, and they have to be viewed in their wider historical perspective. Without this perspective, the current debate in Israel about relations with the Palestinians cannot be adequately understood.

In this broader context, the seminal role of the 1967 Six-Day War is central. Besides its enormous military, strategic, and political consequences, the war had a transformative impact on many aspects of Israel's life and political discourse—though it took some time for this to be realized and internalized. First and foremost, it reversed the outcome of one of the foundational disputes within the Zionist movement, which since the 1947–48 War of Independence had appeared settled.

The major political divide between the left and right within the Jewish community in British Mandatory Palestine and the Zionist movement stemmed from their differing views on the territorial expanse of the future Jewish state. This came to a head in the wake of a 1937 report of a Royal Commission (the Peel Commission) sent to Palestine by the British government to determine the political future of the country. After listening to representatives of both the Arab and the Jewish communities, the Commission came to the conclusion that the clash between the two, and their disparate and conflicting narratives and political aims, would make it impossible to find a common basis for a future independent, unitary country: the Jews, who made up at that time about a third of the population, would not accept a minority status in an Arab majority independent country, while the Arab majority would not accede to the Jewish minority's demand for free Jewish immigration—a challenge which became more and more acute due to the rise of Nazism in Germany and increased pressure of Jews, mainly in Central and Eastern Europe, to flee persecution and discrimination.

Hence in its Report, the Peel Commission proposed the partitioning of Mandatory Palestine into two states, one Jewish and one Arab (with a special status for Jerusalem). This was the first time the idea of partition had been raised, and while the onset of World War II effectively tabled the matter, after 1945 it resurfaced, as the enormity of the Holocaust and the future of the survivors gave it renewed urgency. Britain handed over the decision about the future of Palestine to the newly founded United Nations, and the result was the UN General Assembly Resolution of November 29, 1947. Jointly supported by both the United States and the Soviet Union, which had both adopted the principle of partition first raised by the Peel Commission ten years earlier, the resolution endorsed the establishment of two independent states, one Jewish and one Arab, in the territory of the British Mandate of Palestine.

For the Arabs, both in Palestine and in the surrounding Arab countries—most of them by then members of the United Nations—it was a bitter defeat of their claims that Palestine was as Arab as Egypt or Syria or Iraq and that the Jews had no right for national self-determination. For the Zionists, the legitimization of the right of the Jewish people to self-determination and sovereignty in what it considered its homeland, albeit in only a part of that homeland's territory, was the movement's most spectacular victory to date. But the victory was not without its complexities. From the time of the Peel Commission's Report to the passing of the UN Resolution, the idea of partition deeply divided the Jewish community in Palestine—the *Yishuv*—and the world Zionist movement.

The Zionist right-wing, led by Jabotinsky's Revisionist movement (the ancestor of the present Likud Party), vehemently rejected partition, claiming the whole of Palestine belonged to the Jewish people. By contrast, the position of the Zionist left and center—the socialist and the liberal parties—was more ambivalent. As a matter of principle, they maintained the legitimacy of the Zionist claim to the whole of the land, but under the leadership of the President of the World Zionist Organization Chaim Weizmann and the Chairman of the Jewish Agency for Palestine David Ben Gurion, they ultimately accepted the idea of partition.

In the heated and often bitterly acrimonious debates which engulfed the Zionist movement in the years 1937–1947—the most tragic and terrible decade in Jewish history—two arguments eventually emerged which swayed the majority of Jews in Palestine to accept, with a mixture of exultation and despair, the idea of partition. One was a humanistic, universalistic argument, the other an argument out of *Realpolitik*. Far from opposing one another, they coalesced into a powerful force for accepting the compromise of partition.

The universalistic argument was simple and straightforward: the claim for a Jewish state was founded on the right for national self-determination. But a universal right is just that: once you claim for your own people the rights of self-determination, independence, statehood, and sovereignty, you cannot deny them to other people. You cannot claim that the Jews have a right not to live under Arab rule and that the Arabs do not possess the similar right not to live under Jewish rule. In other words, once Zionism's left and center claimed the right to self-determination for the Jews in Palestine, partition became integral to the realization of that claim.

The *Realpolitik* argument for partition was equally clear: the establishment of a Jewish state could not be achieved without international political, diplomatic, juridical, and perhaps even military support. And with a clear Arab majority in the Mandate—the Arabs in 1947 numbering around 1.1 million people and the Jews about six hundred thousand—there would be no international support for a Zionist claim over the whole country, or, put another way, for Jewish rule over the Arab majority. Securing international support and legitimacy for a Jewish state could be achieved only if the Zionist movement accepted partition and limited itself to Jewish sovereignty in some part of the historical Land of Israel.

The combination of these two arguments made it possible for the Jewish community in Palestine to accept partition and move, on May 14, 1948, toward the establishment of an independent State of Israel based on the partition plan. Thus the Jewish community gained, immediately on declaring its independence, recognition by both the United States and the USSR and, later on, acceptance as member of the United Nations.

The tragedy was that the Arab side did not go through a parallel set of internal debates; its rejection of Jewish statehood was absolute and uncompromising. The Arabs of Palestine, and then the surrounding Arab countries, went to war not only against the nascent Jewish state but also against the UN partition plan—the only case in history in which member states of the United Nations went to war against a UN General Assembly resolution. The consequences for the Palestinian Arabs were catastrophic: military defeat and the flight, displacement, and expulsion of hundreds of thousands of people. A Palestinian Arab state was not established, and the Palestinian Arab regions (the West Bank and Gaza) were occupied, respectively, by Jordan and Egypt. It is tempting to ponder the counterfactual. If the Palestinian Arabs and the Arab nations had gone through an internal debate similar to that of the Jews and accepted the idea of partition, perhaps there would not have been a war in 1947–48 or a Palestinian *nakba* ("Catastrophe") or refugees or almost seven decades of further wars and terrorism. Politically and morally the Middle East would have been a very different region.

From the Israeli perspective, the outcome of the 1948 war seemed to bring an end to the internal debate about partition: a Jewish state has been established, it won the war for its existence, it achieved international recognition and legitimacy, it became a haven for the survivors of the Holocaust and for the Mizrahi Jews who were fleeing or being expelled from Arab countries. Despite major economic and social difficulties (mass immigration coupled with a heavy defense burden) and the permanent threat of war with its Arab neighbors, Israel became a success story and the focus of identity and pride for Jewish communities all over the world. The Labor Party and its liberal coalition partners saw their moderate, compromise-oriented policies vindicated. The Revisionist right-wing party, then called *Herut* ("Freedom"), under its leader Menachem Begin, lost eight parliamentary elections in a row between 1949 and 1973.

While Begin's party, inspired by Jabotinsky's ideas, never formally gave up its ideological opposition to partition and continued to maintain the traditional claim to an "Undivided Homeland," for all practical purposes this claim almost completely disappeared from its policy positions. While in the 1950s Herut initiated mass protests, some of them rather radical and threatening violence, against the Reparations Agreement with Germany, it never organized similar protests against the acceptance of the 1949 Armistice's de facto borders ("The Green Line") which left not only the West Bank ("Judea and Samaria") outside Israel but also left the Old City of Jerusalem under Jordanian occupation. Nor did the right-wing between 1949 and 1967 advocate an Israeli sponsored war to "liberate" the Old City of Jerusalem, Hebron, or Jericho, the location of many of the sites symbolic of Jewish history and memory— the Wailing Wall, the Tomb of the Patriarchs, and Rachel's Tomb, among others.

Moreover, it is conceivable that had the Arab countries at any time prior to 1967 agreed to a peace treaty with Israel based on the 1949 Armistice, there would have been an overwhelming majority in the Knesset—and the country—in favor of it. Herut may have offered up some fiery speeches but as the minority party would have ultimately accepted any deal. In short, the years after the UN

Resolution and the War of Independence brought to an effective end the debate about partition.

The 1967 Six-Day War changed everything.

So decisive was the Israeli victory—it stunned not only its enemies but Israelis themselves and Jews all over the world—that the whole of the historical Land of Israel, from the Jordan River to the sea, was now for the first time under Jewish control. The long-term consequences of this reality were not widely imagined at the time.

The immediate period after the war was characterized mainly by two phenomena: first, the desire of most Israelis to visit the historical sites in the biblical lands of Judea and Samaria; and second, a seemingly contradictory mixture of hope that now, finally, the Arab states would bow to the reality of Israel's existence and move toward peace and reconciliation, with fear that Israel would be pushed back from these regions, as it had been from Sinai and Gaza after the 1956 war. Neither the hope nor the fear became reality. What appeared to be temporary Israeli control of the West Bank and Gaza slowly became entrenched.

Even secular Israelis, then and still in the majority, were deeply moved when visiting the Wailing Wall, which they saw not as a religious site but as a symbolic remnant of the nation's historical statehood, lost in the hopeless struggle against the Roman Empire almost two thousand years prior. Moshe Dayan, the embodiment of Israel's victory—and a typical Israeli secular sabra—declared in the heady days of the summer of 1967 that "we have returned to Anatot [the birthplace of the prophet Jeremiah] and the other sites of our historical homeland not in order to forsake them again."

Thus the debate about partition was resumed, under completely different conditions. It is one thing to agree to give up a claim to a part of your homeland when you are weak, stateless, and a supplicant at the court of international politics. It is quite another to give up part of your homeland when you have gained possession of it in a war, even if that war started as a defensive operation and was never intended to win new territory.

In public opinion more than in government circles, what was initially viewed as a temporary strategic standoff led to a new vision of what the country should look like. The longer the stalemate lasted, buttressed by the Arab refusal to negotiate with Israel, the more legitimate the new reality became. While the government remained committed to negotiations about the future of the occupied territories even after the Arab League's September

1967 Khartoum Declaration of the "Three Noes"—"No negotiations with Israel, no peace with Israel, no recognition of Israel"—popular movements sprang up, including the Movement for the Complete Land of Israel and the beginnings of the settlement movement. These and other groups adopted new nomenclature, using "Judea and Samaria" instead of "West Bank," and the "Land" of Israel instead of the "State" of Israel. One of Israel's most astute writers, Shabtai Tevet, the biographer of Ben Gurion and Dayan, referred to this shift as the "Cursed Blessing."

For Begin, it was anything but cursed. The nationalist Revisionist party was revived. Partition appeared now as something of the past, swept away by Arab intransigence and Israel military might. One of the most radical right-wing leaders, the charismatic Geula Cohen, once wistfully admitted how 1967 totally changed the political spectrum of the country: "Before 1967, we appeared irrelevant. How could you talk about our rights to Hebron and Jericho to new immigrants who were desperately trying to find their way from Tel Aviv to Haifa? Now we are not marginal or irrelevant anymore: we are the bedrock of reality."

The Labor Party, which had led all Israeli coalition governments from 1948 to 1967, was generally credited for independence and for maintaining and guarding the country's security and defense. Its leaders—Ben Gurion, Moshe Sharett, Golda Meir—were considered the state's Founding Fathers and Mothers, while the party's younger generation, including Dayan, Shimon Peres, and Abba Eban, were viewed as their rightful successors. Yet now, Begin, until recently considered not only an outsider but also an irrelevant anachronism, appeared to be a visionary. He could criticize Labor's willingness to negotiate the return of the territories ("Land for Peace") as an example of weakness, if not treason.

There were also subtler but no less significant changes in Israeli politics during this period. One of the coalition partners of the ruling Labor Party was the National Religious Party (NRP), the party of religious Zionism. From Zionism's beginnings, many religious Jews have been ambivalent about the movement; they considered its attempt to establish a Jewish state in the Promised Land by human agency an apostasy, a revolt against Divine Providence, a secular "pushing of the End Days" (*dehikat ha-ketz*), possibly leading to false messianism. So when the first religious Zionist group appeared in the early twentieth century, it was careful to distinguish between the attempt to encourage immigration to Palestine and to achieve a Jewish political presence there on the one hand, and the messianic vision of divine redemption, which should be left to the Almighty in His own good time, on the other. Consequently, the NRP always sat within the more moderate wing of the Zionist movement, accepting partition as the most that could be achieved in the here-and-now. Even during the internal struggle within the Labor-led government, it always supported the more moderate Foreign Minister Moshe Sharett against the more activist Ben Gurion. Its social policies, inspired by biblical precepts to support the weak against the strong, made sense within its coalition alliance with the Labor Party. In a way it was a social-democratic party with a *kippa*.

For the NRP, especially its younger members, the 1967 victory and the resulting access to the historical sites of Judaism—preceded by weeks of almost-genocidal Arab rhetoric—were a providential sign. The establishment of the State of Israel in 1948, and its incredible feat of arms in 1967, were now construed as a clear indication they were living at the threshold of the messianic age. The result was the settlers' movement, spearheaded by the intellectual elite of *Gush Emunim* ("The Bloc of the Faithful"), which saw its mission as ensuring—sometimes against the will of the secular-led government—that the newly conquered territories would never be returned to Arab rule. The teachings of Rabbi Kook on the mystical holiness of the Land of Israel became the cornerstone of the movement's ideology. At times, the movement overlooked the more moderate elements in his thought, in particular his warnings against Jewish statehood in an unredeemed world.

In 1977, the NRP, from its inception a natural ally of Labor, became a willing partner in a Likud-led coalition. Not only that, it joined the Begin-led government as its most radically nationalist partner. It retains this distinction under its current name, The Jewish Home. It is now led by Naftali Bennett, who epitomizes its combination of religious zealotry and radical nationalism.

It has sometimes been pointed out that the initial setbacks of the Israeli army in the opening stages of the 1973 Yom Kippur War helped to discredit the ruling Labor Party and its leaders. This is unquestionably true; the war forced the resignation of Prime Minister Golda Meir, Defense Minister Moshe Dayan, and Foreign Minister Abba Eban. The opposition, under Menachem Begin, as well as popular demonstrations, obviously benefited from the almost total elimination of Labor's leadership, until then held as symbolizing the country's achievements. Yet still, the much deeper processes at work are what changed the political discourse of the country, even if they were not perceived at the time by many observers and even by the main political actors themselves.

* * *

ON GAINING INDEPENDENCE IN 1948, Israel's population was around six hundred thousand. By the end of 2015, that number stood at 8.5 million, 6.3 million of them Jews. No country has experienced such an increase over a comparable period of time. Most of it is due to the mass immigration of Jews from more than a hundred countries around the world. On a practical level, this is the main achievement of Zionist ideology, after the establishment of the state.

Since 1948, there have been three major sources of this immigration: immediately after independence, most immigrants were Holocaust survivors, chiefly from Poland, Romania, Hungary, and Czechoslovakia and Yugoslavia, many of whom found themselves stuck after the war in Displaced Persons camps in Germany, unwilling or unable to return to their home countries. In the last years of British rule in Palestine, many tried to reach the country but had been stopped by the British ban on Jewish immigration: more than fifty thousand Jews were captured on the high seas by the Royal Navy and interred in Cyprus, then a Crown Colony. Only after the establishment of Israel in 1948 were they freed and allowed to move to Israel.

The second wave of immigrants, starting in the 1950s, came from Arab countries, where the conditions of the Jewish communities after 1948 became difficult and in many cases intolerable. The millennia-old Jewish communities in Iraq, Libya, and Yemen immigrated almost in their entirety to Israel, and the majority of the Jews in Syria, Egypt, Tunisia, Algeria, and Morocco emigrated too. Most went to Israel, but some went elsewhere; many Francophone Jews from North Africa found refuge in metropolitan France, for instance. Many Jews also left Turkey and Iran—Muslim but not Arab countries—for Israel. Like the Holocaust survivors from Europe, most of these new arrivals were utterly destitute, barred from taking any of their possessions with them.

In the 1970s the Soviet Union slowly began to allow its Jewish citizens to immigrate to Israel. By the 1990s, after perestroika and the final dissolution of the Soviet Union, almost a million Soviet Jews immigrated. Later on, about one hundred thousand Ethiopian Jews also arrived to Israel, adding a totally new racial dimension to Israeli Jewish society.

Immigration on this scale put enormous pressures on Israel and also led to alienation among the new arrivals, who found themselves in an almost totally foreign environment. The transition made by Jews coming from Middle Eastern countries—the Mizrahim—was especially difficult, as many of them moved almost overnight from poor, almost premodern societies to a modern and developing one.

These successive waves of immigration have been one of the major causes of the shift in Israel's political center of gravity. Israel's Law of Return grants every Jewish person the right to immigrate to Israel. Its Citizenship Law, meanwhile, grants immigrants immediate citizenship, including the right to vote—and run for office—in both national and municipal elections. This is how a political elite composed almost exclusively of Eastern European immigrants and their descendants has been replaced by a new group of politicians who reflects these sweeping demographic changes. The number of MKs, or ministers and mayors of Middle Eastern or recent Russian background, today corresponds to their proportion in the nation's overall population. In a profound sense, this is another major achievement of Zionism, of course.

Just as the original immigrants to Palestine brought with them memories of the non-Jewish societies from which they had come, so have the immigrants from Middle Eastern countries. Thus, just as the worldviews of Israelis of Polish extraction were in many cases shaped by Polish anti-Semitism, so Jews from Yemen or Morocco remember, both personally and communally, oppression and persecution by Arabs. It should not come as a surprise that for many Middle Eastern Jews, their approach to the Palestinians is conditioned by their families' and communities' experiences in Arab societies. As a social activist of Middle Eastern background once memorably stated, if Israel was surrounded by twenty Ukrainian states, not many Eastern European Jews would be enthusiastic about the right of Ukrainians to self-determination.

Moreover, many Middle Eastern immigrants and their descendants, while not fanatically religious—fanatical Jewish religiosity is usually found among certain European, Ashkenazi Orthodox groups—tend to be more traditional than the average European immigrant. While most of the latter came from nations, communities, and families influenced by the Enlightenment's legacy, many Middle Eastern Jews came from Arab Muslim societies which did not go through similar processes of modernization and secularization. They show more deference to their elders and adopt a more conservative approach to political issues, especially regarding the national conflict between Jews and Arabs.

Thus many Middle Eastern Jews in Israel have felt more comfortable with the right-wing nationalist Likud than with the secular, more universalist left-wing parties. In Israel today, the majority of the (dwindling) Labor Party voters are mainly secular Ashkenazi Jews, while the bedrock of Likud consists of Middle Eastern Jews, even if the party's leadership was in the 1970s—and still is to a certain degree—primarily of European background. Meanwhile, the major Sephardi religious party, Shas, also represents more nationalistic tendencies.

The electoral impact of the Russian immigration has been similar, though for quite different reasons. Most Soviet immigrants are urban, middle-class professionals, often with impressive academic credentials. Their contribution to Israel's scientific, high-tech, artistic, and medical life has been an unqualified boon. But their impact on the country's politics has been more complex.

Most Russian immigrants are not religious; half a century of Soviet militant atheism left its mark. And because of high rates of intermarriage with non-Jews during the Soviet period, many Russian immigrants, though entitled to the citizenship privileges based in the Law of Return, may not be Jewish by any religious definition. Yet they come from a culture with a heavy emphasis on a strong central state; though they prefer not to live under Putin, for many of them, Putin is the kind of leader they admire. And because many of these immigrants have been subjected to Soviet propaganda which depicted the Arabs favorably and the Jews unfavorably, their dissent from Soviet ideology also meant that they reversed the Soviet equation: they came to believe, broadly put, that the Jews are right, and the Palestinian Arabs are wrong.

This phenomenon came to the fore in the 1990s, when one of the more famous Soviet Jewish dissidents, Nathan Sharansky, ran for Knesset elections as head of a small "Russian" party (eventually he joined the Likud). In arguing against giving up occupied

Palestinian territories, he recalled that Russia, despite its enormous expanse, insists on not relinquishing the three small Japanese Kurile Islands captured after World War II—so why should Israel give up Judea and Samaria, especially as they are so deeply linked to Jewish history? Most Israelis had never heard of the Kurile Islands matter, but nevertheless, and incredible as it may sound, these islands have played a role in the Israeli debate over the future of the West Bank and the country's relation to the Palestinian.

Most former Soviet Jews now living in Israel vote either for the Likud or for other right-wing parties, like Avigdor Lieberman's "Israel Is Our Home" party which is even more radically nationalist than the Likud. Lieberman is himself secular: at the core of his political ideology is not religion but the Russian legacy of statism. While studies show that the longer immigrants from the former Soviet Union have been in Israel, the more likely they are to shift to more centrist positions, they still appear by and large not to support liberal and left-wing positions.

* * *

TWO FURTHER DEVELOPMENTS HAVE impacted Israel's move to a more conservative set of attitudes and policies.

The first is the creeping impact of living under the continuous threat of terrorism. While Israel has achieved peace with Egypt and Jordan and the threat of conventional attacks by Arab armies has abated, decades of Palestinian terrorism aimed at civilians, not only in the occupied territories but also in Israel proper, has increased feelings of insecurity, fear, and hatred. Just as terrorist attacks in the United States, England, and France have shaken Americans' and Europeans' sense of security and greatly strengthened right-wing, xenophobic, and sometimes racist political parties, a similar hardening of attitudes occurred in Israel. When terrorists who blow themselves up in cafeterias, bars, and other civilian centers are hailed as martyrs in Palestinian society and occasionally by Palestinians authorities, the sense that all Israelis—and the very existence of Israel—are under siege greatly diminishes the willingness of many Israelis to take risks in favor of Palestinian self-determination. This is true even of many Israelis who denounce the continued occupation of Palestinian territories but are skeptical about the chances of peaceful coexistence. The siege mentality also explains what may be viewed as a paradox or an internal contradiction: while a majority of Israelis support the two-state solution, a majority at the same time feel that it may not be feasible in the foreseeable future.

The second development is likewise related to a global phenomenon: the weakening over the past decades of social-democratic parties and ties to the welfare state in many Western democracies. Historically, Labor's hegemony in Israeli politics was seen as part of international, post–World War II consensus on socially oriented economic policies that sought greater equality and solidarity.

With the rise of Thatcherite and Reaganite market fundamentalism, a harsh neocapitalism captured the political arena of many Western democracies. Social democracy and the welfare state have suffered political and electoral defeats in one country after another, and the ideal of social solidarity has been replaced in many countries by a new glorification of free enterprise, privatization, unbridled individualism, and unfettered competition. Israel exemplifies this shift, as evidenced by the diminished role of the kibbutzim and the once powerful Histadruth Labor Federation. The Tel Aviv Stock Exchange has flourished in the newly globalized economy, and privatization has become an almost messianic credo. Benjamin Netanyahu, educated in the United States in the Reagan years, became a symbol not only of a more nationalist policy but also of the adoption of a neocapitalist vision of Israel in a technologically oriented global economy. The success of Israel's hi-tech industry seems to have justified viewing the country as a so-called Start-Up Nation. Meanwhile, solidarity, social justice, and economic equality have taken a back seat.

The result has been a move away from the strong communitarian elements central to traditional Zionist thought. It was not only socialists, including Hess, Syrikin, Borochov, and Ben Gurion, who insisted that Jewish nation building in Palestine had to go hand in hand with a revolution in the social makeup of the Jewish people. Even a bourgeois liberal like Herzl realized that an unrestrained free market economy would be incompatible with the Zionist project: nation building, he argued, needed solidarity and social responsibility, not cutthroat competition, hence a strong public sector and socially oriented policies. It was these elements of Zionism which got slowly attenuated and sometimes even eroded under the combined impact of the global and local developments which have characterized Israeli policies in the last decades under successive Likud governments.

The combination of these various developments had a far-reaching impact on the country's image abroad, too: many Diaspora Jews do not look up anymore to Israel as a model which they cannot realize in their own countries of residence; and progressive and social democratic Western youth do not flock anymore to kibbutzim to experience a life of communal and egalitarian solidarity. The reality of Israeli rule over millions of Palestinians trumps the vision of a just society which should strive to be—as Ben Gurion once said—"A Light unto the Nations." In many cases, the Israeli nation appears to be on the defensive, not as a window toward a better, more just new social world. Future elections may bring a change in the profile of the Israeli government—but it will not be easy to unmake the fundamental changes which have shaped Israel the last fifty years.

And yet.

As with everything else in Israel, the reality is much more complicated and paradoxical, and these developments do not constitute an overall picture of the country.

When Israel was established in 1948 it was a poor, small country, whose very existence was in jeopardy. Few at that time would have believed that seventy years later its Jewish population would have multiplied tenfold; that its main export would shift from citrus to cutting-edge high technology; that the standard of living of most of its citizens would equal that of the populations in the most advanced countries in the West; and that a number of Arab states, not the Jewish homeland, would be on the verge of collapsing, existentially threatened by internal crises and external aggression.

Beyond the challenges arising from the country's failure to achieve reconciliation with the Palestinians, Israel has undergone a number of significant social and political changes which have enhanced its liberal character. The independent and activist Israeli Supreme Court has greatly deepened and enhanced the texture of Israeli democracy. Even lacking a written formal constitution, the Court has adopted decisions decreeing that human rights trump majoritarian parliamentary decisions. In some cases, it has annulled legislation it found to be at odds with constitutional standards of the rule of law, human rights, and transparency. Attempts by right-wing parliamentarians to counter such judicial decisions have failed. The court has issued progressive decisions on questions about same sex unions, adoption, conversion, and religious pluralism. While the Orthodox Chief Rabbinate still holds a monopoly on matters relating to the personal status of Israeli Jews, Conservative and Reform Jews now enjoy much more public recognition and greater standing than in the first decades of the country's existence.

While many bemoan the decline of the Labor movement's thirty years' political hegemony since the victory of Begin's Likud in the 1977 elections, it should be recalled that Labor had dominated the leadership of the Jewish community in Palestine since the mid-1930s. Israel was never a one-party state—even at the height of his popularity Ben Gurion needed coalition partners to gain a parliamentary majority. But for one party to dominate the country's politics in an uninterrupted way for decades had negative consequences: a sometimes ossified patronage system, exclusion of political opponents, arrogance, and built-in corruption. Many observers have pointed out the parallels with India's Congress Party.

Since 1977, Israeli politics have been cyclical, in the manner of most democratic countries: right-wing government followed by left-wing government, national coalitions, and occasional minority governments. The result was a contentious, raucous, and open national politics. If until 1977 no one could imagine the country not being led by the Labor Party, it is now difficult to imagine the return of an entrenched hegemonic party. Now every party lives under the constant threat of a continuous election campaign. Today, the right-wing has an obvious edge but is internally divided and still faces a formidable opposition. Future election outcomes are unpredictable, and Likud-led coalitions have proved to be far from stable.

The failure to find compromise between Israel and the Palestinians forms the backdrop against which Israeli Arab citizens (in Israel proper, not in the occupied territories) live as a minority in the Jewish nation state. But their social and political situation has changed dramatically. In the 1950s, those Palestinian Arabs who had not fled or been expelled in the 1947–48 war were a defeated, mainly agrarian population living under conditions of a harsh military administration. Today, thanks to natural increase and partial family unifications through the return of refugees, they compose almost 20 percent of the country's citizens. While their first parliamentary representatives were mostly meek and subservient elders, there are now 17 Arab members in the 120-member Knesset, the majority of whom belong to a united Common List encompassing four Arab parties, from communists to Islamic fundamentalists, who jointly take a radical Arab nationalist position.

Arab students, who make up between 10 and 20 percent of the student bodies at various universities, are politically and socially active in ways that many in the Jewish majority find hostile. Yet their voice is heard, and Arab university graduates can be found today in all walks of Israeli life—medicine, academia, the arts, journalism, the judiciary, and even, sometimes quite prominently, the army. The judge who sentenced a former Israeli president and a former Israeli prime minister to prison terms (for accusations of rape and corruption, respectively) is an Arab, as was one of the justices in the Supreme Court which denied their appeals. Discrimination continues, in government allocation for education and housing, for instance. But the position of Israel's Arab population has fundamentally changed. Once marginalized and neglected, they are now at the center of the nation's public discourse.

When an Arab Israeli poet wrote during one of the Arab–Israeli wars that "my country is at war with my people," he revealed an experience unprecedented in any other modern democratic country. The Israeli Arab population is not just a minority population (as is the Turkish-origin population in, say, Germany) but an ethnic minority in a nation-state that has been at war with the larger ethnic, cultural, and national community of which this minority is a part. While an Israeli–Palestinian peace still eludes the Jewish state, Israel is today much more liberal and pluralistic than it ever was in its pre-1967 halcyon days.

Despite the current right-wing hegemony, attitudes toward the Palestinians have unquestionably changed since the founding of the state. After all, it was a Labor-led government under Prime Minister Golda Meir that claimed that "there is no Palestinian people" because it preferred to reach an agreement with King Hussein of Jordan ("the Jordanian option") rather than negotiate with the PLO, which at the time was identified with terrorism, airplane hijacking, and utter nonacceptance of Israel. Eventually Labor changed its position and was cruelly criticized for it by the Likud and other right-wing parties.

Yet the most significant development in the last few years is that it is now a Likud Prime Minister who is committed, albeit reluctantly, to a two-state solution. Since his June 2009 Bar-Ilan speech, Benjamin Netanyahu has maintained that his government accepts a two-state solution—a major shift, not wholly accepted by many of his coalition partners (and even if it can be argued that some of Netanyahu's own policies do not promote this position). Nor did such a shift lead to meaningful negotiations with the Palestinian Authority; the gaps between Israel and the Palestinians on some of the core issues (borders, settlements, Jerusalem, refugees, security) remain as deep as ever. Yet there is, at least on a normative level, a framework that could make compromise possible, because the utter denial on the part of the Likud of the claim of the Palestinians to statehood is no longer a cornerstone of the Netanyahu government's stated policy. And it should not be overlooked that despite the lack of an Israeli–Palestinian agreement, the peace treaties with Egypt and Jordan have remained solid, despite the current turmoil in the Arab world.

All these developments, some of them contradictory, are of course also central to relations between Israel and the Diaspora. Though Israel succeeded in becoming the normative focus of contemporary Jewish identity, there is no doubt that this status has been diminished. Some of the harshest critics of current Israeli policies regarding the Palestinians come from Diaspora Jews. Paradoxically, this may point to the continuing salience of Israel in how Diaspora Jews shape their self-identity.

Because this rift relates to the Israeli government policies toward the Palestinians, moderation and an orientation toward compromise is crucial to the maintenance of close relations between the Jewish state and the Jewish Diaspora. Those in Israel who support the retention of the Whole of the Land of Israel (*Eretz Yisrael ha-shelema*) should be aware of the fact that by clinging to real estate (historical and even holy as it may be) they damage the soul of the Jewish people and make overall Jewish solidarity with Israel more difficult. Some on the Israeli right are beginning to realize this.

Despite this complex picture, by any criterion, Israel is an incredible success story: its survival and flourishing is an extraordinary example of the victory of the human spirit over harsh realities. But if current developments continue, some aspects of the original Zionist dream may be in jeopardy. Hubris and disregard for the rights of the other could threaten the moral foundations of the whole enterprise. Ben Gurion might have been exaggerating when he expressed the hope that Israel should be a Light unto the Nations. It should first and foremost be a Light unto Itself: when Israel looks into the mirror and judges itself by its own moral criteria, the nation—and Jews all over the world—should be proud of it. This, perhaps, may be the modern, secular meaning of being the Promised Land.

NOTES

INTRODUCTION

1. Karl Marx, certainly no great friend of things Jewish, was among the first thinkers to bring out the ambivalence of the modern Jew's situation in post-Emancipation liberal society. Marx's reflections on the meaning of Sunday as the official day of rest in secular French schools are much more perceptive than the more naive beliefs of many proponents of Emancipation. "Now according to liberal theory, Jews and Christians are equal, but according to this practice [of having the public schools open on Saturday], Christians have a privilege over Jews; for otherwise how could the Sunday of the Christians have a place in a law made for all Frenchmen? Should not the Jewish Sabbath have the same right?" See Karl Marx, *The Holy Family*, trans. R. Dixon (Moscow, 1956), p. 155.

2. Because nationalism did not appear in the Arab world until the twentieth century, relationships between Jews and Muslims there were not affected by this phenomenon until much later. Thus, with the emergence of Iraqi nationalism in the 1940s under Rashid Ali el-Kailani, Abdul Nasser's radical nationalism in the 1950s, *Istiqlal* nationalism in Morocco around the same time, and Algerian independence, the same developments which had occurred in Europe in the nineteenth century now upset the traditional unequal equilibrium of Jewish existence in Muslim countries. New definitions of identity—secular and nationalist—appeared within both the Arab and Jewish populations. It just happened one century later.

3. For some recent studies on the emergence of Zionism, see Walter Laqueur, *A History of Zionism* (New York, 1972); David Vital, *The Origins of Zionism* (Oxford, 1975). Cf. also Arthur Hertzberg's comprehensive "Introduction" to his anthology, *The Zionist Idea*, rev. ed. (New York, 1969), pp. 15–100.

CHAPTER 1

1. There is no English translation of Krochmal's writings, and very little has been written about him in any language. For a concise account

of his thought, see Nathan Rotenstreich, *Jewish Philosophy in Modern Times* (New York, Chicago, and San Francisco, 1968), chap. 5. See also S. Schechter, *Rabbi Nachman Krochmal and the "Perplexities of the Time"* (London, 1887); J. L. Landau, *Nachman Krochmal—Ein Hegelianer* (Berlin, 1904); Simon Rawidowicz, "War Nachman Krochmal Hegelianer?" in *Hebrew Union College Annual,* vol. 5 (Cincinnati, 1928), pp. 534–82.

2. Letteris's account is reprinted in Y. Kaufmann, *Likutei Ranak* [A Krochmal Selection] (Haifa, 1950), pp. 24–25. (Ranak is the acronym by which Krochmal is usually referred to in Hebrew.) When Hegel's disciples issued their master's first edition of *Werke* in the 1830s, Krochmal was one of the original subscribers, and his name appears in a special appendix to that edition.

3. Nachman Krochmal, "Moreh Nevuchei Ha-zman," in *Kitvei Krochmal* [Krochmal's Works], rev. ed., ed. S. Rawidowicz (London, 1961), p. 35.

4. Ibid., pp. 35–36.

5. G. W. F. Hegel, *The Philosophy of History,* rev. ed., trans. J. Sibree (New York, 1956), pp. 195, 198.

6. Krochmal, "Moreh Nevuchei Ha-zman," p. 29.

7. Ibid., p. 40.

CHAPTER 2

1. The historical perspective of this transformation is most imaginatively discussed in Hans Kohn, *The Idea of Nationalism* (New York, 1961).

2. For an English translation, see Heinrich Graetz, *History of the Jews,* 6 vols. (reprint ed., Philadelphia, 1967).

3. The original was published in *Zeitschrift für die Wissenschaft des Judentums,* ed. Leopold Zunz. A new edition, with an introduction by the writer Lion Feuchtwanger, was issued by Schocken in Berlin in 1936 and became immensely popular among Jews who were aroused to the meaning of their own identity by Nazi persecution.

4. Heinrich Graetz, *The Structure of Jewish History,* trans. Ismar Schorsch (New York, 1975), p. 65.

5. Ibid., p. 67.

6. Ibid., p. 69.

7. Ibid., p. 70.

8. Ibid., pp. 70–71.

9. Ibid., p. 71.

10. Ibid., p. 71.

11. Ibid.

12. In espousing such a future-oriented consciousness for the Jews, Graetz is clearly deviating from Hegel's philosophy of history, which explicitly avoided this dimension. The future was introduced as a dimension of historical writing into the Hegelian school by Hegel's Polish disciple,

Count August von Cieszkowski, who also greatly influenced Moses Hess's writing. There is no direct evidence linking Graetz to Cieszkowski, but it is highly probable that in the intellectual atmosphere of Berlin Graetz became aware of his *Prolegomena zur Historosophie*. For a recent translation of Cieszkowski, see *Selected Writings of August Cieszkowski*, with an introduction by André Liebich (Cambridge, 1979); see also André Liebich, *Between Ideology and Utopia* (Dordrecht, 1979), for a fascinating study of Cieszkowski's contribution to social, nationalist, and religious thought.

13. Graetz, *Structure*, p. 73.
14. Ibid., p. 92.
15. Ibid., p. 95.
16. Ibid., pp. 113–14.
17. Ibid., p. 114.
18. Ibid., p. 120.

CHAPTER 3

1. For a most comprehensive biographical study of Hess, see Edmund Silberner, *Moses Hess: Geschichte seines Lebens* (Leiden, 1966); also Theodor Zlocisti, *Moses Hess: Vorkämpfer des Sozialismus und Zionismus* (Berlin, 1921). In English, see Isaiah Berlin's magisterial essay "The Life and Opinions of Moses Hess," in his *Against the Current* (reprint ed., New York, 1980), pp. 213–51; also David McLellan, *The Young Hegelians and Karl Marx* (London, 1969), pp. 137–59.

2. Friedrich Engels, "Progress of Social Reform on the Continent," in Karl Marx and Friedrich Engels, *Collected Works* (New York, 1976), vol. 3, p. 406.

3. See especially his *Philosophie der Tat*, translated as "The Philosophy of the Act," in Albert Fried and Ronald Saunders, eds., *Socialist Thought* (Garden City, 1964), pp. 249–75.

4. Moses Hess, *Die heilige Geschichte der Menschheit von einem Jünger Spinozas* (Stuttgart, 1837). The reference to Spinoza is of great symbolic significance (see p. 40).

5. Moses Hess, *Philosophische und sozialistische Schriften*, ed. A. Cornu and W. Mönke (East Berlin, 1961), pp. 71–72.

6. Ibid., p. 65. In 1840 Hess wrote an introduction to a work he never completed, called "Die ideale Grunglagen des Neuen Jerusalems" [The Ideal Foundations of the New Jerusalem]. A copy is in the Zionist Central Archives in Jerusalem.

7. See Karl Marx, *Early Writings*, trans. T. B. Bottomore (London, 1963), pp. 1–40.

8. Moses Hess, "Über das Geldwesen," in *Philosophische*, pp. 329–48.

9. Moses Hess, *Rom und Jerusalem—Die letzte Nationalitätenfrage*, rev. ed. (Tel Aviv, 1935), p. 5.

10. Ibid., p. 10.

11. Ibid., pp. 57–70. The use of his given name, Moses, was very indicative of the changes in Hess's own self-awareness. During the years preceding the publication of *Rome and Jerusalem*, Hess tried to push that name, with its obvious Jewish connotation, into the background. Thus he published under the names M. Hess, Moritz Hess, and, after he moved to Paris, also Maurice Hess. With the publication of *Rome and Jerusalem*, he readopted with relish the original Moses, and in the book mentions his pride in assuming his real name again, adding that he would have been even happier if his name were Itzig (Ibid., p. 56).

12. Ibid., pp. 127–31.
13. Ibid., pp. 135–36.
14. Ibid., p. 13.
15. Ibid., p. 221.
16. Ibid., pp. 219 ff.
17. Ibid., pp. 112–13, 237–40.

CHAPTER 4

1. A very early bilingual edition of one of Alkalai's writings was published in Hebrew and English under the title *Harbinger of Good Tidings* (London, 1852).
2. In rabbinical tradition, Alkalai incorporated his given name (Yehuda-Judah) into the title of his book.
3. Arthur Hertzberg, *The Zionist Idea*, rev. ed. (New York, 1969), p. 105.
4. Ibid., p. 106. The number *seventy* refers to the traditional Hebrew expression of "seventy peoples and tongues," which means the whole world, as distinct from the Jews.
5. Ibid.
6. Ibid. I have rendered my own translation of this paragraph, which remains somewhat unclear in Hertzberg's version. The idea that girls as well as boys should be taught Hebrew was as revolutionary and novel as the very idea that the teachers and students should converse in the Holy Language.
7. Ibid., p. 107.
8. Ibid., pp. 106–107.
9. Ibid., p. 114.
10. All these images are derived from the traditional Jewish literature about the coming of the Messiah.
11. Hertzberg, *The Zionist Idea*, p. 111.
12. Ibid., pp. 111–12.
13. Ibid., pp. 112–13.
14. Ibid., p. 113.
15. Ibid., p. 114.
16. Quoted in Moses Hess, *Rom und Jerusalem—Die letzte Nationalitätenfrage*, rev. ed. (Tel Aviv, 1935), p. 243.

CHAPTER 5

1. Arthur Hertzberg, *The Zionist Idea*, rev. ed. (New York, 1969), p. 146.
2. Ibid., p. 147. The term *Torah* should be understood here in its generic sense, that is, a corpus of learning or an intellectual tradition, and not in the narrower religious sense of the Mosaic law.
3. For Smolenskin's polemic against the Reform movement, see his essay, "The *Haskala* of Berlin," in Hertzberg, pp. 153–57.
4. Arthur Hertzberg, "Let Us Search Our Ways," in Hertzberg, p. 149.
5. Ibid.
6. Ibid., p. 151.
7. Ibid.
8. Ibid., p. 152.
9. Ibid., pp. 152–53.

CHAPTER 6

1. Moshe Leib Lilienblum, "The Way of Return," in Arthur Hertzberg, *The Zionist Idea*, rev. ed. (New York, 1969), pp. 169–70.
2. Lilienblum, "Let Us Not Confuse the Issues," in Hertzberg, p. 172.
3. Ibid., pp. 170–72.
4. Ibid., p. 168.
5. Wilhelm Marr's book, *The Victory of Judaism over Germanism*, which became the most influential racial anti-Semitic tract, was published in 1879.
6. Moshe Leib Lilienblum, "The Future of Our People," in Hertzberg, pp. 173–74. To those who maintained that nationalism was disappearing, Lilienblum pointed out that even the least nationalistic European nations, England and France, were not ready to give up their claims to Egypt and Alsace-Lorraine, respectively (p. 175).
7. Ibid., p. 173. The syndrome of accusing Jews of seemingly contradictory associations, here pointed out by Lilienblum, continues in the twentieth century. Nazism accused the Jews of being agents of both Finance Capitalism and International Bolshevism; in the Soviet Union, Jews were accused in the 1950s as "rootless cosmopolitans," and today they are branded as "chauvinistic Zionists." And in contemporary semifascist Argentina, the Jewish bourgeoisie is attacked by leftists and Peronists alike for exploiting the masses; the sons and daughters of the same bourgeoisie, on the other hand, sometimes tend to be active in left-wing movements and are accused by the military establishment of being agents of communism and cosmopolitan antinational forces.
8. Ibid., p. 174.
9. Ibid., p. 177.
10. Ibid., pp. 175–76.
11. Ibid., p. 177.

CHAPTER 7

1. The full title was *Auto-Emancipation—ein Mahnruf an seine Stammesgenossen. Von einem russischen Juden* (Berlin, 1882).

2. Leo Pinsker, *Auto-Emancipation*, trans. D. S. Blondheim, ed. A. S. Super (London, 1932), pp. 4, 32.

3. Ibid., p. 6.

4. Ibid., p. 8.

5. Ibid., p. 13. Lilienblum developed a similar analysis. Pinsker's essay was the first to be published, but it would be idle to speculate who was the first to describe this phenomenon. Such ideas were widespread and could be viewed as part of the *Zeitgeist* as perceived by many Jewish intellectuals.

6. Ibid., p. 14.

7. Ibid., p. 17.

8. Ibid., p. 18, 22.

9. Ibid., pp. 24–25.

10. Ibid., p. 24.

11. Ibid., p. 26. The idea of a National Assembly was raised quite early in the writings of Alkalai (p. 51). Pinsker died before the first Zionist Congress, but at his initiative the various groups of Hovevei Zion (Lovers of Zion) convened in Kattowitz in 1884. The Kattowitz Conference set up a structure which greatly facilitated some of Herzl's groundwork for the Zionist Congress.

12. Pinsker, pp. 24–30.

13. Ibid., p. 26.

14. Ibid., p. 28.

15. Ibid., p. 26.

16. Ibid., p. 22.

17. Ibid., pp. 22–23.

18. Ibid., p. 29. Pinsker's language is intentionally vague on the exact political status here envisaged, but the example before his eyes was the autonomous pashalik of Mount Lebanon, whose Christian Maronite population achieved guarantees from the Great Powers for its special status within the Turkish Empire.

CHAPTER 8

1. For a life of Ben Yehuda, see Robert St. John, *Tongue of the Prophets: The Life Story of Eliezer Ben Yehuda* (London, 1952).

2. This had been Smolenskin's position prior to the 1881 disturbances (see pp. 60–62). After 1881–82 he moved to a more "materialist" position, advocating mass immigration to Palestine.

3. Eliezer Ben Yehuda, "A Letter to the Editor of *Hashahar*," in Arthur Hertzberg, *The Zionist Idea*, rev. ed. (New York, 1969), p. 164.

4. Ibid.
5. Ibid., p. 165.

CHAPTER 9

1. For a fascinating biographical study of Herzl in his Vienna surroundings, see Amos Elon, *Herzl* (New York, 1975). For a more conventional study, see Alex Bein, *Theodor Herzl—A Biography*, trans. Maurice Samuel (Cleveland, 1962).

2. "The New Ghetto," in Ludwig Lewison, ed., *Theodor Herzl: A Portrait for His Age* (Cleveland and New York, 1955), p. 165.

3. A Hebrew translation of Herzl's Paris dispatches has recently been published: Theodor Herzl, *Mi-Boulanger ad Dreyfus* [From Boulanger to Dreyfus], 3 vols., ed. Alex Bein and Moshe Schaerf (Jerusalem, 1974). The dispatches on anti-Semitism in France are in vol. 1, pp. 105–50, and vol. 3, pp. 1059–66. Many of these dispatches were also collected by Herzl in his volume *Palais Bourbon: Bilder aus dem französischen Parlamentsleben* (Leipzig, 1895).

4. Theodor Herzl, *The Jewish State*, 5th ed., trans. Sylvia d'Avigdor (London, 1967), pp. 25–26.

5. Theodor Herzl, *Old-New Land*, trans. Lotta Levensohn, preface by Stephen S. Wise (New York, 1941), pp. 65–66.

6. Just how painful this conclusion must have been for a person of Herzl's background, steeped as he was in European bourgeois culture, can be see from his remark about the languages to be spoken in the Jewish state. Herzl does not envisage a possible revival of Hebrew ("Who amongst us has a sufficient acquaintance with Hebrew to ask for a railway ticket in that language?"); rather, "every man can preserve the language in which his thoughts are at home. . . . We shall remain in the new country what we are here, and we shall never cease to cherish with sadness the memory of the native land out of which we have been driven" (*The Jewish State*, p. 70).

7. Herzl, *The Jewish State*, p. 7.

8. The title *Altneuland* echoes the utopian socialist novel *Freiland* (Freeland), written by Herzl's Viennese contemporary and colleague Dr. Theodor Hertzka and published in 1890. The social arrangements of Herzl's society closely resemble those of Frieland, and Herzl mentions Hertzka's name several times both in *The Jewish State* and in *Altneuland.* Herzl relates that the name occurred to him as a variation on the name of the famous and magnificent Prague synagogue, the *Altneuschul* (Old-New Synagogue), which symbolized for so many emancipated Central European Jews both the continuity and the mystical splendor of Jewish existence.

9. Herzl, *The Jewish State*, p. 70.
10. Ibid., p. 33 ff.
11. Ibid., pp. 37–39.

12. Ibid., p. 72. The English translation mistakenly refers here to a "badge of honour" instead of a "badge of labour." Herzl originally proposed this design of the Seven Golden Stars of Labor as a flag for the Zionist Organization, but a group of English Zionists, who came from a business background, objected to the socialist implications of the design. Eventually Herzl gave in, and the blue-and-white flag with the Star of David was adopted as the Zionist flag and later as the flag of the State of Israel.

13. Herzl, *Old-New Land*, p. 86.

14. Ibid., p. 143.

15. Ibid., pp. 145, 152.

16. Ibid., p. 87.

17. Ibid., p. 79.

18. Ibid., p. 78.

19. Ibid., p. 122.

20. This Dr. Geyer ("vulture"), Herzl ironically remarks, was originally a fanatical anti-Zionist; he later became reconciled to Zionism, yet brought with him his uncompromising attitude to his new creed. Herzl's strongly anticlerical views emerge vividly in his characterization of Geyer.

CHAPTER 10

1. For Nordau's autobiographical sketch, see Max Nordau, *Zionistische Schriften*, 2d ed. (Berlin, 1923), pp. 484–86.

2. "Address at the First Zionist Congress," in Max Nordau, *To His People*, ed. B. Netanyahu (New York, 1941), p. 64.

3. Ibid., p. 66.

4. Ibid., pp. 66–67.

5. Ibid., p. 67.

6. Ibid., pp. 68–69.

7. Ibid., p. 70.

8. Nordau, "Eine Geschichte der Israeliten," in *Zionistische Schriften*, p. 400.

9. Nordau, *To His People*, pp. 70–71.

10. Max Nordau, *Ktavim Zioniyim*, ed. B. Netanyahu (Jerusalem, 1960), vol. 2, p. 29.

11. Ibid., p. 92.

12. Ibid., p. 93.

13. Ibid., p. 101.

14. Ibid., p. 27.

15. Ibid.

16. Ibid.

17. Ibid., p. 26.

18. Ibid.

19. Letter to Herzl, July 17, 1903, in Michael Heymann, ed., *The Minutes of the Zionist General Council: The Uganda Controversy* (Jerusalem,

1977), p. 122. The cultural context of political life, sometimes so lacking in Herzl, thus became very pronounced in Nordau, who was always much more critical than Herzl of European fin-de-siècle culture and its atomized individualism.

20. "On the Maccabean War and the Boer War," in *Ktavim*, vol. 2, pp. 75–76. The speech was reported in *Die Welt*, Dec. 28, 1900.

CHAPTER 11

1. Ahad Ha'am, *Nationalism and the Jewish Ethic*, ed. and with an introduction by Hans Kohn (New York, 1962), pp. 34–43.

2. Ahad Ha'am, "The Jewish State and the Jewish Problem," in *Nationalism*, p. 73.

3. Ibid., pp. 74–75.

4. Ibid., p. 77.

5. Ibid., pp. 78–79.

6. Ibid., p. 80.

7. Ibid., pp. 80–81. Ahad Ha'am remarks in a footnote attached to this paragraph that the quoted phrases are taken from notes he made of some speeches delivered at the first Zionist Congress in Basle.

8. Ibid., pp. 81–82.

9. Ahad Ha'am, "Flesh and Spirit," in *Nationalism*, pp. 202–203.

10. Ibid., p. 203. The reference is to Rabban Yohanan Ben Zakkai, who left Jerusalem when it was besieged by the Romans under Vespasian and Titus and received from them permission to maintain a center for Jewish learning in the town of Yavneh (Jabneh), which thus became the focus for Jewish culture after the destruction of the Temple. Its name became synonymous with the spiritual, rather than the political, content of Judaism.

11. Ibid., pp. 203–204. For this see also Hans Kohn's "Introduction," *Nationalism*, pp. 7–33. See also Leon Simon's "Introduction" of Ahad Ha'am's *Selected Essays*, rev. ed. (Philadelphia and Cleveland, 1962), pp. 11–40.

12. Ahad Ha'am, "Emet me-Eretz Israel," in *Kol Kitvei Ahad Ha'am* [Ahad Ha'am: Complete Works], ed. H. Y. Roth (Tel Aviv, 1946), p. 23.

13. Ibid., p. 24.

14. Ibid.

15. Ibid., p. 29.

CHAPTER 12

1. Together with a most valuable personal memoir selected writings of Syrkin were edited by his daughter, Marie Syrkin, under the title *Nachman Syrkin: Socialist, Zionist* (New York, 1961).

2. Nachman Syrkin, "The Jewish Problem and the Jewish State," in Arthur Hertzberg, *The Zionist Idea*, rev. ed. (New York, 1969), p. 333.

3. Ibid., p. 334.

4. Ibid., p. 335. The last reference is to Lessing's didactic Enlightenment play *Nathan der Weise*.

5. Ibid., p. 338.

6. Ibid., p. 339.

7. Ibid., pp. 338–39.

8. Ibid., pp. 339–40. It is easy to imagine such a profile being written in the 1920s of the Nazi leadership. The term *Catilinian* does not appear in the English translation and has been added here directly from the German original.

9. Ibid., p. 340.

10. Ibid.

11. Ibid., pp. 340–41.

12. Ibid., p. 341.

13. Ibid., p. 342.

14. Ibid., pp. 342–43.

15. Bruno Kreisky's complex and tortured attitude to Israel should also be understood against the background of this polemical history within the socialist movement.

16. Syrkin, "The Jewish Problem," in Hertzberg, p. 344.

17. Ibid.

18. Ibid., p. 347.

19. Ibid., p. 349.

20. Ibid., p. 350.

21. Ibid.

CHAPTER 13

1. For a history of the Bund, see Henry J. Tobias, *The Jewish Bund in Russia* (Stanford, 1972).

2. See Israel Kolatt, "Zionist Marxism," in S. Avineri, ed., *Varieties of Marxism* (The Hague, 1977), pp. 227–70.

3. For a collection of some of the main writings of the Austro-Marxists, see T. Bottomore and Patrick Goode, eds., *Austro-Marxism* (Oxford, 1978).

4. Ber Borochov, *The National Question and the Class Struggle*, trans. L. Jessel (Chicago, 1935), p. 4.

5. Ibid., p. 6.

6. Ibid., pp. 42–43.

7. Ibid., p. 43.

8. Ibid., p. 44.

9. Ibid., p. 36.

10. Ibid., p. 16.

11. Ber Borochov, "Our Platform," in Arthur Hertzberg, *The Zionist Idea*, rev. ed. (New York, 1969), p. 360.

12. Ibid.
13. Ibid., p. 361.
14. Ibid.
15. Ibid., p. 362.
16. Ibid., pp. 363–64. There is no doubt that Borochov's lack of acquaintance with the pluralistic and multiethnic structure of American society led him, in this instance, to reach conclusions which were not borne out by later historical developments. Nevertheless, Borochov's analysis, for all its inaccuracies, left an indelible mark on the thinking of a whole generation of Jewish radicals in Eastern Europe, the United States, and Palestine.
17. Ibid., p. 364.
18. Ibid., p. 365.
19. Ibid., pp. 365–66.
20. Ibid., p. 366.

CHAPTER 14

1. For some of the philosophical aspects of Gordon's thought, see Nathan Rotenstreich, *Jewish Philosophy in Modern Times* (New York, Chicago, and San Francisco, 1968), pp. 239–52.
2. A. D. Gordon, "Some Observations," in Arthur Hertzberg, *The Zionist Idea*, rev. ed. (New York, 1969), p. 375.
3. Ibid., p. 376.
4. Ibid., p. 377.
5. Ibid., p. 376.
6. Ibid., p. 377.
7. Gordon, "Labour," in *Selected Essays*, trans. F. Burnce, rev. ed. (New York, 1973), pp. 51–52. The phrases in brackets do not appear in the English translation and have been directly translated from the Hebrew original.
8. Ibid., p. 52.
9. Ibid.
10. Ibid., pp. 54–55.
11. Ibid., pp. 55–56. This was the intellectual background for Gordon's insistence that the new Jewish villages in Palestine should be maintained by Jewish labor, otherwise a reemergence of a *Galut*-like alienation from physical labor would occur. Gordon was also much concerned with the dangers of Jewish-Arab confrontation, and following Ahad Ha'am he warned against belittling the scope of Arab nationalism in Palestine. In his essays on "Human Nation," he wrote, "The Arabs have the attributes and qualities of a living nation but not of a free people. They live on the land; they till the soil; they speak a national language inherently their own, and so on. Their claim is, therefore, marked by the form and significance of a demand made by a living people. . . . While we discuss whether there is or

is not an Arab national movement, life actively moves it forward. . . . We run ourselves into serious danger if we fail to recognize this vital fact, if we deceive ourselves into the belief that [Arab nationalism] is merely the scheme of a few *effendis* and nothing more" (*Selected Essays*, pp. 26–27).

12. Hertzberg, *The Zionist Idea*, p. 381.

13. Ibid., p. 382.

CHAPTER 15

1. The full text of Jabotinsky's testament is to be found in Zeev Jabotinsky, *Ktavim* [Works], vol. 17 (Jerusalem and Tel Aviv, 1947), p. 18.

2. Zeev Jabotinsky, *Ktavim*, vol. 1, p. 18. For a highly partisan, though generally reliable, biography of Jabotinsky, see Joseph B. Schechtman, *The Vladimir Jabotinsky Story*, 2 vols. (New York, 1956).

3. Jabotinsky, *Ktavim*, vol. 1, p. 16.

4. Ibid., p. 27.

5. Ibid.

6. Ibid., pp. 28–29.

7. Ibid., vol. 9, p. 261.

8. Ibid. The biblical quotation is from Exodus 23:9.

9. Jabotinsky, *Ktavim*, vol. 9, p. 265.

10. This pen name, which became of symbolic importance after 1948 when an armament ship was brought by the Irgun to Israel and a confrontation ensued with the newly established government of David Ben Gurion, had an amusing origin. In his *Autobiography* Jabotinsky candidly admits, "I chose this name due to a funny mistake. At that time my Italian was still shaky, and I thought that the term means a 'crane'—only later did I discover that its real meaning is 'swing'" (*Ktavim*, vol. 1, p. 35).

11. For Jabotinsky's objection to the settlement of Tel Hai, see the verbatim report of the discussion in the Zionist leadership as reported in Gershon Rivlin, ed., *Moreshet Tel Hai* [The Heritage of Tel Hai] (Tel Aviv, 1948), pp. 88–89.

12. Jabotinsky, *Ktavim*, vol. 9, p. 126.

13. Ibid., pp. 126–27.

14. Ibid., p. 128.

15. Ibid.

16. Ibid., pp. 129–30.

17. Ibid., p. 161.

18. Ibid., p. 153.

19. Ibid., p. 154.

20. Ibid., vol. 7, p. 164.

21. Ibid., p. 140.

22. Ibid., vol. 11, p. 319.

23. Ibid., p. 320.

24. Ibid., p. 43.

25. Ibid., vol. 9, p. 87.

26. Vladimir Jabotinsky, *Samson the Nazirite*, trans. Cyrus Brooks (London, 1930), pp. 179–80. In the Hebrew translation of the novel, the *right*-arm salute of the massed Philistines became a *left*-hand salute. Somehow the Hebrew translator must have found the obvious analogy too hard to swallow and tried to make the whole scene a little more palatable to a literary audience whose sensitivity to such spectacles was naturally very high. There is, however, no note in the Hebrew translation that a change has been made from the Russian original. See Zeev Jabotinsky, *Shimshon*, trans. B. Krupnik (Berlin and Tel Aviv, 1930), p. 205.

27. Zeev Jabotinsky, *Al Hadar* [On Glory], ed. M. Jesreeli (Tel Aviv, 1961), p. 31.

28. Jabotinsky, *Ktavim*, vol. 9, p. 239.

29. Ibid., vol. 11, p. 135.

30. Ibid., p. 138.

31. Ibid., vol. 9, p. 209.

32. Ibid., p. 216.

33. Ibid., vol. 7, p. 221. Such a view on the "European" character of the Jewish people obviously overlooks the cultural heritage of the Jewish communities in Arab and Muslim countries and certainly belittles their contribution to the totality of the Jewish experience. But here, as in other instances, Jabotinsky's insistence on the supremacy of Europe is central to his thinking both in general and in Jewish matters.

34. Ibid., vol. 11, p. 219.

35. Ibid., p. 213.

36. Arthur Hertzberg, *The Zionist Idea*, rev. ed. (New York, 1969), p. 562.

37. Jabotinsky, *Ktavim*, vol. 11, p. 90.

38. Ibid., p. 293.

39. Ibid.

40. Hertzberg, *The Zionist Idea*, p. 568.

41. Ibid., p. 565.

42. Ibid., p. 560.

CHAPTER 16

1. On Pines, see Arthur Hertzberg, *The Zionist Idea*, rev. ed. (New York, 1969), pp. 406–15.

2. Ibid., p. 402.

3. For an excellent account of Kook's religious ideas, see Ben-Zion Bokser's "Introduction" to his edition of Abraham Isaac Kook, *The Lights of Penitence* (New York and Toronto, 1976), pp. 1–33.

4. Abraham Isaac Kook, "The Land of Israel," in Hertzberg, p. 419.

5. Ibid., pp. 420–21.

6. Ibid., pp. 419–20.

7. Kook, "Lights for Rebirth," in Hertzberg, p. 430. Here and in the following quotations, the translation has been slightly amended to conform more accurately to the original Hebrew text.

8. Ibid.

9. Kook, "The Rebirth of Israel," in Hertzberg, p. 426.

10. Kook, "The War," in Hertzberg, p. 423. Some of those who nowadays call themselves Rabbi Kook's disciples (like the Gush Emunim activists, for example) conveniently overlook this universalistic dimension in his thought. That they thus belittle the greatness of the man whom they call their mentor is just another instance of a very common irony in the history of ideas.

11. Ibid., p. 422.

12. Ibid.

13. Ibid., p. 423.

CHAPTER 17

1. Of the numerous biographies of Ben Gurion, the most balanced is Michael Bar-Zohar, *Ben-Gurion*, trans. Peretz Kidron (London, 1978).

2. David Ben-Gurion, *Mi-maamad le-am* [From Class to Nation], rev. ed. (Tel Aviv, 1974), pp. 196–97. Ben Gurion's usage of *Hebrew* rather than *Jewish*, in referring to the new community in Palestine, is indicative of this feeling of breaking with the exilic tradition.

3. Ibid., p. 252.

4. Yaacov Becker, ed., *Mishnato shel David Ben Gurion* [The Teaching of David Ben Gurion] (Tel Aviv, 1958), vol. 2, pp. 525–26.

5. Karl Marx, *Early Writings*, trans. T. B. Bottomore (London, 1963), pp. 55–56.

6. Becker, *Mishnato Shel David Ben Gurion*, vol. 1, pp. 190–91.

7. Ben-Gurion, *Mi-maamad le-am*, p. 250.

8. Ibid., p. 187. This insistence on all labor in the new homeland of the Jewish people being done by Jews also led to Ben Gurion's insistence on a clear Jewish majority in the Jewish state and a readiness not to claim those areas of the Land of Israel that were heavily populated by Arabs. Hence his acceptance of partition in 1947–48 and his readiness, after 1967, to give up the densely populated territories of the West Bank and Gaza. A large Arab population in Israel would become an Arab proletariat in a society where most Jews would shy away from physical labor and primary production; thus the sociological achievement of the Zionist revolution would be reversed.

9. Ibid., p. 220.

10. Becker, *Mishnato shel David Ben Gurion*, vol. 2, p. 363.

11. Ibid., pp. 372–73.

12. Ibid., pp. 496–97.

EPILOGUE

1. This does not mean that Israel is a substitute for Jewish religion, only that functionally it plays a role similar to that of religion in pre-Emancipation days. For Jews today who are still religious in the traditional sense, religion has a deep collective existential meaning. But since not all Jews can identify today with the religious symbols, religion is merely a partial focus of identity, and Israel, more than any other factor, now plays this unifying role.

INDEX

Nati Shohat

Shlomo Avineri is a professor of political science at the Hebrew University of Jerusalem and a member of the Israel Academy of Sciences and Humanities. His studies of Hegel, Marx, and Herzl have been translated into many languages. Avineri was the director-general of Israel's Ministry of Foreign Affairs from 1975 to 1977 in the government of Prime Minister Yitzhak Rabin. He writes frequently for *Haaretz* and lives in Jerusalem.